Ethical Branding a

MW00416473

Ethical Branding and Marketing: Cases and Lessons provides current perspectives on fascinating global cases focusing on the specific combination of the two fields of "ethics" and "branding," on their relationship, and on how that joint perspective shapes brands, companies, business strategies, and the market itself.

In a contemporary environment of "truthiness" and fake news, it is more important than ever to review core principles of ethics and to reassess how these principles apply to today's branding and marketing practices. This book addresses practices in ethical branding and corporate culture. It includes such topics as truth, integrity, value, vulnerability, and differentiation. Collectively, these cases provide a contemporary overview of intriguing scenarios and best practices in ethical branding.

The book provides the reader with real, updated insight into ethical decision-making; helps students integrate ethics, branding strategy, and real life, complex situations into an effective learning process; and provides the reader with up-to-date ethical branding cases from around the world.

Hagai Gringarten, M.B.A., Ph.D., is a Professor and a branding expert. He teaches branding and marketing at St. Thomas University's Gus Machado School of Business, and he is a Visiting Professor at Harbin Finance University in China. He has served as president of the American Marketing Association South Florida chapter and co-authored a bestselling book about coffee. He also pursued postgraduate studies at Harvard Graduate School of Business and the Kellogg School of Management. Dr. Gringarten serves as a faculty advisor to the American Marketing Association chapter at STU and is the founder and Editor-in-Chief of the *Journal of Multidisciplinary Research*, a peer-reviewed academic journal. He is also co-founder and faculty advisor of the *Journal of Student Research* and serves on the editorial board of the *Journal of International & Interdisciplinary Business Research*, a California State University system publication.

Raúl Fernández-Calienes, the Reverend Professor, Ph.D., teaches at St. Thomas University, where he is Adjunct Professor of Management Ethics in the Gus Machado School of Business, Senior Research Fellow at the Human Rights Institute, and formerly Visiting Associate Professor in the School of Law. He is Managing Editor of the peer-reviewed *Journal of Multidisciplinary Research* and a past Deputy Editor of the American Bar Association's *International Law Year in Review*.

Routledge Advances in Management and Business Studies

For more information about this series, please visit www.routledge.com/
Routledge-Advances-in-Management-and-Business-Studies/book-series/
SE0305

Ethical Branding and Marketing

Cases and Lessons

Edited by Hagai Gringarten and
Raúl Fernández-Calienes

Routledge
Taylor & Francis Group

LONDON AND NEW YORK

First published 2019 by Routledge

2 Park Square, Milton Park, Abingdon, Oxon, OX14 4RN

605 Third Avenue, New York, NY 10017

Routledge is an imprint of the Taylor & Francis Group, an informa business

First issued in paperback 2020

Library of Congress Cataloging-in-Publication Data
Names: Gringarten, Hagai, editor. | Fernâandez-Calienes, Raúl, editor.
Title: Ethical branding and marketing : cases and lessons / edited by Hagai Gringarten and Raúl Fernâandez-Calienes.
Description: New York, NY : Routledge, 2019. |
Series: Routledge advances in management and business studies | Includes index.
Identifiers: LCCN 2019004478
Subjects: LCSH: Marketing—Moral and ethical aspects. | Branding (Marketing)—Moral and ethical aspects.
Classification: LCC HF5415 .E7959 2019 | DDC 174/.4—dc23
LC record available at https://lccn.loc.gov/2019004478

ISBN: 978-1-138-33727-5 (hbk)
ISBN: 978-0-367-78647-2 (pbk)

Typeset in Sabon
by codeMantra

Dedicated with much love, admiration, and appreciation to my parents Eliezer and Henia Gringarten, who taught me the value of integrity, dignity, responsibility, and fidelity.

Dr. Hagai Gringarten

Dedicado con mucho amor a mis padres, quienes me enseñaron a vivir en fe y obediencia a Dios para el beneficio de la humanidad.

Dr. Raúl Fernández-Calienes

Contents

List of "Check Your Understanding"

Administrative Law
Anthrax
Bayer AG
Bayer Corporation
Bioterrorism
Brand Personality
Cipro
Conflict Management in Franchising
Corporate Social Responsibility
Cyborg
Dummy Variable Creation
Economic Downturns
Education Supply
Ethical Approach
Executive Functions
Fiduciary Standard
Great Communicator
Guild
Gunboat Diplomacy
Happiness
Industry Comparisons
Judicial Review
Katrina
Loneliness
The Medieval Period
Mentors
Multinational Enterprises
National Pharmaceutical Stockpile
Open Institutions
Opium
Orientalism
Private Governance
Private Law
Privatization

Preface

The *Ethical Branding* book is unique because it is ethical branding focused. It provides current perspectives on fascinating global cases. The approach is to focus on the specific combination of the two fields of "ethics" and "branding," on their relationship, and on how that joint perspective shapes brands, companies, business strategies, and the market itself.

In a contemporary environment of "truthiness" and fake news, it is more important than ever to review core principles of ethics and to reassess how these principles apply to today's branding and marketing practices. This book addresses practices in ethical branding and corporate culture. It includes such topics as truth, integrity, value, vulnerability, and differentiation. Collectively, these cases provide a contemporary overview of intriguing scenarios and best practices in ethical branding.

The book's themes include ethics, branding, marketing, business, business communications, and business history. Its objectives include the following:

- provide the reader with real, updated insight into ethical decision-making;
- help students integrate ethics, branding strategy, and real life, complex situations into an effective learning process; and
- provide the reader with up-to-date ethical branding cases from around the world.

This book will have international appeal, not only in primarily English-speaking countries but also in nations known for commerce, trade, marketing, and other aspects of business – nations such as Brazil, China, India, Singapore, and others.

Background

Increasingly, firms realize that branding is one of the most valuable intangible assets that firms have (Holt, 2003; Keller & Sood, 2003; Kellogg, 2010).

In his forward to *Kellogg on Branding* (Tybout & Calkins, 2005), Kotler argued that in this day and age of the quiet revolution of the digital age, change accelerated to levels never before experienced. There are only two answers to the marketing challenges of today: One is to know the customer, and the other is to differentiate through branding.

Kotler and Keller (2009) defined branding as "endowing products and services with the power of a brand" (p. 142). They noted that branding is the act of creating differences between products. While many researchers try to reach a consensus on defining the term brand, branding is being redefined continually.

The American Marketing Association (2009) defines brand as "A name, term, design, symbol, or any other feature that identifies one seller's good or service as distinct from those of other sellers" (n.p.).

Velasquez (2012) defines "business ethics" as "a specialized study of moral right and wrong that focuses on business institutions, organizations, and behavior (p. 15).

The combination of these two terms would seem, then, to be a major element of contemporary business operations – and study. Yet, in practice, one finds a gap in the literature.

As important as branding ethics may appear to be, the terminology within recent university and business school textbooks in these fields is incomplete. A review of some of the leading texts on business ethics shows that the words "branding," "branding ethics," and "ethical branding" do not appear in the index (see, e.g., Audi, 2009; Boatright & Smith, 2017; Stanwick & Stanwick, 2009; Velasquez, 2012). Even a little analysis reveals the gap, a missing step in the process of thinking about – and acting – in relation to ethical branding. The fact of this gap is part of the origins of the present work.

How to Use this Book (Teaching Notes)

Ethical Branding can be of use in many different settings. For scholars, it offers new and unique sources of information and material for research and writing. For instructors, it provides a single work that centralizes data, cases, and examples. For students, it unites streams of thought and experience into a united whole that facilitates understanding of relevant fields. It also provides Discussion Questions that bring together various aspects of the cases for engagement and decision-making in response as well as for developing critical thinking skills.

This book is a solid complement for instructors and students in the field of marketing and business, serving as an updated addition and supplement to the subject.

Through specific pedagogical features, the book highlights a best practices approach, so students, instructors, and others can access the book more easily and efficiently.

Organization of the Book

Ethical Branding is organized alphabetically by author's last name. Each chapter includes pedagogical features such as *Abstracts, Keywords, Cite-Ready References, DOI Numbers, Further Readings, TOC-RSS Feeds, Links,* and *Indexes.* In addition, the book includes a section entitled *Check Your Understanding,* which provides brief definitions or comments in boxes on the margins to highlight and communicate important elements to the reader. Each chapter also includes Discussion Questions that can serve as a method of assessment or a way to start conversation about the relevant themes and topics.

References

American Marketing Association. (2009). Branding definition. Retrieved from https://www.ama.org/resources/Pages/Dictionary.aspx

Audi, R. (2009). *Business ethics and ethical business.* New York, NY: Oxford University Press.

Boatright, J. R., & Smith, J. D. (2017). *Ethics and the conduct of business* (8th ed.). Boston, MA: Pearson.

Holt, D. B. (2003, March 11). What becomes an icon most? *Harvard Business Review, 81,* 1–12.

Keller, K. L., & Sood, S. (2003). Brand equity dilution. *MIT Sloan Management Review, 45,* 12–15.

Kellogg School of Management. (2010, May 23–26). *Kellogg on branding: Creating, building, and rejuvenating your brand, Kellogg School of Management's executive course on branding.* Evanston, IL: Northwestern University.

Kotler, P., & Keller, K. L. (2009). *Marketing management* (4th ed). Upper Saddle River, NJ: Pearson Prentice-Hall.

Stanwick, P. A., & Stanwick, S. D. (2009). *Understanding business ethics.* Upper Saddle River, NJ: Pearson Prentice Hall.

Tybout, A. M., & Calkins, T. (2005). *Kellogg on branding* (1st ed). Hoboken, NJ: John Wiley & Sons.

Velasquez, M. C. (2012). *Business ethics: Concepts and cases* (7th ed.). Boston, MA: Pearson.

Acknowledgements

The editors would like to acknowledge with gratitude the patience of our families, the dedication of each of the contributing authors, and the great support for this project of Brianna Ascher, Mary Del Plato, and the whole Routledge team.

1 Older Adults, Aggressive Marketing, and Unethical Behavior
A Sure Road to Financial Fraud?

Ya'akov M. Bayer

Introduction

Telemarketing is a method of direct marketing and sales by telephone. Although many of the telephone calls are legitimate sales, telemarketing fraud has become a common phenomenon in recent years (Johnson, 2003).[1] Although estimates indicate that fraudulent telemarketing does enormous damage, relatively little empirical research has focused exclusively on deceitful telephone sales in recent years. With the rise of online commerce, the attention of many researchers moved from telemarketing to online fraud, but recent studies have shown that large-scale telemarketing scams continue to be significant (Policastro & Payne, 2015). According to the National Consumers League (2014), 36% of the complaints about fraud in the USA in 2013 concerned telephone transactions.

Economic scams affect many groups in the population, but studies show that older people are more likely to be targets of deception, theft, fraud, and consumer scams (Sanger, 1999; Hines, 2001; Titus & Gover, 2001; Hafemeister, 2002; Johnson, 2003; Klaus, 2005). Estimates of the scope of exploitation of the elderly point to enormous sums. In one estimate in the USA alone, the damage from economic exploitation and deception of elderly people, by all means, was $2.9 billion per year (MetLife Mature Market Institute, 2011). It is reasonable to assume the proportion of elderly people suffering fraud is even higher than the estimate because seniors are less likely to report fraud than younger people (Pak & Shadel, 2011). The injury elderly people suffer in cases of fraud also may be more severe than that of younger victims because they likely have less time and opportunity to recoup the loss. Losing the money that they saved for their later years represents serious harm, and many remain financially disadvantaged (Dessin, 2000; Jackson & Hafemeister, 2011; Smith, 1999). According to Smith (1999), the psychological and emotional impact of fraud is more severe in the elderly than in young people. In many cases, falling for a deception damages their self-image, independence, and self-confidence (Choi, Kulick, & Mayer, 1999) and sometimes leads to genuine mental distress (Deem, 2000).

The issue of fraud and how the elderly cope with it is increasingly important in light of the accelerated growth of the elderly population, increasing life expectancy in Western society (Kinsella & Velkoff, 2001), and forecasts that economic fraud against the elderly is likely to increase because of both population growth and the substantial capital a large segment of the older population hold (Wasik, 2000). On occasion, the fact that fraudulent telemarketers target senior citizens, and the harm this causes, enters the public's awareness. Some Western countries have taken initiatives to combat the phenomenon with both legislation and public relations campaigns (AARP, 2003; Aziz, Bolick, Kleinman, & Shadel, 2000; Mears, Reisig, Scaggs, & Holtfrete, 2016). However, despite its importance and great awareness of the subject, few studies have focused on factors that make seniors more vulnerable to telemarketing fraud (Sykes & Matza, 1957; Dessin, 2000; Payne & Strasser, 2012). This chapter provides an overview of telemarketing fraud and attempts to trace the main reasons that may make the elderly a preferred target of fraud.

Telemarketing

The System and Its Characteristics

Technological advances in recent decades have brought about a real revolution in the economic behavior of markets for goods and services. The changes in the field of communications and the ability to transfer money electronically have created a reality in which significant economic activity is carried out remotely, by telephone or via the Internet. Many companies use call centers to market their goods and services, and this method has become popular in most areas of commerce. However, in a remote, computerized world in which it is possible to create fictitious identities and transfer funds between distant individuals and companies, innovation has generated many possibilities for abusing these mechanisms (Stephens, 2002). Within this remote, alienated framework, interpersonal relationships, and the resultant ability to identify the true intentions of the other side have reduced greatly. The exploitation of psychological weaknesses, biases, or information gaps has become an integral part of marketing processes for goods and services. Faced with an opportunity to rake in a large profit, even by exploiting human weaknesses and biases, a company usually will act to realize those

---

Check Your Understanding

Telemarketing

Telemarketing is a method for the direct marketing and selling of products and services by telephone, in which agents call potential customers, on their home or cellular phone, and offer them a product or service.

profits.[2] In many cases, those that do not are unsuccessful in competitive markets and fail to survive overtime (Akerlof & Shiller, 2015). Thus, the free market, as a whole, rewards the exploitation of human weaknesses and biases for selling products and services.

In this reality, in which emotional manipulation and psychological tactics that exploit the consumer's impulses, weaknesses, and emotions are an accepted norm, the boundary between fraud and seemingly legitimate sale tactics is sometimes blurred. In the absence of clear and effective regulation, the shift from legitimate marketing to exploiting and deceiving weak populations can depend on how carefully organizations maintain ethical standards, how they interpret these rules, and how managers and employees apply them. Companies that engage in legitimate commerce may engage in illegal activities, aggressive marketing, deception, and even customer fraud. In some cases, organizations begin as legitimate businesses and later begin operating fraudulently (Van Raaij, 2016).

Fraudulent Companies' Use of Telemarketing: "Maximizing Profits" without Ethical Boundaries

Fraudulent companies are companies whose *modus operandi* is based on deception, exploitation, and institutionalized manipulation designed to collect money from their victims. The frauds include a wide variety of methods and misrepresentations, some selling a product and other not (Titus, 2001). Fraudulent organizations often operate in the same manner as other telemarketing organizations (Doocey et al., 2001) Many have the characteristics of a formal, organized company with departments, sales targets, administrative hierarchy, and orderly salary payments (Shover, Coffey, & Sanders, 2004). Employees of these organizations usually begin as salespeople with wages based on a set percentage of their sales. A group of salespeople works intensively making telephone calls to potential customers in an effort to make sales. The quantity and size of the transactions employees close are a major variable in determining their salary and promotion to higher positions (Shover, Coffey, & Hobbs, 2003; Shover et al., 2004). Fraudulent companies are in constant danger of closing and ceasing operations due to law enforcement activity. This causes occupational instability for their employees and is a further incentive for them to maximize the deceit to the extent possible, as long as the company exists and the employee has employment.

The many phone calls – from lists and at a distance, without direct, unmediated interaction – are an important component of the mechanism that facilitates scams by countenancing estrangement, emotional detachment, and impersonality of the victim who can be transformed into a "target" and part of the "job." The victim becomes just "another line on the list," without identity or reality. This makes it possible for salespeople to push aside any emotional burden and pangs of guilt they might have, and it supports a structured process of fraud. Companies and employees attempt to normalize the deception while deriving their self-legitimization from the normative mechanisms of competition that have made exploiting weakness, psychological manipulation, and information gaps integral parts of everyday commerce and blame the victims for the success of the fraud due to their stupidity, greed, or incompetence (Shover et al., 2004).

These work environments blur the ethical moral boundaries of the salespeople. These distortions are not exclusive to fraudulent companies, and some of them may exist in legitimate companies, whose representatives also may be defrauding customers.

Fraudulent companies often use sophisticated methods and set a very wide range of "traps" for customers, making it likely that all potential customers will encounter attempts at fraud and possibly become victims. Because telemarketers understand that some populations are easier to deceive, and present greater chances to turn a significant profit with a lower risk of being caught, many fraudulent companies use "phishing" methods to locate "preferred" victims of fraud. Companies build or buy consumer information lists that include data on potential customers such as income, vulnerabilities, compulsive consumption, interest in marketers' inquiries, success of previous frauds, and people susceptible to fraud for various reasons (Aziz et al., 2000; Gross, 1999; Shover et al., 2004). They then construct manipulative mechanisms and fraudulent methods that are adapted to the weaknesses of the target population along with presentations of appropriate information deliberately designed to mislead and exploit weaknesses (Doocey et al., 2001).

In light of the above, it is more likely that populations with vulnerabilities or characteristics that swindlers can exploit will suffer harm, and there is a greater chance that significant damage will result from the fraud. The elderly are a prominent group within the wide range of target populations that fraudulent firms prefer (Hafemeister, 2002; Hines, 2001; Johnson, 2003; Klaus, 2005).

Using Telemarketing to Defraud the Elderly

Group Characteristics of the Elderly

The age that defines a person as "elderly" varies according to the context, for example, retirement or defining the services provided to the population, etc. Researchers believe there is indeed a great deal of variation in age-related processes of change that affect various areas of functioning among different populations of the elderly. These processes occur in varying intensities and at different times, and definitions must account for this heterogeneity (Nelson & Dannefer, 1992). The definitions in studies dealing with economic fraud also vary, but most of them focus on age 60 and older.

The elderly population suffers from stereotypical views that completely encompass all individuals of advanced age, with the assumption they have lost their functional abilities, are weak, and are senile, lacking skills, outdated in their thinking, and unfit to function properly. As a result, the elderly are not treated according to their personal situation, abilities, or characteristics but are collectively, comprehensively cataloged without reference to their particular traits (Doron, 2013). This phenomenon is "ageism" and is common in many societies.

The Problem of Defrauding the Elderly through Telemarketing

Of all the populations that fraudulent companies pursue, the elderly are a preferred target (DeLiema, Deevy, Lusardi, & Mitchell, 2017). According to the American Association of Retired Persons (AARP) (1999), 56% of the potential victims targeted by fraudulent companies were aged 50 and over. According to the Federal Bureau of Investigations (FBI), 80% of fraudulent telemarketing companies focus on defrauding elderly people (Lee & Geistfeld, 1999). The ageist perception of the elderly as weak and incompetent leads to them receiving frequent calls in the belief that the chances of successfully deceiving them is higher than those for other populations; in the eyes of fraudulent companies, they are "easy prey" (Friedman, 1992; Smith, 1999; Dymek, Atchison, Harrell, & Marson, 2001). In addition, swindlers tend to think older people are more likely to own their home, have savings plans, assets, and good credit ratings. Therefore, they assume they will be able to reap higher profits from their fraud (DeLiema et al., 2017; Friedman, 1992; Hough, 2004; Simross, 1994). In many cases, they construct claims to "justify" deception of the elderly, for example, asserting the elderly have no future, so they do not need the money, what they already have ought to be sufficient, that elders have excessive amounts savings, and so on (Shover et al., 2003). In this way, regardless of the vulnerabilities some elderly people do have and that are exploited, just belonging to this group increases their chances of becoming a target of fraud, which in turn increase the odds of them being victims of fraud. In many cases, the "phishing" lists of fraudulent companies include not only age but also a wide cross-section of traits that make a person more likely to become a "successful" victim. Companies share lists of "fraud-prone" older people, and once one company has identified an elderly person, his or her details become a kind of "asset" that swindlers pass around the market (Shover et al., 2003).

Studies show there is no single profile of elderly people who fall victim to fraud. This is partly because swindlers adapt the fraudulent methods, tricks, and deceits to the target audience of the particular scam and vary accordingly. Therefore, individuals who succumb to one type of fraud have different traits from those who succumb to another type (Pak & Shadel, 2011). This makes it difficult to fight the phenomenon and to identify the elderly people who are prone to fraud.

The personal and social processes that sometimes accompany aging do make some elderly people more likely to become victims of fraud. Although these characteristics are common among elderly people, they are not unique to the elderly, and any person with these traits might become a preferred target for fraud. For example, loneliness and cognitive impairment, the topic of the next section, also can occur in younger populations, where they have similar implications as those in contexts of aging.

Telemarketing Fraud and Processes that Accompany Aging

Telephone Accessibility: Loneliness and Trust

Check Your Understanding

Loneliness

Loneliness is a social-emotional state that expresses a lack of belonging, distance from people or a human environment, and often a strong yearning for connection with others. The feeling of loneliness does not require a person to be alone, but may be the result of a life without satisfying social relationships.

Fraudulent telemarketing requires communication between the victim and the swindler. Answering the telephone and being willing to talk to the telemarketer helps "open the door" for the swindlers, and is a necessary condition for fraud. According to Lee and Geistfeld (1999), elderly people tend to answer telemarketing calls and are more willing to listen to telemarketers than young people. Many studies consider loneliness and social isolation the main cause of elderly people's openness to telephone conversations in general and telemarketers in particular, thereby increasing their chances of conversing with a swindler (Alves & Wilson, 2008; Cross, 2016; Kang & Ridgway, 1996). Older people living alone are more likely to be victims of economic fraud; social isolation and a sense of loneliness correlate with a greater chance of being victims of fraud (Choi, Kulick, & Mayer, 1999; Podnieks, 1993).

A feeling of loneliness is a common phenomenon in old age, and studies have found a connection between aging and loneliness, a phenomenon extremely common at very advanced ages (Pinquart & Sorensen, 2001). Explanations for the solitude older people experience include, *inter alia*, the social and physical changes they often experience. Life events that accompany aging such as retirement, physical and functional deterioration, widowhood, physical disability, and the death of family members or close friends all can contribute to the sense of loneliness and social isolation (Lichtenberg, Stickney, & Paulson, 2013). Social isolation makes people feel disconnected from peers and other support systems, increasing the likelihood that they will respond to telemarketers who give them time and attention (Friedman, 1992; Kang & Ridgway, 1996). In many cases, elderly people who lack ordinary social connections, such as family and friends, use social contact with marketers, salespeople, and other commercial contacts as substitute relationships (Kang & Ridgway, 1996). Thus, loneliness and social isolation may impair the quality of elderly people's decision-making, and make it possible for swindlers to exploit their social needs in order to defraud them (Lee & Soberon-Ferrer, 1997).

> **Check Your Understanding**
>
> *Social Isolation*
>
> *Social isolation* is a state of little or no interaction between a person and his or her social environment.

Social isolation sometimes contributes to the success of fraud by creating information gaps. According to Lee and Soberon-Ferrer (1997), social relationships provide senior citizens not only with communal support but also with sources of information about products and services that might protect them from consumer fraud. When it is difficult to obtain information from sources accessible by computer or smartphone, social connections may be the main source of information.

The literature maintains that "opening of the door" to telemarketers is sometimes connected to additional factors, including as attributing importance to phone calls, politeness, and the difficulty of ending conversations with telemarketers (Simross, 1994). Moreover, older people have more leisure time than young people (Werner, 1997). Some researchers also claim that older people tend to be more trusting of people, and this applies to salespeople as well (Hough, 2004; Simross, 1994). Therefore, many seniors are willing to be more trusting of others and approach marketers' offers naively, which helps make them easy targets for telemarketing scams (Hough, 2004).

The Elderly, Decision-Making, and Declining Cognitive Abilities

In order to avoid telemarketing fraud, the customer must be able to understand the information received, remember details of the offer, process vital information, retrieve relevant information, ask appropriate questions, integrate the information, and evaluate what is being offered. Individuals with limited cognitive abilities may fail in some or all parts of this process, have difficulty in dealing with the information to which they are exposed during consumer activities, and thus be more vulnerable to consumer fraud. Although low cognitive abilities are often a key factor facilitating fraud (Lee & Geistfeld, 1999; Lord & Kim, 1995; Lee & Soberon-Ferrer, 1997), few empirical studies focus on the relationship between cognitive decline and telemarketing fraud in general, or on the elderly in particular.

Although many seniors maintain good cognitive functioning until a very advanced age (Hedden & Gabrieli, 2004), the cognitive decline that sometimes accompanies aging can affect the quality of older people's economic decision-making and increase their chance of being deceived. Cognitive decline includes a wide range of symptoms associated with the aging process, such as impaired executive cognitive abilities (Grieve, Williams, Paul, Clark, & Gordon, 2007; Lamar, Zonderman, & Resnick, 2002), forgetfulness, lower ability to maintain concentration and focus, decline in problem-solving abilities (Allen, Bruss, Brown, & Damasio, 2005; Fotenos, Snyder, Girton, Morris, & Buckner, 2005), changes in the ability to perform familiar tasks, difficulties in learning new tasks and skills, damage to reality testing, and difficulty in spatial and temporal orientation or the anxieties about losing them (Bosworth, Schaie, & Willis, 1999; McNeal et al., 2001; Ofstedal, Zimmer, & Lin, 1999; Rahkonen et al., 2001). Elderly people, especially the oldest-old (aged 75 and over), often suffer from irreversible loss of sensory function, such as vision and hearing, slow functioning of the central nervous system, and a decrease in memory functions (Hultsch, Hertzog, & Dixon, 1990). Older adults also have deficiencies in various tasks requiring cued recall memory and associative memory (Kausler, 1994; Chalfonte & Johnson, 1996; Naveh-Benjamin, 2000; Castel, 2005).

Studies show the cognitive decline that accompanies the aging process often leads to poor decision-making (Band, Ridderinkhof, & Segalowitz, 2002). The decline in executive functions, a key factor in decision-making, negatively affects the quality of decision-making (Raz, Gunning-Dixon, Head, Dupuis, & Acker, 1998; West, 1996) and the ability to perform mathematical operations (Bull & Scerif, 2001; Van der Ven, Kroesbergen, Boom, & Leseman, 2012). Working memory capacity determines performance on both ordinary calculations and more complex mathematical processes done in writing (Geary, 1993). These cognitive impairments and their impact on the quality of decision-making also may be detrimental to activities essential for proper economic conduct, such as valuation of products, retrieval of comparative prices, speed of information processing, and weighting data, which are critical for coping with complex consumer decisions. Lusardi, Mitchell, and Curto (2014) found older individuals generally, and especially those aged 75 and older, are less able to cope with economic sophistication and failed to make good economic choices in asset valuation, financial risk assessment, investment selection, and tariff assessment. Fraudsters are aware of these weaknesses and construct their scams to take advantage of the cognitive weaknesses some elderly people experience.

Studies show that executive functions are a limited resource and that prolonged use reduces their quality and, therefore, the quality of economic decisions (Bayer & Osher, 2018; Bayer, Ruffle, Zultan, & Dwolatzky, 2018). Long, persuasive conversations that include many details make it difficult for some elderly people to concentrate, remember, process information, and deal with the telemarketers' offers. The embarrassment that sometimes accompanies having difficulty understanding a transaction or remembering details also may contribute to an elderly person's acquiescence and the success of the fraud. In this context, swindlers sometimes also use deliberate deceptions to take advantage of memory deficits and some elderly people's reticence to internalize that they do not remember well or remember some things incorrectly (Jacoby, Bishara, Hessels, & Toth, 2005).

Check Your Understanding

Executive Functions

Executive functions are responsible for the regulation, integration, transformation, and design of a wide range of cognitive resources while these are in use. Executive functions are not expressed in individual behaviors but in a wide range of functions. The quality of a person's executive functions significantly affects his problem-solving and decision-making abilities.

The traits in this description intensified when elderly people suffer from disease that impairs their cognitive abilities, or discretion, or both, and increases their vulnerability to consumer fraud. In addition, illness also may affect the preferences and behavior of elderly people. Bayer, Ruffle et al. (2018) show the morbidity of mild cognitive impairment (MCI) in the elderly may lead to a change in consumption habits. Their study further shows that MCI correlates with taking more financial risks, a factor the literature described as influencing the possibility of being a victim of economic exploitation (Holtfreter, Reisig, & Pratt, 2008; Peterson et al., 2014; Wood, Liu, Hanoch, & Estevez-Cores, 2016). A poor emotional state also may be a point of exploitation for fraud; sometimes, elderly people are targeted deliberately when they are emotionally vulnerable. For example, many elderly people suffer from depression (Barcelos-Ferreira, Nakano, Steffens, & Bottino, 2013), which the literature shows may influence the quality of their economic decisions (Bayer, Shtudiner, Suhorukov, & Grisaru, 2018; Harlé, Allen, & Sanfey, 2010).

The disease severely affecting cognitive abilities, as in people with dementia and Alzheimer's disease, reinforces this situation. In light of the increase in life expectancy, and the growing number of elderly people, in the last few decades, there has been a rapid increase in the number of elderly people suffering from these diseases (Hebert, Scherr, Bienias, Bennett, & Evans, 2003). The onset of Alzheimer's dementia is usually an impairment of memory and the ability to learn new information. Over time, there is extreme deterioration of other cognitive abilities, including the ability to concentrate, plan, and solve problems, draw conclusions, reason, communicate with others, exercise judgment, or orient themselves in space (Burns & Iliffe, 2009). At those stages of the disease when the elderly person still can function and communicate on the requisite level, swindlers may exploit the situation fraudulently.

Behavior After and During Fraud: Failure to Report and Underestimating the Phenomenon's Severity

Despite telemarketing scams' prevalence and the damage they cause, society and academic literature pay little attention to this form of exploiting the elderly. In many cases, society does not treat the problem of defrauding the elderly as a serious problem, and sometimes society and the authorities even attribute a degree of guilt to the victim (Gross, 1999; Shichor, Sechrest, & Doocy, 2001). Authorities often treat it as less severe than violent crimes (Deem, Murray, Gaboury, & Edmunds, 2002).

Many elderly people who have been defrauded do not tell their families or report to enforcement agencies (Deem, 2000; Friedman, 1992; Johnson, 2003; Lee & Geistfeld, 1999; Wasik, 2000), which means the exact scope of the phenomenon and resultant damages is unknown. Studies have found that older individuals are more likely to be unsure about the legality of salespeople's business practices than the rest of the population and, therefore, tend not to report or identify frauds (AARP, 1996). Even in cases when it is clear to an older person that they have been defraud, many tend not to file a report because of the shame, embarrassment, and humiliation they feel because they were deceived and "fell into a trap." Many seniors say they feel "stupid" and are embarrassed by the fact that they believed the swindlers. Sometimes, they are afraid to report scams they suffered for fear of stigmatization and labeling. This feeling sometimes links to their age, and a feeling that previously "it would not have happened to me," which intensifies the feeling of loss that accompanies old age. Sometimes, elderly people worry that if they tell their family, the family will think they are unable to manage their financial affairs independently, a concern accompanied by fear of deterioration in their situation following the discovery (e.g., being moved to nursing home). Social isolation, limited access to enforcement agencies, mobility problems, communications issues, and the feeling that the complaint will not be handled also contribute to the fact that the elderly fail to report fraud (Crown Prosecution Service, 2013).

Economic scams of this type often do not raise immediate warning signs in the elderly person's environment, which makes it difficult for family members or the social environment to identify them. Many elderly people will report a fraud only after they no longer can face the harassment or when after the economic damage is large and the burden becomes unbearable, which makes it difficult to identify and stop the fraud when it is still possible to minimize the damage. If telemarketing fraud continues and involves scams that dilute the elderly person's financial resources over time, rather than immediately, relatives or others will find it difficult to detect unusual activity or identify it as fraud (Quinn & Tomita, 1997). If fraud is not reported and is difficult to detect in early stage, the damage may be on-going and substantial. The delay impedes locating and punishing offenders. Fraudulent companies are aware that offences against the elderly are reported less frequently, and of the fact that elderly people sometimes find it difficult to remember details about the swindler or provide investigators with sufficiently detailed information if the matter does reach the authorities. These factors reduce the risk they take when defrauding elderly people.

Discussion and Conclusions

Is Aggressive Marketing to the Elderly a Sure Path to Financial Fraud?

In a reality in which skilled, sophisticated swindlers are a telephone call away from their victims, fraud becomes a risk that hangs over the heads of all consumers. From a stereotypical perspective that considers older people "easy prey," many swindlers prefer to focus on scams that target the elderly in general, and the frail elderly in particular. For some elderly people, traits associated with old age may make it easier for fraudulent companies to commit fraud, while being more likely to avoid punishment, and be able to continue operating.

Is every encounter between an elderly person and a fraudulent company a sure path to victimizing the elderly person victim? The answer is definitely "No." Many elderly people function independently and know how to deal with swindlers who try to deceive them. However, the encounter between fraudulent companies and certain elderly people may indeed entail a high risk of economic and psychological harm. How do you differentiate between these? The lack of in-depth studies examining the relationship between old age and its characteristics, and telemarketing scams and their characteristics, makes it difficult to make this distinction and develop effective tools for identifying those older people who are at greater risk. There are senior citizens who live independent lives and do not suffer from illness, extreme cognitive decline, or loneliness and social isolation. It can be difficult to distinguish between these people, who can deal with swindlers and avoid being defrauded, and those elderly people for whom any encounter is a sure recipe for becoming a victim of significant fraud. This makes it challenging for individuals or agencies to intervene without harming the independence of the elderly. Therefore, research that might provide tools for early detection of potential victims and individualized preventive measures would make an important contribution to reducing the scourge of fraud that targets the elderly.

In the absence of effective tools for pinpointing the individuals who are prone to fraud, broad policy measures sometimes protect all elderly people from contact with telemarketing companies, such as "do not call" lists that block elderly people's phone numbers from telemarketers, or having family members, support services, or other agencies involved in the management of elderly people's financial affairs. These methods are fraught with dilemmas about their legitimacy and how best to prevent fraud of the elderly. On one hand, access to telemarketing facilitates and enables exploitation of the elderly, but on the other hand, telemarketing does help many elderly people access services and products, and allows them contact with companies, without making the effort required to leave the house. Preferably, elderly people should be able to choose between these options themselves. A broad generalization that keeps elderly people from purchasing over the telephone prevents them from managing their money independently and privately. Any measure that does not also limit other populations may result in age discrimination, impairment of elderly people's autonomy, and their right to manage their lives independently. The desire to protect senior citizens from fraud and exploitation must be in balance with maintaining their independence and dignity, taking their wishes into account, even if this sometimes involves certain risks. Attempts to help the elderly easily can undermine the basic right of every person to make their own decisions, even if at times they may appear to other people as bad decisions.

Many countries are fighting the phenomenon of fraud targeting the elderly through legislation that allows them to change their decision after being given sufficient time to reconsider and consult with others. These arrangements give people over a certain age a longer period to reassess and cancel telephone transactions than younger people. These methods, assuming they do not cause the deprivation of the elderly person and exclusion from certain products, are a positive step because a large share of the fraud is the result of manipulations and situations that disrupt the elderly person's ability to make informed decisions at a given moment. Granting seniors additional time for calm deliberation gives them the opportunity to reconsider. However, these initiatives often are too complex for some consumers, and it seems highly sophisticated swindlers will find ways to overcome these barriers.

Several countries are trying to combat elder fraud by holding the parties involved in the payment – that is, the banks and credit card companies – responsible and requiring them to give refunds in cases in which they likely could have identified irregular transactions and thereby prevent the fraud. The possibility of financial impact on these intermediaries could lead to their greater involvement, attention, and sensitivity, thereby helping to reduce and detect fraud.

Finally, people should remember that despite the ugliness and wide-spread distribution of this phenomenon, the majority of society rejects and condemns such behavior toward the elderly. Therefore, it is important to develop awareness of possible fraud among the elderly, their families, support agencies, authorities, financial institutions, and institutions that provide services to the elderly and the general population, which may help to identify and reduce this ugly phenomenon.

Discussion Questions

1   Is it legitimate to approach lonely or socially isolated individuals and use their need for social interaction to sell products?
2   Where is the boundary for legitimate and illegitimate use of consumers' impulses, weaknesses, and cognitive biases?
3   Do you believe that, in order to combat the phenomenon of telemarketing fraud, it is necessary to reduce the access of the elderly to telemarketers, even at the cost of harming their independence?

To Cite This Chapter

Bayer, Y. M. (2018). Older adults, aggressive marketing, and unethical behavior: A sure road to financial fraud? In H. Gringarten, & R. Fernández-Calienes (Eds.). *Ethical branding and marketing: Cases and lessons* (pp. 1–18). Routledge Management and Business Studies Series. London and New York: Routledge.

Acknowledgements

The author is grateful to Professor Zeev Kaplan, Dr. Zeev Shtudiner, and Ms. Moria Malka-Siso for their assistance and the wise comments that contributed to the writing of this chapter.

Notes

1 Some recent studies do not differentiate between telemarketing fraud and other types of fraud (e.g., online scams, etc.), making it difficult to pinpoint the extent of this phenomenon alone. Anderson (2013) estimated that in 2011, close to 11% of all people in the USA were victims of some type of financial fraud. Doocey, Shichor, Sechrest, and Geis (2001) estimate the annual loss from telemarketing fraud in the USA is about $40 billion.
2 Akerlof and Shiller (2015) consider this process as "the phishing equilibrium."

References

AARP: American Association of Retired Persons. (1996). *Telemarketing fraud victimization of older Americans*. Washington, DC: AARP Foundation.

AARP: American Association of Retired Persons. (1999). *Facts about fraudulent telemarketing*. Washington, DC: AARP Foundation.

AARP: American Association of Retired Persons. (2003). *Off the hook: Reducing participation in telemarketing fraud*. Washington, DC: AARP Foundation.

Akerlof, G. A., & Shiller, R. J. (2015). *Phishing for phools: The economics of manipulation and deception*. Princeton, NJ: Princeton University Press.

Allen, J. S., Bruss, J., Brown, C. K., & Damasio, H. (2005). Normal neuro-anatomical variation due to age: The major lobes and a parcellation of the temporal region. *Neurobiology of Aging, 26*(9), 1245–1260.

Alves, L. M., & Wilson, S. R. (2008). The effects of loneliness on telemarketing fraud vulnerability among older adults. *Journal of Elder Abuse & Neglect, 20*(1), 63–85.

Anderson, K. B. (2013). *Consumer fraud in the United States, 2011: The third FTC survey*. Washington, DC: Federal Trade Commission.

Aziz, S. J., Bolick, D. C., Kleinman, M. T., & Shadel, D. P. (2000). The national telemarketing victim call center: Combating telemarketing fraud in the United States. *Journal of Elder Abuse & Neglect, 12*(2), 93–98. doi:10.1300/J084v12n02-10

Band, G. P., Ridderinkhof, K. R., & Segalowitz, S. (2002). Explaining neuro-cognitive aging: Is one factor enough? *Brain and Cognition, 49*(3), 259–267.

Barcelos-Ferreira, R., Nakano, E. Y., Steffens, D. C., & Bottino, C. M. (2013). Quality of life and physical activity associated to lower prevalence of depression in community-dwelling elderly subjects from Sao Paulo. *Journal of Affective Disorders, 150*, 616–622.

Bayer, Y. M., & Osher, Y. (2018). Time preference, executive functions, and ego-depletion: An exploratory study. *Journal of Neuroscience, Psychology, and Economics, 11*(3), 127–134.

Bayer, Y. M., Ruffle, B. J., Zultan, R., & Dwolatzky, T. (2018). Time preferences of older people with mild cognitive impairment. doi:10.2139/ssrn.3183366

Bayer, Y. M., Shtudiner, Z., Suhorukov, O., & and Grisaru, N. (2018). Time and risk preferences, and consumption decisions of patients with clinical depression. Available at doi:10.2139/ssrn.3217632

Bosworth, H. B., Schaie, K. W., & Willis, S. L. (1999). Cognitive and sociodemographic risk factors for mortality in the Seattle Longitudinal Study. *The Journals of Gerontology Series B: Psychological Sciences and Social Sciences, 54*(5), P273–P282.

Bull, R., & Scerif, G. (2001). Executive functioning as a predictor of children's mathematics ability: Inhibition, switching, and working memory. *Developmental Neuropsychology, 19*(3), 273–293.

Burns, A., & Iliffe, S. (2009). Alzheimer's disease. *The BMJ, 338*, b158.

Castel, A. D. (2005). Memory for grocery prices in younger and older adults: The role of schematic support. *Psychology and Aging, 20*(4), 718.

Chalfonte, B. L., & Johnson, M. K. (1996). Feature memory and binding in young and older adults. *Memory & Cognition, 24*, 403–416.

Choi, N. G., Kulick, D. B., & Mayer, J. (1999). Financial exploitation of elders: Analysis of risk factors based on county adult protective services data. *Journal of Elder Abuse & Neglect, 10*(3–4), 39–62.

Cross, C. (2016). "They're very lonely": Understanding the fraud victimization of seniors. *International Journal for Crime, Justice, and Social Democracy, 5*(4), 60–75. Available at SSRN: https://ssrn.com/abstract=2924927

Crown Prosecution Service. (2013, December 12). *Crimes against older people – Prosecution policy*. Updated, 25–26.

Deem, D., Murray, M., Gaboury, M., & Edmunds, C. (2002). *2002 Victim Assistance Academy textbook*. Washington, DC: United States Department of Justice.

Deem, D. L. (2000). Notes from the field: Observations in working with forgotten victims of personal financial crimes. *Journal of Elder Abuse & Neglect*, *12*(2), 33–48.

DeLiema, M., Deevy, M., Lusardi, A., & Mitchell, O. S. (2017). *Exploring the risks and consequences of elder fraud victimization: Evidence from the health and retirement study*. Working Paper, WP 2017–374. Ann Arbor, MI: University of Michigan Retirement Research Center. Retrieved from http://mrrc.isr.umich.edu/wp374/

Dessin, C. L. (2000). Financial abuse of the elderly. *Idaho Law Review*, *36*(2), 203–226.

Doocey, J. H., Shichor, D., Sechrest, D. K., & Geis, G. (2001). Telemarketing fraud: Who are the tricksters and what makes them trick? *Security Journal*, *14*(3), 7–26.

Doron, Y. (2013). *Ageism in Israeli society: The social construction of old age*. Jerusalem, Israel: Van Leer Institute/Hakibbutz Hameuchad Publishing House. [Hebrew].

Dymek, M., Atchison, P., Harrell, L., & Marson, D. C. (2001). Competency to consent to medical treatment in cognitively impaired patients with Parkinson's disease. *Neurology*, *56*, 17–24.

Fotenos, A. F., Snyder, A. Z., Girton, L. E., Morris, J. C., & Buckner, R. L. (2005). Normative estimates of cross-sectional and longitudinal brain volume decline in aging and AD. *Neurology*, *64*(6), 1032–1039.

Friedman, M. (1992). Confidence swindles of older consumers. *The Journal of Consumer Affairs*, *26*(1), 20–46.

Geary, D. C. (1993). Mathematical disabilities: Cognitive, neuropsychological, and genetic components. *Psychological Bulletin*, *114*(2), 345.

Grieve, S., Williams, L., Paul, R., Clark, C., & Gordon, E. (2007). Cognitive aging, executive function, and fractional anisotropy: A diffusion tensor MR imaging study. *American Journal of Neuroradiology*, *28*(2), 226–235.

Gross, E. A. (1999). Elderly victims of telemarketing fraud: Demographic, social, and Psychological factors in victimization and willingness to report. *Dissertation Abstracts International*, *61*(09), 5054.

Hafemeister, T. L. (2002). Financial abuse of the elderly in domestic settings. In R. J. Bonnie & R. B. Wallace (Eds.), *Elder mistreatment: Abuse, neglect, and exploitation in an aging America* (pp. 382–445). Washington, DC: National Academies Press.

Harlé, K. M., Allen, J. J., & Sanfey, A. G. (2010). The impact of depression on social economic decision making. *Journal of Abnormal Psychology*, *119*(2), 440.

Hebert, L. E., Scherr, P. A., Bienias, J. L., Bennett, D. A., & Evans, D. A. (2003). Alzheimer disease in the US population prevalence estimates using the 2000 census. *Archives of Neurology*, *60*(8), 1119–1122. doi:10.1001/archneur.60.8.1119

Hedden, T., & Gabrieli, J. D. E. (2004). Insights into the ageing mind: A view from cognitive neuroscience. *Nature Reviews Neuroscience*, *5*, 87–96.

Hines, J. (2001). Telemarketing fraud upon the elderly: Minimizing its effects through legislation, law enforcement, and education. *Albany Law Journal of Science and Technology, 12*, 839.

Holtfreter, K., Reisig, M. D., & Pratt, T. C. (2008). Low self-control, routine activities, and fraud victimization. *Criminology, 46*, 189–220.

Hough, M. (2004). Exploring elder consumers' interactions with information technology. *Journal of Business & Economics Research, 2*(6), 61–66.

Hultsch, D. F., Hertzog, C., & Dixon, R. A. (1990). Ability correlates of memory performance in adulthood and aging. *Psychology and Aging, 5*(3), 356.

Jackson, S. L., & Hafemeister, T. L. (2011). Risk factors associated with elder abuse: The importance of differentiating by type of elder maltreatment. *Violence and Victims, 26*(6), 738.

Jacoby, L. L., Bishara, A. J., Hessels, S., & Toth, J. P. (2005). Aging, subjective experience, and cognitive control: Dramatic false remembering by older adults. *Journal of Experimental Psychology: General, 134*(2), 131–148.

Johnson, K. D. (2003). *Financial crimes against the elderly.* Washington, DC: United States Department of Justice.

Kang, Y. S., & Ridgway, N. M. (1996). The importance of consumer market interactions as a form of social support for elderly consumers. *Journal of Public Policy & Marketing, 15*(1), 108–117.

Kausler, D. H. (1994). *Learning and memory in normal aging.* New York, NY: Academic Press.

Kinsella, K., & Velkoff, V. (2001). *An aging world* [United States Census Bureau, Series P95/01–1]. Washington, DC: United States Government Printing Office.

Klaus, P. A. (2005). *Crimes against persons age 65 or older, 1993–2002.* Washington, DC: United States Department of Justice, Office of Justice Programs, Bureau of Justice Statistics.

Lamar, M., Zonderman, A. B., & Resnick, S. (2002). Contribution of specific cognitive processes to executive functioning in an aging population. *Neuropsychology, 16*(2), 156.

Lee, J., & Geistfeld, L. V. (1999). Elderly consumers' receptiveness to telemarketing fraud. *Journal of Public Policy and Marketing, 18*(2), 208–217.

Lee, J., & Soberon-Ferrer, H. (1997). Consumer vulnerability to fraud: Influencing factors. *The Journal of Consumer Affairs, 31*(1), 70–89.

Lichtenberg, P. A., Stickney, L., & Paulson D. (2013). Is psychological vulnerability related to the experience of fraud in older adults? *Clinical Gerontologist, 36*, 132–146.

Lord, K. R., & Kim, K. C. (1995). Inoculating consumers against deception: The influence of framing and executional style. *Journal of Consumer Policy, 18*(1), 1–23.

Lusardi, A., Mitchell, O. S., & Curto, V. (2014). Financial literacy and financial sophistication in the older population. *Journal of Pension Economics & Finance, 13*(4), 347–366.

McNeal, M. G., Zareparsi, S., Camicioli, R., Dame, A., Howieson, D., Quinn, J., … Payami, H. (2001). Predictors of healthy brain aging. *The Journals of Gerontology Series A: Biological Sciences and Medical Sciences, 56*(7), B294–B301.

Mears, D. P., Reisig, M. D., Scaggs, S., & Holtfreter, K. (2016). Efforts to reduce consumer fraud victimization among the elderly: The effect of information access on program awareness and contact. *Crime & Delinquency*, 62(9), 1235–1259.

MetLife Mature Market Institute. (2011). *The MetLife study of elder financial abuse: Crimes of occasion, desperation, and predation against America's elders*. New York, NY: MetLife Mature Market Institute. Retrieved from https://www.metlife.com/assets/cao/mmi/publications/studies/2011/mmi-elder-financial-abuse.pdf

National Consumers League. (2014). *Watchdog report: Scammers increasingly relying on internet-enabled phone technology to reach victims*. Retrieved from http://www.nclnet.org/newsroom/press-releases/878-watchdog-report-scammers-increasingly-relying-on-internet-enabled-phone-technology-to-reach-victims

Naveh-Benjamin, M. (2000). Adult age differences in memory performance: Tests of an associative deficit hypothesis. *Journal of Experimental Psychology: Learning, Memory, and Cognition*, 26, 1170–1187.

Nelson, E. A., & Dannefer, D. (1992). Aged heterogeneity: Fact or fiction? The fate of diversity in gerontological research. *The Gerontologist*, 32(1), 17–23.

Ofstedal, M. B., Zimmer, Z. S., & Lin, H. S. (1999). A comparison of correlates of cognitive functioning in older persons in Taiwan and the United States. *The Journals of Gerontology Series B: Psychological Sciences and Social Sciences*, 54(5), S291–S301.

Pak, K., & Shadel, D. (2011). *AARP Foundation national fraud victim study*. Washington, DC: AARP Foundation.

Payne, B. K., & Strasser, S. M. (2012). Financial exploitation of older persons in adult care settings: Comparisons to physical abuse and the justice system's response. *Journal of Elder Abuse & Neglect*, 24(3), 231–250. doi:10.1080/08946566.2011.653315

Peterson, J. C., Burnes, D. P. R., Caccamise, P. L., Mason, A., Henderson, C. R., Jr., Wells, M. T., & Lachs, M. S. (2014). Financial exploitation of older adults: A population based prevalence study. *Journal of General Internal Medicine*, 29, 1615–1623. doi:10.1007/s11606-014-2946-2

Pinquart, M., & Sorensen, S. (2001). Influence on loneliness in older adults: A metaanalysis. *Basic and Applied Social Psychology*, 23(4), 245–266.

Podnieks, E. (1993). National survey on abuse of the elderly in Canada. *Journal of Elder Abuse & Neglect*, 4(1–2), 5–58.

Policastro, C., & Payne, B. K. (2015). Can you hear me now? Telemarketing fraud victimization and lifestyles. *American Journal of Criminal Justice*, 40(3), 620–638.

Quinn, M. J., & Tomita, S. K. (1997). *Elder abuse and neglect: Causes, diagnosis, and interventional strategies* (Vol. 8). New York, NY: Springer Publishing Company.

Rahkonen, T., Eloniemi-Sulkava, U., Halonen, P., Verkkoniemi, A., Niinistö, L., Notkola, I. L., & Sulkava, R. (2001). Delirium in the non-demented oldest old in the general population: Risk factors and prognosis. *International Journal of Geriatric Psychiatry*, 16(4), 415–421.

Raz, N., Gunning-Dixon, F. M., Head, D., Dupuis, J. H., & Acker, J. D. (1998). Neuroanatomical correlates of cognitive aging: Evidence from structural magnetic resonance imaging. *Neuropsychology*, 12(1), 95.

Sanger, D. (1999). Confessions of a phone-scam artist. *Saturday Night, 114*, 86–98.

18   Ya'akov M. Bayer

Shichor, D., Sechrest, D., & Doocy, J. (2001). Victims of investment fraud. In H.
N. Pontell & D. Shichor (Eds.), *Contemporary issues in crime and criminal
justice: Essays in honour of Gilbert Geis* (pp. 81–96). Upper Saddle River,
NJ: Prentice Hall.
Shover, N. (1996). *Great pretenders: Pursuits and careers of persistent thieves.*
Boulder, CO: Westview.
Shover, N., Coffey, G. S., & Hobbs, D. (2003). Crime on the line: Telemarketing
and the changing nature of professional crime. *British Journal of Criminology, 43*(3), 489–505.
Shover, N., Coffey, G. S., & Sanders, C. R. (2004). Dialing for dollars: Opportunities, justifications, and telemarketing fraud. *Qualitative Sociology, 27*(1),
59–75.
Simross, L. (1994, August 12). Smooth operators: Crafty telephone crooks
are bilking Americans out of billions by promising deals too good to be
true. But if you know the scams, you can avoid being a victim. *Los Angeles Times.* Retrieved from http://articles.latimes.com/1994-08-12/news/
ls-26486_1_telemarketing-fraud
Smith, R. G. (1999). Fraud and financial abuse of older persons. *Current Issues
in Crime and Criminal Justice, 11*, 273.
Stephens, G. (2002). Crime in cyberspace. In B. Jacobs (Ed.), *Investigating de-
viance* (pp. 307–312). Los Angeles, CA: Roxbury.
Sykes, G., & Matza, D. (1957). Techniques of neutralization: A theory of delin-
quency. *American Sociological Review, 22*, 667–670.
Titus, R. M. (2001). Personal fraud and its victims. In N. Shover & J. P. Wright
(Eds.), *Crimes of privilege* (pp. 57–66). New York, NY: Oxford University
Press.
Titus, R. M., & Gover, A. R. (2001). Personal fraud: The victims and the scams.
Crime Prevention Studies, 12, 133–151.
Van der Ven, S. H., Kroesbergen, E. H., Boom, J., & Leseman, P. P. (2012). The
development of executive functions and early mathematics: A dynamic rela-
tionship. *British Journal of Educational Psychology, 82*(1), 100–119.
Van Raaij, W. F. (2016). *Understanding consumer financial behavior: Money
management in an age of financial illiteracy.* New York, NY: Palgrave
Macmillan.
Wasik, J. F. (2000). The fleecing of America's elderly. *Consumers Digest, 39*(2),
77–83.
Werner, E. (1997). Financial exploitation of the elderly by telemarketing fraud:
Related factors. *Masters Abstracts International, 35*(06), 1679.
West, R. L. (1996). An application of prefrontal cortex function theory to cog-
nitive aging. *Psychological Bulletin, 120*(2), 272.
Wood, S. A., Liu, P.-J., Hanoch, Y., & Estevez-Cores, S. (2016). Importance
of numeracy as a risk factor for elder financial exploitation in a community
sample. *The Journals of Gerontology Series B: Psychological Sciences and
Social Sciences, 71*, 978–986. doi:10.1093/geronb/gbv041

2 Twitter Me This

Fake News, Real Issues, and the Twitter Presidency

Thomas F. Brezenski

Introduction

Since he became president, Donald Trump has used Twitter more than 2,000 times, waxing eloquent in 280 characters or less on "Crooked Hillary," "Low IQ Crazy Mika," and a host of other issues ranging from the dismissive (a disinvite to a New Year's Eve party) to the deadly serious (a potential nuclear standoff with North Korea). Number 45 tweets so often that there are dual accounts, one for official business (@POTUS) and another for private musings (@realDonaldTrump). In all likelihood, Mr. Trump will be the first US president to have a separate section in his presidential library dedicated solely to his tweets and use of social media.

There is no doubt this is an historic presidency in terms of its transparency and immediacy. It is the presidency of the second wave of Millennials who define and shape the world of social media. No longer do traditional major TV or cable news networks wield the powers of news making and agenda setting. Twitter, Instagram, Snapchat, YouTube, and Facebook have infiltrated the journalistic battlefield and are there to stay. The oligarchies of the major media outlets in the context of what we as news consumers have access to have gone the way of the Roman Empire. President Trump is representative of this new wave of uncensored openness and new social media winning strategies.

The Branding Connection (or Disconnection)

There has been a litany of complaints about the president's use of his private Twitter account since he took office with most stating that, at the very least, it is not befitting of the president to have such a public presence outside of traditional settings such as White House news briefings. Following the Monica Lewinsky affair, President Bill Clinton stated that even presidents had the right to a private life. If so then maybe President Trump has the right to a public one. It is not as if 1600 Pennsylvania Avenue is an impenetrable lead box in terms of the private lives of the First Families. Since the age of television, presidents, First Ladies, and their children have had an impact on public preference and product perception. A classic example is in the world of US sports. Since the Gilded Age, baseball had been "America's Game" played as far back as during lulls in battle during the Civil War. Babe Ruth was as much an "American icon" as George Washington.

Then came the presidential election of 1960 when a tousled young millionaire Senator named John Fitzgerald Kennedy (JFK) from Massachusetts and his cosmopolitan wife Jackie took up residence in the White House. Their summer retreat in Hyannis Port, Massachusetts, and the beaches nearby were spontaneous touch football fields where even famous National Football League (NFL) players received invitations to join in on the fun. The age of Camelot brought about the pillbox hat and a penchant for flinging the pigskin around the front yard like their athletic young president. Today, the Super Bowl is annually the most-watched televised event of the year in the USA, and Super Bowl Sunday is as close to a national holiday as you can get without actually being one. Not to put too fine a point on it, but try to remember the last World Series party you were invited to. The NFL, of course, was thrilled, and is still today, but corporations generally avoid connections of their products and brands with political positions (Matos, Vinauales, & Sheinin, 2017), and presidents certainly put forth their sentiments on political issues. That being said, it is sometimes simply unavoidable for a product to be associated with a particular occupant of the Oval Office, be it positive or negative.

The Kennedy-NFL branding connection was not just a one-shot deal. The US public follows the First Family almost as rabidly in terms of trend as its British counterparts across the Atlantic follow the House of Windsor. Jellybean manufacturers cheered, and gourmet jellybean stores popped up in malls across the country during the presidency of Ronald Reagan when the public came to know he kept a large bowl of jellybeans on his desk in the Oval Office to snack on. Broccoli farmers cringed when President George Bush, Reagan's successor, announced publicly he hated broccoli and refused to eat it. Bill Clinton's yearning for McDonald's Big Macs that dated back to his boyhood days in Hope, Arkansas, probably filled Burger King boardrooms with angst throughout the 1990s. We also gleefully filled out our NCAA[1] Basketball Tournament pool sheets with President Obama for eight years, office policy be damned. President Trump is no different in this regard. The president's private account has

Check Your Understanding

Great Communicator

President Ronald Reagan earned the nickname "The Great Communicator" from the press by his adroit ability to connect with his audience whether it was the White House Press Corps or the average American through his speeches and press conferences.

more than 32 million followers (Burke, 2017). Perhaps, his Twitter usage is the equivalent of that perfect spiral for a touchdown from JFK to RFK[2] on a Massachusetts beach back in 1961.

The president himself is also a product that is subject to branding, and so is the nation he leads and represents. Donald Trump was not the first president to make effective use of social media tools – that would be Barack Obama – but he has been able to brand himself effectively throughout the Republican primaries straight through his general election victory. The parallels of strategy between the two campaigns are striking: Obama clearly went for the Kennedy-esque, offering youth and vigor with the hallmark "Change We Can Believe In," while Trump deftly tapped in to Ronald Reagan's strong-man populist appeal with "Make America Great Again" that echoes in the same timbre as the Great Communicator's hallmark slogan "It's Morning in America." Zavattaro (2010) correctly concluded that presidential politics is now candidate-centered, as opposed to platform-centered. Thus, direct informal presidential communication with the electorate not only is advisable but also may be habitual in the future.

One of the controversies swirling around Trump's tweeting habits is that many critics feel he is harming the US reputation abroad with his actions, especially when he engages in a back-and-forth exchange with a political rival (foreign or domestic) or member of the media. This "reputation" of the USA is just another way of branding (Garbacz-Rawson, 2007) – only it is the nation itself, as opposed to the individual leading it. The "America First" style of nation branding that Trump prefers (tight borders, limited immigration, and projection of economic and military power) enamors him to his base but chafes those who believe that the twenty-first century is an era of globalization. This zero-sum game about where the USA is going, how it is doing, and what it should be is a good deal of what fuels the fire of what we now call the "fake news!" controversy. Trump's political opponents view the White House as a font of untruths and flat-out lies, while the administration sees the mainstream media as manufacturing false information just to stymie the president's agenda and drag down his approval ratings. The president has taken to Twitter at every available opportunity to fire back at who he calls the real purveyors of "fake news," even offering a trophy to the least credible of the lot, by which he means every outlet with the exception of Fox News (Segodnya, 2017).

Many see Trump as machine-gunning the whole media crowd from the stately *New York Times* to the world-renowned CNN[3] with nothing but blanks as these outlets are trusted implicitly to report in an unbiased and

> **Check Your Understanding**
>
> *Zero-Sum Game*
>
> *Zero-Sum Game* is from game theory, a situation in which when one side wins the other side must suffer a loss.

even-handed fashion. There exists, however, evidence to the contrary that provides powder for the president's shells. As it turns out, "fake news" in the mainstream media does exist (Herman, 2017), and it does so in the form of the presentation of misleading information as well as sweeping under the proverbial rug any story that calls into question already accepted dogma. This does not mean that the president has been completely and utterly truthful in every tweet. The *New York Times* is clearly not "failing," and CNN's ratings have not hit "rock-bottom" as the president has either stated implicitly or implied over Twitter. Previous presidents have had testy relations with the press, but few have retaliated with the zeal that Trump has. In examining his personal tweets that generate all the attention (as opposed to the arid official @POTUS versions), not all his tweets are about the so-called "fake media." An excellent question to ask, and one the research here takes up is, what motivates the president to pick up his smartphone? Or, conversely, does anything give Mr. Trump pause on the keyboard? It is these queries that drive the hypotheses behind the model the forthcoming paragraphs will outline.

The President's Use of Twitter: More than Just Combating "Fake News"

Fox News is and has been for years the undisputed king of cable network news, far outstripping its main rivals CNN and MSNBC in the all-important ratings department, and it has done so by boldly branding itself as the go-to channel for conservatives to get their information. Preaching to the choir generates loyal viewership, and Fox News has seen only growth in that department the past decade, no matter which party was in power, and there is no end in sight to its reign at the top of the cable news hierarchy. The president himself is engaging in his own sort of "media branding." He has stated in no uncertain terms that he uses social media as a way to get "the real story" the way he sees it to the people directly, without it being distorted through the lens of a group he sees as obviously hostile to him. President Trump presents himself as a social media Robin Hood emptying his quiver from the Sherwood Forest of the White House lawn, while the Sheriffs of Nottingham of the mainstream media look on in helpless frustration as his Twitter projectiles strike home with unerring accuracy and sharper point. Like the Robin Hood of legend, when the president has aimed his bow directly at his foes he rarely misses the mark in terms of artfully skewering the target. CNN, for example, has been a presidential pincushion in terms of accusations of being the gold standard of fraudulent information. President Trump has even gotten personal with anchors of popular news shows, such as MSNBC's *Morning Joe*. He has belittled its main anchors Joe Scarborough and Mika Brzezinski referring to them in tweets as "Psycho Joe" and "Low IQ Crazy Mika" in a tweet-for-tweet back-and-forth jab fest (Cannon, 2017). Trump had even raised questions about Scarborough's involvement in the death of an intern at his office when he was a member of Congress back in 2001 (Devaney, 2017), even though the coroner ruled it an accidental death due to a heart condition and a subsequent fall. Co-anchor of *Morning Joe* Brzezinski was quick to respond and keep the bonfire going by saying the president was throwing around false conspiracy theories, muffling the first Amendment and acting inappropriately. Scarborough himself simply tweeted that the president was "not well" (Tornoe, 2017). The president, of course, was in fine fettle and probably should have received a thank-you card for all the ratings he generated during the brouhaha as well as helping make MSNBC the cable proxy refuge for wounded liberals still stinging from Hillary Clinton's demoralizing defeat months earlier, as MSNBC enjoyed a surge in total daily viewership exemplified by a 105% increase over 2016 in May 2017 (Associated Press, 2017).

Fox News and President Trump, conversely, enjoy a relationship that a crackerjack marriage counselor would envy. Exclusive interviews, frequent references, tweets of praise for its reporting on specific issues that please him, and appearances on *Fox & Friends* make the White House and Fox News Network one big happy family. Franklin and Eleanor Roosevelt should have had such a close and fruitful political partnership.

CNN, which Trump describes as the most "untrusted source" of news, gets bashed on Twitter its fair share for sure but seems more respected by the president in general by comparison to say, MSNBC. The president will indeed take his twitter potshots at the network on a regular basis, but there will never be a personal attack on an Anderson Cooper. For reasons known only to himself, the president has in no uncertain terms made CNN, by both tweet and implication, the ultimate villain in the "fake news" conflict along with the *New York Times* but has kept his comments relatively impersonal while in the Oval Office.

The Model

The regression model in the present research is based on the premise that the president has partial motivation to tweet from his desire to combat "fake news" as he sees it and, thus, the model has representations of the primary sources of his complaints on the matter, those on cable. Obviously, worrying about "fake news" is not Mr. Trump's sole concern as chief executive, so the model will include other explanatory variables to account for the day-to-day influences that a president is likely to encounter and that encourage him to tweet.

Data

For this analysis, all of Mr. Trump's private account tweets from the day of his inauguration to the last day of 2017 from *All the President's Tweets* from CNN.com comprise the data set. This data set does not take into account all of the president's tweets prior to his inauguration. For the purposes of this research, the private account serves as the source of the data set. For the independent variables representing the three cable news networks in the model, all the weekly prime-time ratings of the 49 weeks from Mr. Trump's inauguration to the end of 2017 represent them numerically in the model. The source of the data set is www.adweek.com/tvnewser. Significant US news events, significant world news events, and unexpected disasters' source is 2017 Current Events\Infoplease, yielding a total of 49 cases ($N = 49$).

The OLS Regression Equation

Number of Tweets On Personal Twitter Account Per Week = a + $b1(CNN)$ + $b2(FoxNews)$ + $b3(MSNBC)$ + $b4(USNewsEvent)$ + $b5(WorldNewsEvent)$ + $b6\ (UnexpectedDisaster)$ + e

Variables in the Equation

The Dependent Variable

The dependent variable, number of Trump's tweets per week on his personal account, is simply the number of times he tweeted on his personal account @realDonaldTrump per week during his presidency in 2017 following his inauguration (see Table A1 of the Appendix).

The Explanatory Variables

CNN

President Trump, as the ex-host of the TV show *The Apprentice*, is a television ratings fiend and extremely knowledgeable as to what makes a television show successful, news show or otherwise. It is almost a lead pipe cinch to conclude that he follows the ratings of the major news networks as he did *The Apprentice* and its time-slot competitors when he was its host. The president makes frequent references to ratings whenever possible, almost exclusively in the negative. CNN has been a target of the president on multiple occasions either by name or in veiled reference (the most "untrusted source in news" as one particularly barbed tweet put it) but has not been the victim of a presidential full frontal smartphone assault as MSNBC has, for example. This is probably in part due to the network's longevity, international reputation and the journalistic chops of its mainstays in addition to its current third place standing in the ratings behind both Fox News and Trump arch-nemesis MSNBC, which makes it less of a threat and tempting target. Or maybe it is the decades of the intro by Darth Vader intoning ominously, "This is CNN." Take your pick. In any event, despite the president's inherent disdain for the network, for the most part the most ardent vitriol is saved for other areas and any splash made by CNN is likely to be met with a shrug and a brush off rather than a volley of tweets unless it is of Watergate or Monica Lewinsky proportions. Thus, it is expected that the relationship between the CNN variable and the number of tweets per week will be (surprisingly) negative.

Fox News Network

Hypothesizing the direction of this variable is easier than picking the winner of a one horse race. As more people watch Fox, the president will certainly laud the success and want to be a part of it. The president loves a winner and the undisputed kings of cable news will have Number 45 in their corner for as long as he is in office unless some cataclysmic change takes place. Fox News has been the right-wing standard-bearer for years on end and any conservative worth their political salt would do back flips to be on friendly terms with a network that reaches into the living rooms of the most conservative homes in the country by a long shot. The president understands this very well and his tweets reflect it, with never a discouraging word, plugs for upcoming Fox News shows and even interviews done by the First Lady. This a relationship that would put family therapists out of business for good and rivals the press relationships that FDR and Reagan had with the press corps during their presidencies. The president makes the most of every opportunity through Twitter to solidify his relationship with the network and will continue to do it often in the future. Without question, it is hypothesized that the Fox News variable will be positively related to Trump's tweeting.

MSNBC

Given the sheer level of animosity and the network's clear role as cable news' foil to Fox News, no matter what fortunes befall MSNBC the president would either deride them as a fluke if a success or twist the knife in further if the opposite were true. This is true ideological polarization at work. If MSNBC were to be in the spotlight for any reason, expect the president's smartphone keyboard to be hot to the touch, especially around 7 a.m., one of his favorite times to tweet and coincidentally the same time as MSNBC's *Morning Joe*, home to his favorite media sparring partners. MSNBC also happens to be the most likely favored network of Hillary Clinton fans who Trump, though he won the election, still hates like poison and takes every opportunity to blame "Crooked Hillary" for everything that's wrong in the world. Although MSNBC is a fledgling network in comparison with CNN and Fox News, its current number two network news ranking and its left-leaning tendencies combined with dealing a healthy dose of criticism of the president on a regular basis would make MSNBC a prime Twitter target for the president and thus the relationship is expected to be positive.

US News Events

From the tragedy of the mass shootings in Las Vegas to the ugliness in Charlottesville to NFL players kneeling during the national anthem, the president has had his say on Twitter, and at length. From a news standpoint, the president is a homebody with his ear to the American soil. No one can accuse the president of being ill-informed of anything that is the hot topic at the office water cooler or at the town diner. No matter what the issue, Mr. Trump knows about it, has an opinion on it, and is more than willing to tweet about it. Just ask NFL Commissioner Roger Goodell. That being said, US News Events is expected to have a positive relationship with the amount of the president's tweeting. A dummy variable was used to capture the effects of this variable, with the case taking on a value of one if a significant event occurred during the time period and zero otherwise.

> **Check Your Understanding**
>
> *Dummy Variable Creation*
>
> *Dummy variable creation* is a statistical method of operationalizing a variable for inclusion in a statistical model that has no numeric value.

World News Events

There is a school of thought in international relations that states that one ought to play one's foreign policy cards close to the vest. President Trump did not attend that school and one can safely make the assumption that he uses tweets as public barometer, media strategy, or as a negotiation tool. His tweets are replete with explicit examples of US foreign policy strategy, especially with reference to North Korea and his special friend Kim Jong-un, whom he has tagged with the moniker "Little Rocket Man." Whether this is playing Texas Hold 'Em with your cards backwards by accident or scaring the living daylights out of your opponent by design no one is quite sure. What is sure is that the Dear Leader of North Korea would be wise to get a Twitter account and join the 32 million others who know that the president is irritated enough with his constant missile testing to mention "the button," which is not a good thing since many believe he will fuse North Korea into a giant pane of glass at the drop of a hat and drop it himself. Thus, this variable will have a positive relationship with the number of weekly presidential tweets. A dummy variable was used to capture the effects of this variable, with the case taking on a value of one if a significant world event occurred during the time period and zero otherwise.

Unexpected Disasters

Though not nearly as bad as the record-breaking year of 2005 when people in hurricane prone areas had to worry

Check Your Understanding

Katrina

Katrina refers to Hurricane Katrina, one of the deadliest natural disasters in US history that struck the US Gulf Coast, causing the most damage to New Orleans, in 2005. The administration of George W. Bush was widely criticized for its lackluster response to the disaster.

about losing their roofs to storms named after college sororities two days before Thanksgiving, the 2017 hurricane season gave us three of the worst natural disasters in decades in Hurricanes Harvey, Irma, and Maria. Texas, Florida, and especially Puerto Rico sustained extensive damage. This was indeed the perfect time for the "Twitter Presidency" to come of age. The president tweeted that he was tracking each storm, when help was on the way and details of his visit to each location. It was a far cry from President George W. Bush who initially just flew over the smoldering Superdome frowning during Katrina in 2005 or a paralyzed Bush I administration during Hurricane Andrew in 1992. The president seemed highly attuned to the plight of the people in each storm's path and heaped praise upon first responders and those who mobilized to get supplies to the storms' victims. Despite the criticism leveled at the president with the response with regard to the recovery from Maria in Puerto Rico, the president's tweets depicted an engaged chief executive well versed in the gravity of each situation. Therefore, the Unexpected Disasters variable will have a positive relationship with the dependent variable. A dummy variable was used to capture the effects of this variable, with the case taking on a value of one if a natural or other disaster occurred during the time period and zero otherwise.

Discussion of Results

The model overall performed fairly well with four of the six explanatory variables reaching significance with an R-square value of .44 (see Table A2 of the Appendix). Two of the cable news media variables came up significant (CNN and Fox News) and in the correct direction as predicted validating those hypotheses. The Beta weights for both are robust indicating impact as well as significance. The failure of the MSNBC variable to reach significance by a long shot and the anemic Beta weight is perhaps the model's major shortcoming. Perhaps, this author placed far too much emphasis on the skirmish between the president and the hosts of MSNBC's *Morning Joe* and overestimated the importance of the network's new found success in the ratings war. More attention should also have probably been paid to the tweet where the president stated that the hosts of *Morning Joe* were not necessarily bad people, just put under pressure by network executives to discredit the president in their reporting. Another surprise in the model was the failure of World News Events to reach significance along with a similarly tepid Beta weight. Given the criticism of the Obama administration with regard to handling ISIS and reports of his own success with rolling the Islamic State back under his watch along with the exchanges with Kim Jong-un that had the nuclear war Chicken Littles out in force, it was a surprise to see this part of the model fail. One would think that these ongoing events would be a major motivating factor for the president to start typing, but surprisingly enough, this was not the case.

Perhaps, though, we are dealing with a president that is more interested and adept at the domestic than the foreign. The two presidencies thesis, in which the presidency is divided into two separate spheres, one foreign and one domestic (Canes-Wrone, Howell, & Lewis, 2008) seems to be in play here. If one examines the president's tweets, there is a distinct domestic bent in terms of subject matter and area. Job creation, the border wall, immigration policy, healthcare, and tax reform are all major issues the president has tweeted on repeatedly during the first year of his presidency with his first major legislative victory being in the domestic area of tax policy. Bill Clinton was no different. The president who turned a major deficit into a surplus in his eight years in office could sport no major foreign policy trophy. Conversely, Ronald Reagan arguably won the Cold War by beating the Russian bear to death with a checkbook but left a budget deficit of historic proportions for his successors to grapple with. Maybe if Clinton and Reagan were president in the age of today's social media, they would have tweeted in the areas of their respective expertise, be it domestic or foreign affairs.

The explanatory variable US News Events performed as expected. Along the lines of the two presidencies thesis discussion in the previous paragraph, if Mr. Trump falls in the category of a president who favors the domestic side of the presidency, then it stands to reason that news on the home front will be his forte. That certainly came through in the model and in the examination of his individual tweets no topic is out of the realm of the president's twitter commentary reach. The best example would be the flap over the kneeling of National Football League players during the playing of the national anthem before games. It was started by former San Francisco 49ers player Colin Kaepernick to protest racial injustice across the USA. Trump sees it as a blatant disrespect for the American flag and all who fought to defend it. Trump's supporters and a good deal of NFL fans agree with him. The president fired off a fusillade of tweets that lasted weeks that called for boycotting of games, refusing to watch games on TV (Trump the ratings maven at his best again) and called out everyone from the NFL commissioner's office on down to individual players. He praised owners who demanded their players stand for the anthem and made sure everyone knew when Vice President Pence walked out of an Indianapolis Colts game when some players took a knee during the anthem. Never has a sitting president become involved in such a way in dealing with a protest during a sporting event. God only knows how he would have dealt with the raised Black Power fists at the 1968 Olympics in Mexico City, but with the 2018 Winter Olympics days away, you can bet the US athletes will be standing rock-steady for our national anthem.

Being commander-in-chief often entails being reassuring-voice-in-chief. This often happens at the spur of the moment, when the president least expects it or finds it politically expedient. Such was the problem in 2017 during the months of August through October when Hurricanes Harvey, Irma, and Maria arrived in the Atlantic basin. A high-energy person thrives under these circumstances and our current president certainly fits the description. That the Unexpected Disasters variable performed best of all with the "heaviest" Beta weight and significance at the $p<.005$ level was not surprising given that Trump seems to feed off of excitement and challenges and the threat of a monster landfalling hurricane certainly provides those. The president turned amateur meteorologist from the outset, tweeting about the storms while they were still well offshore, advising the populace that he was watching them. He did not stop there, tweeting especially during Harvey and Irma in all caps "we are with you" to the people affected as a reminder that they were not old news in the Oval Office. Moreover, it seemed genuine and heartfelt and expressed the sentiments of an entire nation in a single tweet, a significant departure from the politically motivated messages designed to deliver a blow or drive home a point. It was one human being reaching out to others in a firm reassuring tone that in the end, everything was going to be alright, and we were all in this together. For Trump, they were perhaps the finest hours of his presidency to date, eclipsing the tax overhaul victory easily, at least from this vantage point. Crises often bring out the better angels of our nature and this was the case for the president. If one can call the bird that serves as the logo for Twitter a dove, during and following the hurricanes Number 45's tweets were olive branches and rainbows to people who needed to know their president cared.

Suggestions for Future Research

The model here only scratches the surface of this particular line of research. It is groundbreaking, unique, and a worthy addition as a subfield of presidential studies. One thing that intrigued me while conducting this research was the times at which the tweets were sent, especially in response to a particular event. This author would like to see future efforts in this area focus on "time lapse." That is, the time that elapses between a specific event occurring and a tweet on that subject from the president.

The level of immediacy and its interpretation would open up a whole new avenue in how presidential administrations are structured. For example, a long time lapse would allow for consultation with advisors, a polished draft, and the like. An immediate burst would indicate the president's own thoughts "straight off the cuff." Even time of day would be significant. It would be interesting to see how many times the president "tweets from the hip," as opposed to ones with a delayed response time. This could be a measure of how the president is using (or not) his White House staff and Cabinet for advice and would advance the study of White House communication procedural dynamics in the process.

Conclusion

Whether the next president uses social media to the extent that President Trump does is a matter of conjecture, but at this juncture, we are undeniably in the age of the "Twitter Presidency." The battle over whose news is "authentic" and whose news is "fake news" no doubt will continue to rage on and will not be solved by even the best White House correspondent since Helen Thomas or the most eloquent White House Press Secretary since Pierre Salinger. The fact of the matter is we are at the dawn of a new age in presidential politics, where ideas and opinions are delivered through new unfiltered channels to be digested directly by the constituency without any fillers or by-products from the traditional journalistic sources.

The "Twitter Presidency" is alive and well and shows no signs of going the way of the pet rock or the mullet. It undeniably reaches a generation raised on tweets, Instagram posts, Snapchats, and Houseparty hookups and subconsciously makes them part of the political process, whether the action is a nod in agreement, an angry tweet fired back, or a head-shake in dismay. "Fake news" may be a plague upon the land due to it being the lord of lies but the controversy it has created has put a stake through the heart of the monster known as political alienation. Today, social media is electric with political chatter with reference to the president's tweets on both sides of the political aisle with the young leading the way with over 40% of Twitter users between the ages of 18 and 34, according to Statista. That bodes well for our electoral future as that number will undoubtedly rise and more age groups embrace the potential of political efficacy of social media outlets like Twitter. This author is not one of the 40% in that key demographic, but you can follow his tweets at @DrBrez, where all the news is never fake.

Discussion Questions

1   Do you think the "Twitter Presidency" is one-time phenomenon based on the personality of one individual or is it a model for future office holders to follow? Explain.

2   Some say that it is "unbecoming" of a president to utilize social media in the way that President Trump has. Others disagree stating that since George Washington there has been no presidential etiquette rulebook that occupants of the Oval Office must follow. Which statement do you think is most correct, and why?

3   Some have suggested that purveyors of "fake news" be punished in some way for misleading the public, while staunch advocates of the First Amendment's right to free speech say it gives media or social media outlets the right to lie, as long as they do not defame the subject, and it is up to the news consumer to "do his or her homework" and fact-check. Do you think there should be some sort of informal sanction on those who purposely mislead the public, or is everyone responsible for his or her own vetting of any news story? Explain.

4   One of the major criticisms of the "Twitter Presidency" is in the area of foreign policy. Some experts feel the president's tweets give too much information away as to US diplomatic and military strategy, which could have negative consequences should an international crisis arise. Do you think the president jeopardizes national security with the content of his tweets on foreign policy issues? Why, or why not?

5   With the advent of the "Twitter Presidency," some have argued that the position of White House Press Secretary has been diminished significantly, with people paying more attention to the president's tweets than what is said at White House press briefings. Has social media in the White House put the position of Press Secretary on the road to obsolescence? Why, or why not?

To Cite This Chapter

Brezenski, T. F. (2018). Twitter me this: Fake news, real issues, and the Twitter presidency. In H. Gringarten, & R. Fernández-Calienes (Eds.). *Ethical branding and marketing: Cases and lessons* (pp. 19–34). Routledge Management and Business Studies Series. London and New York: Routledge.

Appendix

Table A1 President Donald Trump – Summary of Personal Twitter Account Use – 2017.

Date Range	Number of Personal Account Tweets
01/20 – 01/29	59
01/30 – 02/05	45
02/06 – 02/12	48
02/13 – 02/19	38

(Continued)

Date Range	Number of Personal Account Tweets
02/20 – 02/26	27
02/27 – 03/05	26
03/06 – 03/12	27
03/13 – 03/19	27
03/20 – 03/26	27
03/27 – 04/02	41
04/03 – 04/09	21
04/10 – 04/16	23
04/17 – 04/23	40
04/24 – 04/30	49
05/01 – 05/07	31
05/08 – 05/14	40
05/15 – 05/21	19
05/22 – 05/28	33
05/29 – 06/04	28
06/05 – 06/11	36
06/12 – 06/18	35
06/19 – 06/25	50
06/26 – 07/02	58
07/03 – 07/09	46
07/10 – 07/16	53
07/17 – 07/23	40
07/24 – 07/30	70
07/31 – 08/06	36
08/07 – 08/13	39
08/14 – 08/20	50
08/21 – 08/27	64
08/28 – 09/03	30
09/04 – 09/10	34
09/11 – 09/17	40
09/18 – 09/24	70
09/25 – 10/01	75
10/02 – 10/08	41
10/09 – 10/15	57
10/16 – 10/23	66
10/23 – 10/29	57
10/30 – 11/05	61
11/06 – 11/12	39
11/13 – 11/19	34
11/20 – 11/26	32
11/27 – 12/03	43
12/04 – 12/10	38
12/11 – 12/17	24
12/18 – 12/25	48
12/25 – 12/31	26
$N = 49$	2,041

Table A2 Twitter OLS Regression Model Report.

	B	Beta Weight	T-Value
(Constant)	26.174		
CNNShare	–20.598	–.439	–2.916
FoxShare	9.474	.391	2.384
MSNBCShare	1.527	.047	.352
USNewsEvent	9.242	.331	2.424
WorldNewsEvent	2.913	.104	.838
UnexpectedDisasters	15.092	.452	3.205
R-Square = .441			
N = 49			
Durbin – Watson Test: 1.604			

$p < .01$
$p < .05$
$p < .005$

Notes

1 National Collegiate Athletic Association.
2 Robert Fitzgerald Kennedy, President Kennedy's brother.
3 Cable News Network.

References

Associated Press. (2017, June 6). Politics absolutely fueling cable news surge, but the network evening news. *The Taylorville Illinois Breeze-Courier*. News. Retrieved from infoweb.newsbank.com/resources/doc/nb/news/16625691058BA5B0?p=AWNB

Burke, S. (2017, June 17). How many social followers does Trump actually have? @*CNNTech*. Retrieved from http://money.com/2017/06/17/technology/trump-social-media-followers/index.html

Canes-Wrone, B., Howell, W., & Lewis, D. (2008, January). Toward a broader understanding of presidential power: A reevaluation of the two presidencies thesis. *The Journal of Politics, 70*(1), 1–16. Stable URL: http://www.www.jstor.org/stable/10.1017/ s0022381607080061

Cannon, C. (2017, July 1). Trump's Twitter attack: Cause or effect? *Los Angeles Daily News* Opinion, 1–4. Retrieved from http://proxy.stu.edu:2048/login?url=Https://search.proquest.com.docview/1915019659?accountid=14129

Devaney, J. (2017, November 29). Mika hits Trump over 'Deeply Disturbing' Tweet. *Newsmax.com*. Newsfront. Retrieved from infoweb.newsbank.com/resources/doc/ nb/news/166848204D1CF78?p=AWNB

Garbacz-Rawson, E. A. (2007, July). Perceptions of the United States of America: Exploring the political brand of a nation. *Place Branding and Public Diplomacy, 3*(3), 213–221. doi:10.1057/palgrave.pb.6000067

Herman, E. (2017, July–August). Fake news on Russia and other official enemies. *Monthly Review*. Retrieved from http://search.proquest.com/central/docview/1927794767/8a4fd73A9CFC418EPQ15?accountid=14129

Matos, G., Vinuales, G., & Sheinin, D. (2017, Spring). The power of politics in branding. *Journal of Marketing Theory and Practice, 25*(2), 125–140. doi:10. 1080/10696679.2016.1270768

Segodnya, R. (2017, November 27). Trump offers trophy to 'Most Dishonest' US News network for coverage of his Presidency. *Sputnik-Moscow*, 1–2. Retrieved from http://proxy.stu.edu:2048/login?url=https://search.proquest. com/docview/1968418460?accountid=14129

Tornoe, R. (2017, November 30). Was Trump's morning joe spiked? *Philadelphia Daily News*. Retrieved from http://proxy.stu.edu:2048/login?url=https:// search.proquest.com/docview/1970426871?accountid=14129

Zavattaro, S. (2010, March). Brand Obama: The implications of a branded president. *Administration Theory & Praxis, 32*(1), 123–128. doi:10.2753/ ATP1084-1806320108

3 Ethical Branding in Franchising

Implications for Brand Values and Corporate Culture

Antonella Capriello and Rohail Hassan

Introduction

Branding is an essential element of any franchise agreement, as a brand is a fundamental asset that enables franchise firms to differentiate themselves from competitors (Caves & Murphy, 1976). As Zachary, McKenny, Short, Davis, and Wu (2011) explain, franchise branding is also instrumental in maintaining the internal cohesion of the franchising network through the dissemination of common values. Nyadzayo, Matanda, and Ewing (2011) assert that marketing and branding activities rely on the franchisees' abilities and help franchise to understand, interpret, and share the brand values.

The European Code of Ethics for Franchising highlights that franchising entails not only legal obligations but also ethical obligations with implications on brand values and chain policies (Adler, 2009). The tendency of franchisor and franchisee behaviors toward opportunism requires strengthening ethical policies to perverse cooperation and cohesion in franchising networks (Brookes, Altinay, & Aktas, 2015). Ethical branding and Corporate Social Responsibility in franchising have even more fundamental implications on non-financial performance (Kim & Pennington-Gray, 2017) and may accrue positive perceptions toward a brand with the resulting effects on franchisees' perceptions (Lee et al., 2016). Additionally, Dant, Grünhagen, and Windsperger (2011) underline the emerging discussions on social responsibility in franchising, which summarize the concept of environmental initiates with potential benefits on corporate reputation.

This chapter proposes a conceptual framework for ethical branding in franchising and the outline of the chapter is as follows. With a focus on ethical issues, Section title (Brand Relationship Management and Ethical Issues) describes the factors influencing brand relationship management, Section title (Franchisor Support and Training) identifies the variables affecting brand citizenship behaviors, and Section title (Information and Knowledge Sharing) discusses the implications on brand relationship quality, while Section title (Brand Architecture, Market Areas, and Distribution Channels) presents the elements that influence brand equity.

Section title (Power Relationships and Opportunism) concludes with the conceptual framework for ethical branding.

Brand Relationship Management and Ethical Issues

In the franchisee channels, brand relationships reflect the development and management of the franchisor–franchisee relationship. Key franchising challenges include establishing a franchising network where franchisors foster cooperation, creative actions, and ethical behaviors in franchisees. Literature indicates the variables that influence the brand relationship management construct as information sharing, franchisor support (Terry, 1993), and social interactions (Morgan & Hunt, 1994). Analyzing emerging ethical issues, this section considers the specific variables that affect the nature of brand management relationships.

Franchisor Support and Training

In identifying the processual antecedents of perceived channel conflict in franchising, Weaven, Grace, Frazer, and Giddings (2014) point out franchisees have high expectations with regard to prospective income and franchisor support in relation to marketing and promotional assistance. In the light of transaction cost perspective (Williamson, 1975), Spinelli and Birley (1996) state that franchisee satisfaction–dissatisfaction of the franchisor service provision determine the subsequent behaviors. More specifically, dissatisfied franchisees may involve in unethical behaviors (e.g., reducing service quality or refusing to adopt system standards), failing to meet contractual stipulations and misrepresenting revenues (Grace, Weaven, Frazer, & Giddings, 2014; Morrison, 1997). This behavior will have a negative impact on brand image and inevitably generates litigation with potential implications on the relationship and its termination (Weaven, Grace, Dant, & Brown, 2010).

In a relational exchange perspective, the franchisor's network of relationships is central to sustaining joint constructive dialogue and problem-solving, as franchisors and franchisees perform together to co-create value (Grünhagen & Dorsch, 2003). From a theoretic resource dependency perspective, Harmon and Griffiths (2008) confirm that franchisees assess the value of the resources and services provided in the context of alternative investment opportunities, since franchisees may deem franchisor support inadequate with implications on the franchising relationship trust (Watson & Johnson, 2010).

Information and Knowledge Sharing

Franchising relies on mechanisms to encourage information sharing to assist franchisees in achieving their goals (Mohr & Spekman, 1994), as franchisees require information in connection with expertise and the promised benefits associated with the franchising operations. Based on the ideas of Tikoo (2002), the franchisor has a key role in collecting, synthesizing, and sharing information throughout the entire network. Communication problems and disputes are more persistent and problematic with the shift from founding franchisor to the professional manager (Dant, 1995).

Knowledge sharing is instrumental in brand reputation processes and organizational learning (Koza & Dant, 2007). The dissemination of information may reduce channel members' potential frictions in the goal alignment of the franchise system (Dant & Nasr, 1998).

Brand Architecture, Market Areas, and Distribution Channels

Brand relationship management as a construct includes brand architecture with implications on the product and service provision capacity (Nyadzayo et al., 2011). In light of geographical pressure, brand architecture should also include the design of franchise regions and market zones (Cox & Mason, 2007), since the identified structure has a significant effect on the survival of the system and performance. Cox and Mason (2009) argue that franchisors generally refine and restructure existing territories and market areas with consequences for existing franchisees. Fock (2001) states that the re-designing of the franchise territories could be a significant source of conflict among franchisor and franchisee, reflecting specific ethical issues in connection with the newly designed areas. To attract initial franchisees, Cox and Mason (2009) express the opinion that the franchisor grants exclusive rights to a territory, whilst in the absence of exclusive territorial rights, franchisees may view new franchising outlets in the same area as encroachment. With the development of omni-channel strategies, franchisors need to refocus the content of the franchising agreements. This aspect represents an emerging ethical issue in terms of governing online and offline outlets limiting a potential source of conflict (Pagano & Pardo, 2017).

Power Relationships and Opportunism

Despite the mutual incentive to perform well in a franchising agreement, a two-sided opportunism threat may apparent in the franchisor and franchisee relationship (Lafontaine, 1992). Opportunistic behaviors are harmful and can reduce both wealth creation and distribution in the franchising network with relevant implications on the brand values and reputation building processes (Wathne & Heide, 2000). According to Gassenheimer, Baucus, and Baucus (1996), opportunism can manifest when parties operate in physically different locations, often entailing different challenges and decisions that are not in the favor of the other parties. A franchisor and franchisee perspectives are instrumental to produce a better understanding on the implications of opportunistic behaviors.

Franchisor Opportunism

By designing and offering one-sided contracts, franchisors aim to safeguard their interests (Kashyap, Antia, & Frazier, 2012) and establish their franchisees' obligations in the ongoing relationships. In the resource-scarcity perspective, franchisors act to collect capital (Combs & Ketchen, 2003) and may operate opportunistically by withholding information to persuade prospective franchisees to invest (Ting, Chen, & Bartholomew, 2007). In this pre-contract stage, an information asymmetry is a form of opportunism, as the franchisor may not reveal valuable information. In the post-contract stage, franchisors aim for rapid growth of the franchise and may concede new outlets in an area where a franchisee already serves the market.

Franchisee Opportunism

Franchisees have little possibility to act opportunistically prior to signing the contract with the exception of withholding information in relation to personal details on their characteristics, experience, and financial situation. However, in the course of developing franchising relationships, problems may arise for franchisors (Combs, Michael, & Castrogiovanni, 2004; Lafontaine, 1992) in relation to franchisee opportunistic behaviors, such freeriding on other outlets, failing to pay royalties, damaging a franchisor by releasing proprietary information about a franchise, and not adhering to quality standards (Bradach, 1997; Kidwell, Nygaard, & Silkoset, 2007).

Conflict Management

As Bradford, Stringfellow, and Weitz (2004) explain, conflicts related to the different goals between franchisor and franchisees represent an obstacle for achieving specific objectives. Whereas litigation often results from the franchise system's failure to resolve a dispute internally (Williamson, 1983). In addition, by excluding an arbitration clause from the franchise contract, the franchisor's strategy for resolving disputes may force the parties to settle their disputes by means of protracted court action. This unethical approach favors the franchisors, as franchisees cannot sustain the legal fees and the costs in terms of time. Some franchisors may avoid arbitration when they are unwilling to reconcile with a defiant or confrontational franchisee (Drahozal & Hylton, 2003).

In the ethical branding perspective, as the study of Giddings et al. (2009) identify, a
greater understanding of the
specific features of franchising relationships is critical in
order to manage conflicts in

> **Check Your Understanding**
>
> *Conflict Management in Franchising*
>
> *Conflict Management in Franchising* re-
> lates to the different goals between fran-
> chisor and franchisees.

the franchising network. Franchisors need to acknowledge the worth of
working with franchisees effectively to achieve their common interests
(Giddings et al., 2009), whilst franchisees need to understand the importance of a realistic evaluation of the opportunities since the pre-selection
stages (Brookes, Altinay, Wang, & Yeung, 2016).

Brand Citizenship Behaviors and Ethical Issues

According to Uçanok and Karabati (2013), Brand Citizenship Behaviors
(BCB) focus on the theory of organizational citizenship behavior, which
is the notion that "organizations need to engage their employees in discretionary behaviors more than formal job requirements" (p. 89). The
idea of BCB emphasizes the involvement of employees for the promotion
a brand (Burmann & Zeplin, 2005). Moreover, Nyadzayo et al. (2011)
propose a similar approach in relation to the role of franchisees by discussing the concept of BCB in accordance with a set of identified constructs (such as partner selection process, brand enthusiasm, and brand
advancement) influencing the analyzed dimension. In the below section,
we examine the concept of BCB, with a focus on ethical issues and the
main factors influencing this construct.

Partner Selection and Contract Formulation

Bergen, Dutta, and Walker (1992) reflect on the nature of agency problems in the franchising relationships, since incentives exist for both the
franchisor and the franchisee to misrepresent the nature of business relationships in the pre-contract stage (*ex-ante* adverse selection) and influence their performance obligations (moral hazard) in the post-contract
stage.

However, Altinay, Brookes, and Aktas (2013) argue that prospective franchisees have limited business experience and are skeptical to
seek professional business advice; in those conditions, these franchisees tend to have unrealistic expectations of the future performance
of their business, which may have a negative effect on brand relationship management. Another important ethical issue relates to franchisor behavior whereby under-resourced franchisors recruit franchisees
to maintain cash flow instead of following identified criteria to select
franchisees.

Innovation and Brand Advancement

Innovation and brand advancement are key factors for franchising competitiveness with relevant implications on new markets (Wu, Huang, Tsai, & Chen, 2009) and instrumental to attracting new franchisees for the brand chain (Watson & Stanworth, 2006). Conversely, Weaven et al. (2010) emphasize franchise systems that do not bring innovation tend to have higher levels of conflict. In addition, Watson, Stanworth, Healeas, Purdy, and Stanworth (2005) indicate that innovation and advancement could be a source of conflict between franchisor and franchisees.

According to Kuratko, Hornsby, and Covin (2014), innovation and brand advancement have negative effects when there is no goal alignment with the organizational strategy. In this perspective, brand citizenship behaviors should include franchisees in innovation processes. An ethical issue emerges when new initiatives, or a new image, or both entail financial pressure and marketing funds from the franchisees. In those conditions, corporate communication is instrumental to overcome franchisees' negative perceptions.

Brand Endorsement and Brand Enthusiasm

Brand endorsement refers to the willingness to spread positive word-of-mouth in highly competitive markets (Brocato, Voorhes, & Baker, 2012) by recommending the brand to potential customers. As Nyadzayo et al. (2011) explain, franchisors are a significant role player for positive attitude promotion toward the franchisee brand as they communicate constructive values and create a sense of community. Johnson and Rapp (2010) explain the concept of brand enthusiasm that involves additional initiatives (e.g., local marketing activities through sponsorships and charity events). For ethical branding, this aspect is challenging and implies sharing the ethical values and behaviors across the organization. It also underlines the emerging need to reflect on programs that reward franchisees for their involvement in promoting corporate image consistent with the idea of reinforcing the ethical values.

Brand Relationship Quality and Ethical Issues

Fournier (1994) proposed the concept of Brand Relationship Quality (BRQ), based on customer-based indicator, which is the strength of the relationship between the individual customer and the brand. Similarly, Athanasopoulou (2009) states that BRQ can measure by applying identified constructs: trust, commitment, and satisfaction. Hence, the present section proposes BRQ to measure the strength of brand relationships with a focus on the identified variables expressing the quality of networking processes between the franchisor and the franchisees.

Trust and Commitment

More importantly, Doherty and Alexander (2004) explain the role of trust and commitment to establish long-term relationships since the growth of social interactions in the business intra-system contributes to achieving effective management processes (Yau et al., 2000). As Watson et al. (2005) explain, the key role of sharing information and data is building trust and commitment to the franchisor by managing communication channels.

Commitment also is essential for successful long-term franchising relationships, since it allows partners to preserve the relationship, minimize risk perceptions, and avoid switching behaviors (Dwyer, Schurr, & Oh, 1987). Communication is a crucial ingredient in social relationships to obtain commitment (Mohr & Spekman, 1994), reduce ambiguity and conflict (Nygaard & Dahlstrom, 2002), create synergy between partners, and promote mutual problem-solving (Cummings, 1984).

Franchisee Satisfaction

Geyskens, Steenkamp, and Kumar (1999) claim that franchisee satisfaction consists of an effective condition depending on the quality of franchising relationships. With a focus on ethical issues, Morrison (1996) emphasizes the critical elements of franchise that preserve relationships based on contractual obligations, perceptions of fairness, and goal compatibility. Inequity in the franchisors' levels of control and influence also generates dissatisfaction with franchising agreements (Spinelli & Birley, 1996) and threatens network stability (Morrison, 1997).

An additional factor is the franchising relationship stage: In discussing the antecedent of causes of perceived channel conflict, Weaven et al. (2014) state that development of the franchising business, experienced franchisees may face less value of the franchisor services provided and quality control mechanisms (e.g., allocation of expansion rights) and may become less satisfied. Porter and Renforth (1978) also describe this condition of dissatisfaction that may generate unethical approaches in franchising business with negative effects on future development (Grünhagen & Dorsch, 2003). Satisfaction also is instrumental in enhancing the franchise's corporate reputation, since it favors loyalty and franchisee recommendations to other potential franchisees (Hing, 1995). The communication approach, two-directional communication, and formality have a positive and significant effect on social and economic satisfaction (Lee et al., 2016). According to Morrison (1997), cooperative relationships can stimulate higher performance from franchisees with implications on developing a corporate culture.

Brand Equity, Corporate Culture, and Ethical Issues

In conceptualizing franchising brand equity, Nyadzayo, Matanda, and Ewing (2016) highlight a three-dimensional construct that contains franchisee-perceived relationship value, franchisee-perceived brand image, and franchisee-perceived brand loyalty. In analyzing the implications of ethical issues, brand equity also depends on the Corporate Social Responsibility (CSR) practices in the franchising system. In addition, Perrigot, Oxibar, and Déjean (2015) analyze 117 French franchisors and identify that 86% share information about CSR activity on their website at least one time. They underline that the online communications focus on products (safety), human resources (health, safety, industrial relationships), community involvement (arts, humanitarianism, health), and environment (pollution, recycling, certification, labels). Mandelbaum (2008) highlights the use of their CSR activities for additional reasons in connection with identified benefits (such as investor relationships, cost savings, marketing benefits, community involvement, political and regulatory relations, and risk reduction). From this perspective, Baugh (2010) underlines that all franchisees must engage in the franchisors' CSR activities, which could involve being part of specific CSR committees.

In addition, Rondán-Cataluña, Navarro-García, Gámez-González, and Rodríguez-Rad (2012) recommend that an ethical code should be comprehensive, serious, and compulsory for association members, permitting the association to achieve a high reputation to provide security and confidence to entrepreneurs. According to the Preble and Hoffman (1999) study of 13 ethical policy areas of international ethical codes covering 21 franchising activities in 21 countries, a franchising association code of ethics should include several underlying ethical themes (e.g., maintaining system integrity, good faith behavior, full disclosure, avoiding deception, open communication, fairness, and safeguarding public interest). These codes normally place emphasis on an identified group of stakeholders including franchisors, franchisees, affiliated consultants, franchisor associations, and public interest (consumers, suppliers, and government). In relation to the economic stake in the franchising industry, they cover most stages of the franchising relationship, but a narrow focus on stakeholders with the limitations of ethical guidance and few enforcement provisions (Preble & Hoffman, 1999). In relation to brand equity, franchisors may use their membership in a franchising association as a quality signal to market their system (Adler, 2009). Associations act as an information source for franchisees, sharing responsibilities, the standards and norms of behavior expected in the franchising industry with potential benefits on franchisors' relationships (Lawrence & Kaufman, 2010).

Conclusions

With a focus on ethical issues, this study adopts a relationship perspective in providing a conceptual framework to manage brand relationships and quality signals, develop brand citizenship behaviors, and enhance brand equity in reputation-building processes. These factors underline that ethical business practices do not depend solely on respecting contractual agreement obligations, but also sharing common ethical values and practices by involving stakeholders.

Figure 3.1 highlights four key elements that enhance brand value and interact with the effective management of the relationships among franchisors and franchisees. The proposed framework is instrumental in measuring the potential ethical issues in a stakeholder perspective and underlines the inference on brand values. Brand relationship management focuses on developing a corporate culture based on coordinating and integrating franchisors and franchisees.

Ethical behaviors and policies enable strategically enhancing the franchising corporate culture and brand values. More specifically, as franchisees tend to behave opportunistically, choosing strategies that promote the chain brand values across the network structure are essential to limit these behaviors. The conceptual framework has further implications on franchisor behaviors in selecting new franchisees. As an evidence, in reflecting on the feature of "good franchisor," Bellin (2016) underlines good franchisors' need to select prospective franchisees who understand the nature of contractual obligations, and this approach can contribute effectively to the overall network growth. Consequently, the identified

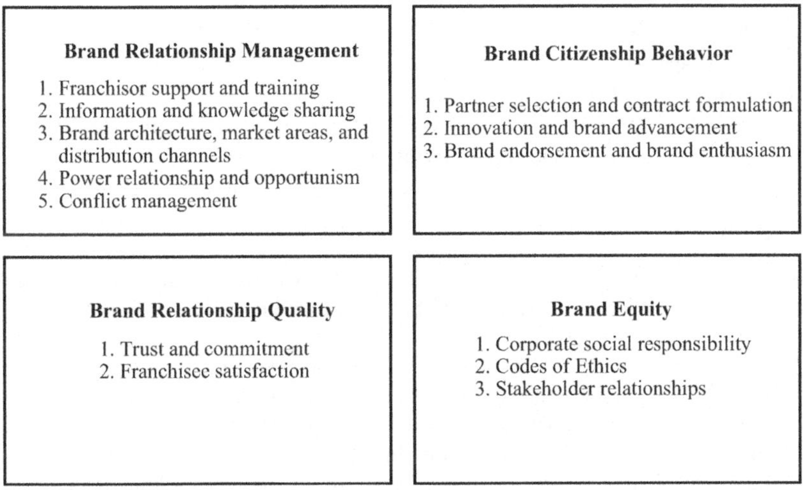

Brand Relationship Management

1. Franchisor support and training
2. Information and knowledge sharing
3. Brand architecture, market areas, and distribution channels
4. Power relationship and opportunism
5. Conflict management

Brand Citizenship Behavior

1. Partner selection and contract formulation
2. Innovation and brand advancement
3. Brand endorsement and brand enthusiasm

Brand Relationship Quality

1. Trust and commitment
2. Franchisee satisfaction

Brand Equity

1. Corporate social responsibility
2. Codes of Ethics
3. Stakeholder relationships

Figure 3.1 Ethical branding in franchising.

factors are instrumental to create an ethical corporate culture with applications in franchisor selection processes. This aspect is particularly relevant considering the social costs of failed franchisees and defensive measures (Bellin, 2015).

Ethical branding also has implications on innovating the corporate culture. Franchisors should provide clear contractual terms and continuous support, share common values, and develop a conflict management system. These ethical approaches can result in satisfied franchisees who avoid opportunism and are actively responsible for the business expansion. An ethical corporate culture based on the described variables can be instrumental in dealing with emerging issues in formulating multi-channel strategies. Empirical evidence could render the conceptual framework more robust to analyze how and under which conditions these factors interact and complete to accrue brand equity.

Discussion Questions

1   Explain brand relationship management in accordance with ethical issues.
2   Discuss the components of brand relationship quality in relation to ethical principles.
3   Analyze brand citizenship behaviors in connection with ethical issues.
4   Discuss the interactions between brand equity and ethics.
5   Reflect on the importance of ethical branding in franchising.

To Cite This Chapter

Capriello, A., & Hassan, R. (2018). Ethical branding in franchising: Implications for brand values and corporate culture. In H. Gringarten, & R. Fernández-Calienes (Eds.). *Ethical branding and marketing: Cases and lessons* (pp. 35–49). Routledge Management and Business Studies Series. London and New York: Routledge.

References

Adler, J. Y. (2009). The ethics of franchising: How codes of ethics compare and what to consider in deciding whether to subscribe to them. *Franchise Law Journal, 29*(2), 74–80.
Altinay, L., Brookes, M., & Aktas, G. (2013). Selecting franchise partners: Tourism franchisee approaches, processes, and criteria. *Tourism Management, 37*, 176–185. doi:10.1016/j.tourman.2013.01.016
Athanasopoulou, P. (2009). Relations hip quality: A critical literature review and research agenda. *European Journal of Marketing, 43*(5/6), 583–610. doi:10.1108/03090560910946945

Baugh, P. (2010). The business case for 'going green.' *Franchising World, 42*(5), 49–50.

Bellin, H. (2015, December). Bad franchisors! *Journal of Marketing Channels, 22*(4), 333–338, doi:10.1080/1046669X.2015.1113486

Bellin, H. (2016, March). Good franchising. *Journal of Marketing Channels, 23*(1–2), 77–80. doi:10.1080/1046669X.2016.1147893

Bergen, M., Dutta, S., & Walker, O. C. (1992, July). Agency relationships in marketing: A review of the implications and applications of agency and related theories. *Journal of Marketing, 56*(3), 1–24. doi:10.2307/1252293

Bradach, J. L. (1997, June). Using the plural form in the management of restaurant chains. *Administrative Science Quarterly, 42*(2), 276–303. doi:10.2307/2393921

Bradford, K. D., Stringfellow, A., & Weitz, B. A. (2004). Managing conflict to improve the effectiveness of retail networks, *Journal of Retailing, 80*(3), 181–195. doi:10.1016/j.jretai.2003.12.002

Brocato, D. E., Voorhees, C. M., & Baker, J. (2012). Understanding the influence of cues from other customers in the service experience: A scale development and validation. *Journal of Retailing, 88*(3), 384–398. doi:10.1016/j.jretai.2012.01.006

Brookes, M., Altinay, L., & Aktas, G. (2015). Opportunistic behavior in hospitality franchisee agreements. *International Journal of Hospitality Management, 46*, 120–129. doi:10.1016/j.ijhm.2015.02.001

Brookes, M., Altinay, L., Wang, X. L., & Yeung, R. (2016). Opportunity identification and evaluation in franchisee business start-ups. *Journal of Service Theory and Practice, 26*(6), 889–910. doi:10.1108/JSTP-04-2015-0089

Burmann, C., & Zeplin, S. J. (2005). Building brand commitment: A behavioral approach to internal brand management. *Journal of Brand Management, 12*(4), 279–300. doi:10.1057/palgrave.bm.2540223

Caves, R., & Murphy, W. (1976). Franchising: Firms, markets, and intangible assets. *Southern Economic Journal, 42*(4), 572–586. doi:10.2307/1056250

Combs, J. G., & Ketchen, D. J. (2003, June). Why do firms use franchising as an entrepreneurial strategy? A meta-analysis. *Journal of Management, 29*(3), 443–465. doi:10.1016/S0149-2063(03)00019-9

Combs, J. G., Michael, S. C., & Castrogiovanni, G. J. (2004, December). Franchising: A review and avenues to greater theoretical diversity. *Journal of Management, 30*(6), 907–931. doi:10.1016/j.jm.2004.06.006

Cox, J., & Mason, C. (2007). Standardization versus adaptation: Geographical pressures to deviate from franchise formats. *Service Industries Journal, 27*(8), 1053–1072. doi:10.1080/02642060701673737

Cox, J. & Mason, C. (2009). Franchise network restructuring: Pressures, constraints and mechanisms. *Entrepreneurship & Regional Development, 21*(5–6), 503–527. doi: 10.1080/08985620802365178

Cummings, T. G. (1984). Transorganizational development. In B. M. Staw & L. L. Cummings (Eds.), *Research in organizational behavior: An annual series of analytical essays and critical reviews* (Vol. 6, pp. 367–422). Greenwich, CT: JAI Press.

Dant, R. P. (1995). Motivation for franchising: Rhetoric versus reality. *International Small Business Journal, 14*(1), 10–32. doi:10.1177/0266242695141001

Dant, R. P., & Nasr, N. I. (1998, January). Control techniques and upward flow of information in franchising in distant markets: Conceptualization and preliminary evidence. *Journal of Business Venturing, 13*(1), 3–28. doi:10.1016/S0883-9026(97)00040-2

Dant, R. P., Grünhagen, M., & Windsperger, J. (2011, September). Franchising research frontiers for the twenty-first century. *Journal of Retailing, 87*(3), 253–268. doi:10.1016/j.jretai.2011.08.002

Doherty, A., & Alexander, N. (2004). Relationship development in international retail franchising: Case study evidence from the UK fashion sector. *European Journal of Marketing, 38*(9/10), 1215–1235. doi:10.1108/03090560410548942

Drahozal, C. R., & Hylton, K. N. (2003, June). The economics of litigation and arbitration: An application to franchise contracts. *The Journal of Legal Studies, 32*(2), 549–584. doi:10.1086/377054

Dwyer, F. R., Schurr, P., & Oh, S. (1987, April). Developing buyer-seller relationships. *Journal of Marketing, 51*(2), 11–27. doi:10.2307/1251126

Fock, H. K. (2001). Retail outlet location decision maker – franchisor or franchisee? *Marketing Intelligence & Planning, 19*(3), 171–178. doi:10.1108/02634500110391717

Fournier, S. (1998, March). Consumers and their brands: Developing relationship theory in consumer research. *Journal of Consumer Research, 24*(4), 343–373. doi:10.1086/209515

Gassenheimer, J. B., Baucus, D. B., &. Baucus, M. S. (1996). Cooperative arrangement among entrepreneurs: An analysis of opportunism and communication in franchise structures. *Journal of Business Research, 36*, 67–79. doi:10.1016/0148-2963(95)00164-6

Geyskens, I., Steenkamp, J.-B. E. M., & Kumar, N. (1999, May). A meta-analysis of satisfaction in marketing channel relationships. *Journal of Marketing Research, 36*(2), 223–238. doi:10.2307/3152095

Giddings, J., Frazer, L., Weaven, S., & Grace, A. (2009). Understanding the dynamics of conflict within business franchise systems. *Australasian Dispute Resolution Journal, 20*(1), 24–32.

Grace, D., Weaven, S., Frazer, L., & Giddings, J. (2013, June). Examining the role of franchisee normative expectations in relationship evaluation. *Journal of Retailing, 89*(2), 219–230. doi:10.1016/j.jretai.2012.12.002

Grünhagen, M., & Dorsch, M. J. (2003, September). Does the franchisor provide value to franchisees? Past, current, and future value assessments of two franchisee types. *Journal of Small Business Management, 41*(4), 366–384. doi:10.1111/1540-627X.00088

Harmon, T. R., & Griffiths, M. A. (2008). Franchisee perceived relationship value. *Journal of Business & Industrial Marketing, 23*(4), 256–263. doi:10.1108/08858620810865834

Hing, N. (1995). Franchisee satisfaction: Contributors and consequences. *Journal of Small Business Management, 33*(2), 12–25.

Johnson, J. W., & Rapp, A. (2010, August). A more comprehensive understanding and measure of customer helping behavior. *Journal of Business Research, 63*(8), 787–792. doi:10.1016/j.jbusres.2008.03.006

Kashyap, V., Antia, K. D., & Frazier, G. L. (2012, April). Contracts, extracontractual incentives, and ex post behavior in franchise channel relationships. *Journal of Marketing Research, 49*(2), 260–276. doi:10.1509/jmr.09.0337

Kidwell, R. E., Nygaard, A., & Silkoset, R. (2007, July). Antecedents and effects of free riding in the franchisor–franchisee relationship. *Journal of Business Venturing*, 22(4), 522–544. doi:10.1016/j.jbusvent.2006.06.002

Kim, M.-S., & Pennington-Gray, L. (2017). Does franchisor ethical value really lead to improvements in financial and non-financial performance? *International Journal of Contemporary Hospitality Management*, 29(10), 2573–2591. doi:10.1108/IJCHM-04-2016-0188

Koza, K. L., & Dant, R. P. (2007, August). Effects of relationship climate, control mechanism, and communications on conflict resolution behavior and performance outcomes. *Journal of Retailing*, 83(3), 279–296. doi:10.1016/j.jretai.2007.03.002

Kuratko, D. F., Hornsby, J. S., & Covin, J. G. (2014, January–February). Diagnosing a firm's internal environment for corporate entrepreneurship. *Business Horizon*, 57(1), 37–47. doi:10.1016/j.bushor.2013.08.009

Lafontaine, F. (1992). Agency theory and franchising: Some empirical results. *The RAND Journal of Economics*, 23(2), 263–283.

Lawrence, B., & Kaufmann, P. J. (2010) Franchisee associations: Strategic focus or response to Franchisor opportunism. *Journal of Marketing Channels*, 17(2), 137–155, doi:10.1080/10466691003635119

Lee, Y.-K., Nor, Y., Choi, J., Kim, S., Han, S., & Lee, J.-H. (2016). Why does franchisor social responsibility really matter? *International Journal of Hospitality Management*, 53, 49–58. doi:10.1016/j.ijhm.2015.10.006

Mandelbaum, D. G. (2008). Seeing green: Environmental friendliness as a business strategy. *Franchising World*, 40(11), 56–58.

Mohr, J., & Spekman, R. (1994, February). Characteristics of partnership success: Partnership attributes, communication behavior, and conflict resolution techniques. *Strategic Management Journal*, 15(2), 135–152. doi:10.1002/smj.4250150205

Morgan, R. M., & Hunt, S. D. (1994, July). The commitment–trust theory of relationship marketing. *Journal of Marketing*, 58(3), 20–38. doi:10.2307/1252308

Morrison, A. J. (1996). Small firm strategic alliances: The UK Hotel Industry. Unpublished Ph.D. Thesis, University of Strathclyde, Strathclyde, England. Retrieved from http://ethos.bl.uk/OrderDetails.do?uin=uk.bl.ethos.308682

Morrison, K. A. (1997). How franchise job satisfaction and personality affects performance, organizational commitment, franchisor relationship, and intention to remain. *Journal of Small Business Management*, 35(3), 39–63.

Nyadzayo, M. W., Matanda, M. J., & Ewing, M. T. (2011, October). Brand relationships and brand equity in franchising. *Industrial Marketing Management*, 40(7), 1103–1115. doi:10.1016/j.indmarman.2011.09.004

Nyadzayo, M. W., Matanda, M. J., & Ewing, M. T. (2016, January). Franchisee-based brand equity: The role of brand relationship quality and brand citizenship behavior. *Industrial Marketing Management*, 52, 163–174. doi:10.1016/j.indmarman.2015.07.008

Nygaard, A., & Dahlstrom, R. (2002, April). Role stress and effectiveness in horizontal alliances. *Journal of Marketing*, 66(2), 61–82. doi:10.1509/jmkg.66.2.61.18474

Perrigot, R., Oxibar, B., & Déjean, F. (2015, April). Corporate social disclosure in the franchising sector: Insights from French franchisors' websites. *Journal of Small Business Management*, 53(2), 321–339. doi:10.1111/jsbm.12074

Porter, J., & Renforth, W. (1978). Franchise agreements: Spotting the important legal issues. *Journal of Small Business Management, 16*(4), 27–31.

Preble, J. F., & Hoffman, R. C. (1999, February). The nature of ethics codes in franchise associations around the globe. *Journal of Business Ethics, 18*(3), 239–253. doi:10.1023/A:1005733003323

Rondán-Cataluña, F. J., Navarro-García, A., Gámez-González, J., & Rodríguez-Rad, C. J. (2012). Content analysis and assessment of international codes of franchising association. *Management Decision, 50*(4), 635–650. doi:10.1108/00251741211220228

Spinelli, S., & Birley, S. (1996, September). Towards a theory of conflict in the franchise system. *Journal of Business Venturing, 11*(5), 329–342. doi:10.1016/0883-9026(96)00049-3

Terry, A. (1993). The distribution of goods and services through business format franchising – (part 2). *Current Commercial Law, 1*(2), 60–65.

Tikoo, S. (2002, Autumn). Franchiser influence strategy use and franchisee experience and dependence. *Journal of Retailing, 78*(3), 183–192. doi:10.1016/S0022-4359(02)00064-7

Ting, S., Chen, C., & Bartholomew, D. E. (2007). An integrated study of entrepreneurs' opportunism. *Journal of Business & Industrial Marketing, 22*(5), 322–335. doi:10.1108/08858620710773459

Uçanok, B., & Karabatı, S. (2013, Spring). The effects of values, work centrality, and organizational commitment on organizational citizenship behaviors: Evidence from Turkish SMEs. *Human Resource Development Quarterly, 24*(1), 89–129. doi:10.1002/hrdq.21156

Wathne, K. H., & Heide, J. B. (2000, October). Opportunism in interfirm relationships: Forms, outcomes, and solutions. *Journal of Marketing, 64*(4), 36–51. doi:10.1509/jmkg.64.4.36.18070

Watson, A., & Johnson, R. (2010). Managing the franchisor–franchisee relationship: A relationship marketing perspective. *Journal of Marketing Channels, 17*(1), 51–68. doi:10.1080/10466690903436305

Watson, A., & Stanworth, J. (2006, September). Franchising and intellectual capital: A franchisee's perspective. *The International Entrepreneurship and Management Journal, 2*(3), 337–349. doi:/10.1007/s11365-006-0005-0

Watson, A., Stanworth, J., Healeas, S., Purdy, D., & Stanworth, C. (2005, January). Retail franchising: An intellectual capital perspective. *Journal of Retailing and Consumer Services, 12*(1), 25–34. doi:10.1016/j.jretconser.2004.02.001

Weaven, S., Frazer, L., & Giddings, J. (2010). New perspectives on the causes of franchising conflict in Australia. *Asia Pacific Journal of Marketing and Logistics, 22*, 135–155. doi:10.1108/13555851011026917

Weaven, S., Grace, D., Dant, R., & Brown, J. R. (2014). Value creation through knowledge management in franchising: A multi-level conceptual framework. *Journal of Services Marketing, 28*(2), 97–104. doi:10.1108/JSM-09-2013-0251

Weaven, S., Grace, D., Frazer, L., & Giddings, J. (2014, March). Processual antecedents of perceived channel in franchising. *Journal of Business Economics and Management, 15*(2), 316–334. doi:10.3846/16111699.2012.711362

Williamson, O. E. (1975). *Markets and hierarchies: Analysis and antitrust implications – A study in the economics of internal organizations.* New York, NY: Free Press, Macmillan.

Williamson, O. E. (1983, September). Credible commitments: Using hostages to support exchange. *American Economic Review, 73*(4), 519–540.

Wu, S. H., Huang, S. C. T., Tsai, C. Y. D., & Chen, Y. C. (2009). Service innovation in franchising convenience store: An exploratory study. *International Journal of Electronic Business Management, 7*(2), 137–148.

Yau, O. H. M., McFetridge, P. R, Chow, R. P. M., Lee, J. S. Y., Sin, L. Y. M., & Tse, A. C. B. (2000). Is relationship marketing for everyone? *European Journal of Marketing, 34* (9/10), 1111–1127. doi:10.1108/03090560010342494

Zachary, M. A., McKenny, A. F., Short, J. C., Davis, K. M., & Wu, D. (2011, August). Franchise branding: An organizational identity perspective. *Journal of the Academy of Marketing Science, 39*(4), 629–645. doi:10.1007/s11747-011-0252-7

4 Lessons from the Housing Crisis Support a Formal Fiduciary Standard in For-Profit Higher Education

Robert J. Foran

Introduction

Many factors contributed to the Great Recession, but the erosion of lending standards in the mortgage industry largely explains the root cause of the severe economic downturn. Over a span of a few years, financial firms made it incrementally easier for more individuals to obtain mortgages to purchase larger and more expensive homes. Between 2006 and 2015, as real estate prices collapsed and the Great Recession ensued, nearly 10 million homeowners directly experienced the hardships of foreclosure, home surrender, or short sale (National Center for Policy Analysis, 2015). Similar to the housing market before the crash, the growth of higher education has introduced more risks to student borrowers. By the end of 2016, the outstanding student loan debt surpassed $1.4 trillion, and while falling, the three-year student loan default rate for all postsecondary students exceeded 10% (National Center for Education Statistics, 2017).

The parallels between the precrisis housing market and the current postsecondary education industry highlight the need to retheorize the relationship between some providers and students. Compared to public and nonprofit institutions, the for-profit cohort records higher incidences of borrowing, larger loan amounts, and substantially higher default rates, outcomes reflective of easy credit, and aggressive marketing by some providers in the group. Following the precedent the expansion of the investment advice fiduciary definition established, this chapter argues for expanding the scope of the fiduciary standard to include for-profit providers of postsecondary education services.

The Parallels between Housing and Education

The Great Recession, technically occurring from December 2007 to June 2009, designates the most severe and lasting economic decline in the postwar period. The Federal Reserve Bank (FRB) reports that, at the trough, employment and output declined by 6.3% and 5.1%, respectively (Federal Reserve Bank of Minneapolis, 2017). Many factors contributed to the prolonged period of retracted economic activity, but the erosion of standards in the mortgage lending industry and the securitization of mortgage debt, substantially explain the root causes of the financial meltdown. As rules relaxed in the mortgage lending industry, more people borrowed more money to purchase larger, more expensive, and, in many cases, multiple homes. The spike in housing prices that followed created a financial bubble, a tipping point in the market. The rapid housing market collapse in 2007 led to a broader withdrawal of available credit. As the unraveling of credit facil-

---

Check Your Understanding

Economic Downturns

Economic downturns: How do the Great Recession and the Great Depression compare?

The Great Recession refers to the decline in worldwide economic activity from 2007 to 2009. In the USA, gross domestic product (GDP) declined by more than 4% and the unemployment rate climbed to 10%. The Great Depression was much longer and deeper. From 1929 to 1939, domestic output fell by more than 40% and unemployment reached 25%.

---

ities roiled the financial markets, the dramatic loss of household wealth further deterred business investment and consumer spending. Amid the loss of business and consumer confidence, the recession deepened.

Output and employment indicators, the very broadest measures of economic activity, fail to capture the extensive suffering inflicted by the economic downturn. The National Center for Policy Analysis reports that nearly 10 million homeowners directly experienced the hardships of foreclosure, home surrender, or short sale between 2006 and 2015, a displacement that exceeded the number recorded for the Great Depression (National Center for Policy Analysis, 2015). To make matters worse, the damaged credit histories of many hindered re-entry into the housing market despite a prolonged period of economic recovery that included extensive job creation and the widespread return of mortgage credit facilities. Over time, individual credit scores improved, easing the burden of borrowing for the homeowners that experienced foreclosures before 2011. Unfortunately, formerly sidelined homeowners faced another hurdle as they attempted to re-enter the housing market. In many regions of the country, returning homebuyers faced steep home prices, as values had substantially rebounded in the interim.

The Great Recession resulted from lax credit and investment standards. Lower borrowing thresholds resulted in unethical decisions by lending agents to extend loans and encourage indebtedness on those foreseeably incapable of repaying. Securitization enabled the seemingly endless supply of credit. The collateral of home mortgage loans backed new bond products that attempted to identify and spread risks across different classes of bond instruments. More types of bonds attracted more investors. The larger volume of bonds sold to investors supported the supply of more mortgage loans to persons less likely to make their payments.

In theory, securitization expanded the availability of mortgage credit for the benefit of consumers. In practice, however, the creation of highly complex financial instruments, or derivatives, served an ulterior function. Besides creating a larger volume of business, the potential larger profit from derivatives depended on their complexity and lack of complete information about them. Some market participants understood the nature of these products and the risks involved, but other investors operated in the dark (Kolb & Overdahl, 2010).

The adoption of more technology in the financial services industry rapidly accelerated from about 1980 (U.S. Congress Office of Technology Assessment, 1984). Easier and less costly means to communicate and trade aided transparency and the timeliness of transactions, expansion of trading volumes, and a reduction in transaction costs. Despite the long-term efficiency trend in the financial markets, the complexity of derivatives presented new and larger information gaps, or belief differences, among the buyers and sellers concerning potential risks and rewards of the investment products. Instances of asymmetrical information, whether unintended or by design, offered new trading opportunities for some parties. For some, these new opportunities filled the loss of revenues in more conventional lines of trading.

Initially welcomed by many market participants, runaway securitization turned out badly. The proliferation of derivatives negatively affected homebuyers, investors, and large banks down the line. Speaking at Carlton University in 2010, Donald Kohn, former Vice Chairman of the Board of Governors at the Federal Reserve Bank, summarized this important development in the financial markets:

> Serious deficiencies with these securitizations, the associated derivative instruments, and the structures that evolved to hold securitized debt were at the heart of the financial crisis. Among other things, the structures exposed the banking system to risks that neither participants in financial markets nor regulators fully appreciated.
>
> (Kohn, 2010, n.p.)

Check Your Understanding

Securitization

Securitization: How does securitization contribute to risks in the financial markets?

Securitization is the practice of pooling debts to construct financial instruments dependent upon the underlying cash flows. The classification of cash flows purports to reduce risks; however, the complexity of the arrangements contributes to uneven information, an impediment to risk assessment.

For example, in January 2008, Bank of America Corporation (BAC), then the largest bank in the USA, completed the purchase of Countrywide Financial Corporation, the most active single-family mortgage loan originator in the USA before the credit crisis. In the early stages of a financial meltdown, BAC viewed the purchase of a weakened Countrywide as an opportunity to become the top provider of home loans in the USA. In retrospect, the $4 billion purchase represented a mere fraction of the tens of billions of dollars in costs the bank ultimately incurred for loan buybacks, write-downs, litigation, and penalties associated with the purchase. As a penalty for mortgage fraud at Countrywide, the Federal courts ruled in favor of the US Department of Justice in a case that described a systematic lack of compliance in loan originations and a perverse employee incentive structure. By *hustling* loan originations, Countrywide produced, packaged, and sold thousands of faulty loans to the super-sized government-backed mortgage companies, Fannie Mae and Freddie Mac. For investigators, the $1.3 billion penalty for BAC highlighted a profit-driven business culture at Countrywide that favored quantity over quality by eliminating quality checkpoints and providing employee incentives for producing more loans (Rakoff, 2014).

The response to the mortgage crisis included federal regulation. One year following the official end of the most severe economic downturn since the Great Depression, then recently elected President Obama signed the Dodd-Frank Wall Street Reform and Protection Act into law. Dodd-Frank legislation authorized the formation of the Financial Stability Oversight Council (FSOC) and the Consumer Financial Protection Bureau (CFPB). The creation of the FSOC introduced regulations for business practices in the financial services industry associated with systemic failure. New rules governed banks and financial service companies deemed too risky, especially when the risks could spill over to the general financial industry. Although stopping short of requiring the reestablishment of a separation of commercial and investment banking activities formerly required by the Glass-Steagall Act of 1933, these new regulations to increase bank reserve requirements and place limits on certain investment categories helped to restore confidence in the financial system. On the consumer side, CFPB focused on ways to protect households from unfair, deceptive, and abusive financial practices in the credit industry.

The national economy recovered. Mortgage foreclosures abated. While other factors also may have contributed to these results, federal regulation contributed with higher standards. For the first quarter of 2017, the Board of Governors reported a national delinquency rate on single-family residential mortgages below 4%, a significant reduction from the peak rate of nearly 12% recorded for the first quarter of 2010 and slightly above the range of 1.5%–3.5% reported from 1991 until the onset of the Great Recession (Federal Reserve Bank of St. Louis, 2017).

The Risks of For-Profit Education

Borrowing for the costs of postsecondary education presents little systemic risk to the financial markets because of the smaller size of the industry. However, housing and education share some important characteristics.

Both industries generate positive spillovers, beneficial economic and social outcomes experienced beyond the firsthand parties to the transaction. Unfortunately, both industries also demonstrate large upfront entry costs that discourage market participation. To realize a larger public benefit, the government looks for ways to encourage broader home ownership as well as educational attainment. Similar to the role of the giant government sponsored housing finance firms, Fannie Mae and Freddie Mac, government subsidies and sponsored credit facilities, chiefly administered through Title IV of the Higher Education Act, encourage broader participation in postsecondary education, especially at for-profit institutions. At present, some 90% of first time, full-time degree and certificate-seeking students at for-profit postsecondary undergraduate institutions receive some type of federal student aid (FSA). The largest share of FSA comes in the form of student loans, primarily administered through the Stafford Loan Program (National Center for Education Statistics, 2017).

By 2014, for-profit college enrollments at all Title IV institutions represented just over 9% of postsecondary enrollments, a slight decrease since 2010 but an increase of approximately six-fold since 1990 (National Center for Education Statistics, 2015). Douglass (2012) associates some for-profit postsecondary enrollment growth with the *Brazilian effect*, the for-profit response to unmet public demand in developing countries. In the USA, the view of unmet public demand provides ongoing support for the amended Servicemen's Readjustment Act of 1944 (GI Bill), which prompted a resurgence of for-profit education firms in the decade following WWII (Connell, 2016). Widely considered a positive development, the GI Bill continues to enjoy broad public support for easing the transition of former military service personnel in the post 9/11 era.

The tuition credits and other education benefits from the GI Bill also create important revenue sources for for-profit postsecondary education program providers. In practice, the push to access a larger share of this reliable revenue stream contributes to the development of misaligned incentive structures among some providers. For-profit postsecondary education providers typically employ few full-time faculty but large numbers of recruiters. In extreme cases, for-profit institutions report a recruiter to staff ratio in excess of 10:1 (Beaver, 2017). Others employ aggressive and allegedly deceptive marketing schemes, such as the *pain funnel*. In the pain funnel, prospective

---

Check Your Understanding

Education Supply

Education supply: What initiative provided a jump-start for for-profit education?

At the end of World War II, Congress passed the G. I. Bill or the Serviceman's Readjustment Act of 1944 to help returning war veterans readjust to civilian life. GI education benefits prompted a rapid expansion of postsecondary education in the USA. Although substantively amended over the years, the law enjoys ongoing political and social support. The education benefits offer a reliable revenue source for postsecondary education companies.

students submit to a series of escalating questions that probe for disappointments and failures. Once revealed, recruiters exploit those vulnerabilities to obtain educational program commitments, enabled through credit, with promises to a pathway to success and happiness.

For instance, with the acquisition of Daniel Webster College in 2009, ITT Education Services, Inc. (ITT) served almost 80,000 students, spent about $250 million on marketing, and recorded almost $500 million in profits. In the following year, with almost 90,000 students and an even larger marketing budget, revenues increased to $1.6 billion, and profits rose to more than $600 million (US Senate Committee on Health, Education, Labor, & Pensions, 2012). Appel and Taylor (2015) describe the marketing materials ITT and others used as "a visual guide to help recruiters exploit prospective students' vulnerabilities" (p. 33).

In addition to the revenue enhancement potential of opportunistic marketing, cost-reduction strategies carry important implications for the for-profit education model. Overall, the expenses for student services, academic support, and instructional support, expenses not associated with instruction but including expenditures for advertising, recruitment, and management salaries, exceed 60% at for-profits. In contrast, for-profits only allocate approximately 25% of all expenses to instruction and a mere $19 per full-time enrollment for research and services to the public (National Center for Education Statistics, 2017).

Rules and regulations surrounding the flow of funds to the for-profit education market eroded alongside the deterioration of standards at banks and mortgage lenders. In 1998, the amended Higher Education Act of 1965 increased the limit of government-sourced revenues at proprietary education service providers from 85% to 90%. The new so-called *90/10 rule* required for-profits to derive a mere 10% of fiscal year revenues from sources independent of FSA programs. Unfortunately, the Higher Education Opportunity Act passed in 2008 further weakened the rules by allowing institutions that do not meet the rule to participate in Title IV programs during the following year, with provisional eligibility for two years thereafter (U.S. Congress, 2013).

Looking at full-time undergraduate students at for-profit institutions, only 23% that enrolled in a program for

---

Check Your Understanding

Industry Comparisons

Industry comparisons: What aspects are common to buying a home, investing for retirement, and pursuing a college education?

The three transactions typically represent large financial commitments that have long-term implications for employment income, wealth accumulation, and standard of living. Consumers rely on a series of professionals to guide them through these choices. Real estate agents, mortgage brokers, and lawyers assist in home purchases. Financial consultants advise on retirement plans. College admissions and course counsellors lead students through educational choices.

the first time in 2009 earned a degree or certificate within six years (National Center for Education Statistics, 2015). Despite a much lower graduation rate than their counterparts at nonprofit institutions, students attending for-profit colleges and universities paid more tuition and accumulated more debt (Lynch, Engle, & Cruz, 2010). In 2012, 40% of public four-year-dependent students graduated with no student loan debt, whereas nearly 85% of students that completed a for-profit bachelor's degree program borrowed and almost two-thirds of the for-profit graduates owed more than $27,980 (Association of Public and Land-Grant Universities, 2012).

A comparison of the housing industry before the Great Recession and the contemporary for-profit postsecondary education marketplace reveals similar outcomes. Prior to 2008, relaxed lending standards and securitization promoted a larger mortgage-lending marketplace. However, unethical business practices and risks expanded alongside the increase. In the months leading up to the crash, borrowers, lenders, and investors did not fully understand the hazards.

In postsecondary education, the rapid increase in for-profit enrollments, which subsidies and easier access to credit facilities encouraged, coincides with a dramatic increase in outstanding student loans and loan defaults. Similar to housing, for-profit postsecondary education demonstrates some unethical business practices and insufficient consideration for the risks of student borrowing. Misrepresentations of job prospects, false documentation of income data on FSA forms, inaccurate attendance records, and reports of faulty test scores by some providers likely contribute to the increase in enrollment of financially and academically underqualified students at some for-profits (Association of Public and Land-Grant Universities, 2012). With regard to ITT, the congressional oversight committee concluded the following:

> ITT is one of the most expensive companies examined by the committee, and it is not clear that the value of the education justifies the cost. The cost of attending ITT is so high that the company has created its own loan program to enable students to borrow money in excess of federal lending limits. While the retention rates for both the Associate and the Bachelor's program are slightly better than average, the company has a high rate of student loan default, with 26% of students defaulting within 3 years of entering repayment. This likely reflects the high cost of the programs offered, and an inability on the part of some students to find jobs that allow them to repay the debt they incur. The company makes this work by utilizing some of the most disturbing recruiting tactics among the companies examined, and by taking very creative approaches to complying with the 90/10 limitation on revenue received from FSA programs.
>
> (U.S. Senate Committee on Health, Education, Labor, & Pensions, 2012)

Richard Cordray, first director of the Consumer Financial Protection Bureau (CFPB), correctly connected housing and for-profit education marketplace developments. "Like the mortgage market in the lead-up to the financial crisis, the for-profit college industry may be experiencing misaligned incentives. These colleges benefit when students take out large amounts of loans, regardless of the students' long-term success" (Cordray, 2014). This public scrutiny has supported a number of regulatory actions.

Education Oversight Initiatives

In 2010, The Dodd-Frank Wall Street Reform and Consumer Protection Act empowered the CFPB to pursue actions against unfair, deceptive, or abusive practices of financial institutions. In conjunction, the US Department of Education (ED), under the Obama administration, created a pathway to protect students against the misconduct of postsecondary educational institutions. The *Borrower Defense* (BD) initiative provides for loan repayment forgiveness, reimbursements for prior loan payments, and Pell Grant semester eligibility restorations when schools deceive students about educational services secured through a federal student loan or violate state law directly related to the federal student loan (Federal Student Aid Office, n.d.). Although strengthened in 2016, the new administration appears ready to amend the regulations intended to protect students from institutional misconduct in these areas.

Nonetheless, the still binding Executive Order (EO) 13607 of 2012 promotes eight so-called *principles of excellence* through new regulations to increase substantive and procedural protections for military personnel, veterans, and respective family members against the aggressive and deceptive tactics some education program providers pursue (Obama, 2012). In particular, all proprietary postsecondary schools serving these populations must now report program costs, graduation rates, graduate earnings, and debt accumulations. The more recent Gainful Employment (GE) regulations apply to vocational programs at proprietary schools, and some non-degree or certificate programs at all colleges (U.S. Department of Education, 2015). According to GE rules, programs risk losing the ability to participate in taxpayer funded FSA when a typical graduate incurs an annual loan payment that represents more than 20% of discretionary or 8% of total annual income. In retrospect, the last reporting GE required indicates that two-thirds of the 21 programs at ITT Technical Institute of Indianapolis, Indiana, required loan repayments that exceeded 20% of post-completion discretionary incomes (Federal Student Aid Office, 2016). Similar to BD, the future of enforcement of EO and GE regulations remains unclear under the new administration (U.S. Department of Education, 2017).

Despite the potential for regulatory setbacks, government oversight has changed the marketplace. In 2014, Corinthian Colleges, Inc., one of the major for-profit publicly traded education firms, closed after ED suspended the company from FSA eligibility. Later that year, the CFPB filed a lawsuit against ITT, which alleged that the for-profit misled students about future job prospects and pressured students into predatory loans that were likely to default and credits that would not transfer. In the third quarter of 2016, ITT closed, leaving students and, to some extent, taxpayers saddled with $500 million dollars in student loan debts. A few days later, the CFPB issued a consent order that forced Bridgeport Education to pay refunds and discharge student debts to settle claims of deceptive marketing and a faulty in-house student loan program (Consumer Financial Protection Bureau, 2016; cf., U.S. Department of Justice, 2015). These actions represent progress; however, a more comprehensive framework is required.

A Path toward More Ethical Industry Conduct

In the development of the common law in the USA, the courts have applied fiduciary duties in a variety of settings. These duties, often invoked in commercial settings, constrain "parties who otherwise are free to pursue of prefer their own interests" (DeMott, 2006, p. 926). Duties compel entrusted parties to always place the interests of the shareholders or clients first. Specifically, they constrain parties who otherwise are free to enhance their profits at the expense of the shareholders or clients. In practice, the invocation of fiduciary duties of care and loyalty prohibit a range of business misconduct. The application of these duties is not always consistent. The factual nuances in specific cases contribute to the variety of interpretation under the common law. However, instances of deception and fraud in the marketplace represent clear examples of a breach of those duties. Moreover, when these breaches are widespread and egregious, they may prompt a regulatory response, similar to the actions of CFPB in the housing and for-profit education industries. The President by executive order, the legislature, or a regulatory agency may enact fiduciary duties, independent of the remedies common law courts afford.

Historically, the corporate fiduciary duties arose to curb rent seeking by managers in corporations. Corporate officers and directors could too easily turn corporate opportunities and management privileges to their personal benefit or to the benefit of non-shareholders. The courts developed fiduciary duties as obligations on management in favor of shareholders. The stalwart free-market supporter, Milton Friedman (1962), famously argued the shareholder perspective as follows:

> ...there is one and only one social responsibility of business to use its resources and engage in activities designed to increase its profits so long as it stays in the rules of the game, which is to say, engages in open and free competition, without deception or fraud.

(p. 133)

Stakeholder theory expanded the range of beneficiaries of fiduciary duties. It introduced legitimate consideration of the interests of other groups, persons, and entities vital to the success of the company (Freeman, 1984). Generally, early applications of stakeholder theory, absent considerations for the value of intrinsic social functions, largely helped for-profits to see how considering the needs of others would help to improve bottom lines. Later, emphasizing Kant's principle of respect for persons, stakeholder theory invoked a moral obligation to act in the interests of others. Thus, a management theory for corporate performance enhancement became a component of an ethical theory of corporate governance, or Corporate Social Responsibility (CSR). The evolved perspective requires consideration of the interest of all persons, groups, and entities, not just those vital to the success of the company (Freeman, Harrison, Wicks, Parmar, & de Colle, 2010).

CSR resonates in many corporate halls. However, talk and practice often diverge, especially if the former alone serves the immediate goal of public relations. Unfortunately, for-profit postsecondary education program outcomes, similar to the housing industry record before the Great Recession, reveal the shortcomings of some industry practices under existing corporate governance structures. Outcomes indicate that many students incur substantial debt to cover the high upfront costs to a large number of for-profit programs with a record of poor outcomes, and, far too often, many go into default. Moreover, a growing record of deception and fraud in the industry, which regulators compile, bolsters the argument that this marketplace, not unlike the mortgage lending industry before the Great Recession, reflects widespread breach of duties at the top of the hierarchy.

Student loan default rates declined after 2010, but remain high compared to the national mortgage delinquency rate. Student loans assumed for private non-profit undergraduate degree programs currently experience default rates of 8%; whereas, the student loan default rate for loans associated with completing proprietary undergraduate degree programs remains above 15%, nearly one-third higher than the default rate for loans to earn degrees at public four-year institutions and almost quadruple the current national mortgage delinquency rate (National Student Loan Data System, 2016). Although new oversight in the for-profit education market represents progress, current regulations do not completely restore, or make all eligible students whole, who have suffered from unethical corporate practices. In addition, the risks of regulatory backtracking follow the recent change in political leadership and the continued efforts of industry lobbyists. Together, the complexity of education decision-making, the heavy reliance students place on the greater knowledge of providers, and the meaningful long-term implications of poor outcomes highlight the inadequacies of the existing regulatory framework. The lack of sufficient consideration for the interest of students, persons vital to the success of the providers, suggests a need to retheorize the relationship between for-profit education providers and students. This chapter advocates adoption of a formal fiduciary standard to the relationship among students, for-profit providers, and the government. A policy initiative to extend the fiduciary rule highlights the deeply rooted structural importance of education and the failure of some for-profits to consider the needs of students and the public at-large.

The Duties of a Fiduciary

In professional roles involving high-reliance by the public for complex decision-making with long-term implications, fiduciaries like physicians, lawyers, and bank trust officers must disclose potential conflicts of interest, disciplinary records, and information about their qualifications, services, and fees. For accountants, for example, the fiduciary test is functional. It depends on the context. Accountants owe a fiduciary duty to their clients, especially when the relationship involves great trust and heavy reliance on business expertise, or when an accountant provides advice as a registered investment advisor. However, when their task involves an audit of the client, accountants owe a fiduciary duty to the public as well.

As another model, the Employee Retirement Income Security Act of 1974 (ERISA) requires all persons with control or authority over the management or administration of an employee benefit plan or its assets to meet certain fiduciary criteria (US Department of Labor, n.d.). Setting the standard of fiduciary conduct, ERISA governs all employee benefit plans to guard the interests of members and their beneficiaries with provisions for access to federal courts and the determination of remedies for breach of duty.

ERISA replaces the Welfare and Pension Plans Disclosure Act (WPPDA). Disclosure, the primary focus of WPPDA, remains a cornerstone of ERISA. Originating in the common law of trusts, disclosure requires fiduciaries to share all information needed to reach an informed decision. Fiduciaries must respond to the requests of participants and beneficiaries, or initiate the research, vetting, and full disclosure of information relevant and pertinent to the plan and its participants.

Expanding the scope of retirement plan oversight, ERISA adds duties of care, monitoring, prudence, and, especially, loyalty. The duty of loyalty complements the duty of disclosure. ERISA laws require plan administrators, as fiduciaries, to act solely for the benefit of the members of plans and their beneficiaries. ERISA section 404(a)(1), frequently referred to as the *exclusive benefit rule*, prohibits self-dealing and the placement of third-party interests over that of a plan participant or beneficiary. It requires the fiduciary to perform his or her duties to the retirement plan exclusively in the interests of the members and their beneficiaries, and for the exclusive purpose of providing benefits to the members and their beneficiaries.

With respect to the duty of care, specifically, employers must earmark employee retirement funds and hold the assets in accounts that are separate from the assets of the business to help safeguard against misappropriations and business failures. The distinct separation of company and plan assets keeps the retirement plan assets outside the reach of the company's creditors in the event

> ### Check Your Understanding
>
> #### Fiduciary Standard
>
> *Fiduciary standard: Is your best friend your fiduciary?*
>
> Your best friend is not your fiduciary, unless he or she additionally fills an important role such as your attorney, investment adviser, trustee, doctor, or the director or officer of a company in which you hold shares. Fiduciary duties impose obligations of loyalty and care on a person or entity. A fiduciary must place the interests of beneficiaries, clients, and shareholders first, above his or her own. Although we may hope a friend is always loyal, the law does not impose or expect this duty.

the business declares bankruptcy. As an added aspect of care, ERISA directs fiduciaries to monitor the performance, fee schedules, actual fees charged, and all changes to policies, procedures, and practices of plan service providers.

Before ERISA, employees and their beneficiaries enjoyed few protections or remedies when employers declared bankruptcy, borrowed from or pledged plan assets for collateral, or imprudently invested pension funds. ERISA section 404(a)(1)(B) specifies that a fiduciary must act "with the care, skill, prudence and diligence under the circumstances then prevailing that a prudent man acting in a like capacity and familiar with such matters would use in the conduct of an enterprise of a like character and with like aims." Now known as the *prudent person rule*, the fiduciary must weigh investment decisions on behalf of the beneficiaries against those of a hypothetical prudent person to manage risks. The duty of prudence implies a careful, sober, and judicious approach to relevant discovery and decision-making, which in many instances includes considerations on providing for the future. The determination of prudence is case-specific. Before the investment of plan funds or the sale of plan assets, the duty of prudence requires considerations for risk of loss, expected rates of return, and the role that the investment fulfills in the plan's portfolio of investments, for example, diversification and liquidity.

Additionally, the Obama administration expanded the investment advice fiduciary definition to promote more accountability and transparency in the retirement account services industry. Under the prior, more limited definition, only fee-based advisers filled the role of fiduciary. Brokers, insurance agents, and investment salespeople merely strived to meet investment suitability criteria, which created potential conflicts of interests such as recommending products with higher commissions, fees, and kickbacks. Administered by the US Department of Labor, the so-called *fiduciary rule* legally and ethically binds brokers and financial advisers to meet the fiduciary standards imposed under ERISA when transacting for retirement accounts (U.S. Department of Labor, 2016, 2017). Any financial professional investing or providing investment advice for retirement plans now must consider what is best for clients with regard to retirement investments. Extending the fiduciary standard strictly forbids conflicts of interest and hidden fees. Brokers and agents now must go beyond the determination of the mere appropriateness of an investment to place the needs of their clients first, ahead of any considerations for commissions.

Duties of Loyalty and Care in Higher Education

Posing the question of fiduciary rules easily transfers to the education context. Do considerations of the intrinsic importance of education and the record of for-profit providers support another extension of the fiduciary rule? At a basic level, a fiduciary relationship requires elements of entrustment, disproportionate power and control, and self-interest subordination to protect the interest of the beneficiaries (Scharffs & Welch, 2005). Students rely on the greater knowledge, skills, and power of providers to navigate the complexities of education decision-making. They ultimately pay for the high costs of postsecondary education access directly, upfront and deferred through borrowing, and indirectly through work-study trade-offs and aid tapping. The for-profit providers are in the position of identifying revenue sources available to students through FSA programs, exhaustible property-like interests intrinsically associated with improving livelihoods and social welfare, and make determinations with respect to these resources.

Students must thus entrust providers, the holders of power and control in the relationship, to represent their interests in the access and use of their entitlements. Unfortunately, too many providers place far too little emphasis upon the interests of their students, the stakeholder group most vital to the success of the company. The design of a new relationship to limit the discretion of providers requires the construction of a framework of substantive and formal duties. These consist principally of duties of loyalty, disclosure, and care. The proposal also must contemplate considerations of focus, duration, scope, and remedy (Chodos, 2011).

Under fiduciary law, the duties of loyalty and care act as primary regulatory instruments (Frankel, 1998). Loyalty sounds straightforward; however, the goals to increase revenues and profits conflict with the delivery of consistent and objective advice to students. In such contexts, studies from other industries suggest the faultiness of incentive-based advice (Mullainathan, Noth, & Schoar, 2011).

Already in place for the benefit of military personnel and veterans, Part (c) of EO 13607 provides for a type of duty of loyalty. It forbids fraudulent and aggressive recruitment practices and payment of incentive compensation. Instead, marketing materials ought to reflect the results of a thorough investigation of the relevant questions, such as program costs, completion and job placement rates, and the projected growth of labor demand in the fields related to the program.

In addition to certain already prohibited practices, minimizing the risks of breach of duty of loyalty calls for internal barriers and the engagement of independent agents. In particular, a record of self-dealing by some providers suggests the need for an independent clearing-house, which the industry would fund, to collect, organize, and distribute information on all for-profit education programs to facilitate program comparisons. Clearly, more standardized information on programs, costs, and outcomes facilitates improved decision-making among students.

Duties of disclosure would require a fiduciary to share all information pertinent to informed decision-making. *Borrower Defense* (BD) already has increased disclosure requirements for the for-profits by requiring proprietary schools with high student loan default rates to include a plain-language warning in their advertising and promotional materials. GE regulations also require more disclosure with added penalties for failing to meet standards. To some extent, the emphasis on disclosure requirements in BD and GE regulations mirror the regulatory environment of employee-sponsored retirement plans before ERISA. In addition, the eight principles of excellence, which Section title (The Parallels between Housing and Education) of EO 13607 outline, apply regulations, for institutions servicing military service personnel, veterans, and respective family members, which approach the level of a fiduciary standard (Obama, 2012).

Parts (a) and (b) of EO 13607 further strengthen disclosure by requiring providers to give prospective students the total costs of programs and the portions of the costs that the federal education benefits cover. Providers must disclose the availability and eligibility for FSA, before the assumption of private student loans, estimated debt accumulations to complete the programs, and details about student program outcomes to facilitate program and institutional comparisons. To some extent, EO 13607 addresses the duty of care. Part (g) requires educational plans that outline "all the requirements necessary to graduate and the expected timeline of completion," and Part (h) requires dedicated access to academic and financial counseling services to help with "the successful completion of their studies and with their job searches." Other parts establish rules for new program offerings and clarify refund and re-admittance policies for service members, veterans, and respective family members.

Unfortunately, some of the existing regulations only direct institutions with regard to the needs of military service personnel, veterans, and family members. These would need to be extended to all students. At a minimum, all the for-profits must begin efforts to determine the suitability of an educational program for specific students. This requires that providers obtain knowledge of each student's academic and financial preparedness. In this context, the Association of Public and Land-Grant Universities proposes the development of institution-specific student risk indices to incorporate predictors of academic and financial success (Tanner, 2012).

Duties to students begin with marketing and recruitment. Once enrolled in a program, students depend on the school to act in good faith and with their interests in mind. In the course of earning a degree, many students assume large debts. Therefore, fiduciary duties must continue during the loan repayment period for indebted students. The scope of the duties and the degree of breach should inform the remedy. The extent of trust, the size of the power differential, and the long-term importance of education outcomes suggest a high level of duty to students.

In terms of potential penalties, existing regulations mainly reflect efforts to increase disclosure. BD provides a limited pathway to debt forgiveness, loan payment refunds, and aid reinstatements; however, these remedies stop short of the assessment of penalties for actual damages and restitution. In many cases, students endure an opportunity cost for ill-advised educational programs that include a substantial allocation of time and foregone earnings. Even if new laws permit students to seek further recourse, remedies like FSA ineligibility for the institution and restitution of tuition for students likely would bankrupt individual institutions. It would leave them without the necessary resources to settle individual student claims. Therefore, other options need consideration. One possibility is for-profits paying a tax per full-time student equivalent to fund a separate reserve account for the benefit of potential student claims.

Conclusion

This essay merely begins to sketch out a path to higher ethical standards by means of extending fiduciary duties to the education sector. A formal fiduciary framework in the for-profit postsecondary education industry limits the discretion of providers around formative duties and highlights the importance of a fundamental structural role formerly filled at public and non-profit institutions. The recommendation to increase the substantive and procedural protections for students afforded by the fiduciary framework avoids the simplistic recommendation to end eligibility for government-backed educational assistance in the for-profit postsecondary industry. An up-front call to end eligibility at for-profit providers in favor of public and non-profits fails to recognize that, as an industry, for-profits increase access and demonstrate a record of quickly responding to the perceived needs of industries in an era of rapid structural economic change. Sadly, in some form and to some extent, some of the unwanted behaviors at for-profits exist in the public and non-profits as well. As such, this chapter suggests the continuing exploration of a fiduciary framework for other relationships related to the overall supply of postsecondary education.

Discussion Questions

1   What practices in for-profit education create ethical risks?
2   How do conflicts of interest in the financial services industry compare to the for-profit education industry?
3   Which fiduciary duties should for-profit education providers perform?
4   What are the possible remedies when for-profit education firms commit a breach of duty?

To Cite This Chapter

Foran, R. J. (2018). Lessons from the housing crisis support a formal fiduciary standard in for-profit higher education. In H. Gringarten, & R. Fernández-Calienes (Eds.). *Ethical branding and marketing: Cases and lessons* (pp. 50–68). Routledge Management and Business Studies Series. London and New York: Routledge.

References

Appel, H., & Taylor, A. (2015). Education with a debt sentence: For-profit colleges as American dream crushers and factories of debt. *New Labor Forum, 24*(1), 31–36. doi:10.1177/1095796014562860.

Beaver, W. (2017, January/February). The rise and fall of for-profit higher education. *Academe, 103*(1), 32–37.

Chodos, R. (2011). The nature of fiduciary law and its relationship to other legal doctrines and categories. *Boston University Law Review, 91*(3), 837–848.

Connell, K. W. (2016). *Degrees of deception: America's for-profit higher education fraud* (Reprinted ed.). Lanham, MD: Rowman and Littlefield Publishers.

Consumer Financial Protection Bureau. (2016, September 12). *Consent order in the matter of: Bridgeport Education, Inc.* Retrieved July 24, 2017, from Consumer Financial Protection Bureau: http://files.consumerfinance.gov/f/documents/092016_cfpb_BridgepointConsentOrder.pdf

Cordray, R. (2014, February 26). *CFPB sues for-profit college chain ITT for predatory lending.* Retrieved July 10, 2017, from Consumer Financial Protection Bureau: https://www.consumerfinance.gov/about-us/newsroom/cfpb-sues-for-profit-college-chain-itt-for-predatory-lending/

DeMott, D. A. (2006). Breach of fiduciary duty: On justifiable expectations of loyalty and their consequences. *Arizona Law Review, 48*(4), 925–956.

Douglass, J. A. (2012, June). The rise of the for-profit sector in U.S. higher education and the Brazilian effect. *The European Journal of Education Research, 47*(2), 242–259. doi:10.1111/j.1465-3435.2012.01521.x

Federal Reserve Bank of Minneapolis. (2017). *The recession and recovery in perspective.* Retrieved July 20, 2017, from Federal Reserve Bank of Minneapolis: https://www.minneapolisfed.org/publications/special-studies/recession-in-perspective

Federal Reserve Bank of St. Louis. (2017, June 16). *Economic data: Delinquencies and delinquency rates.* Retrieved August 20, 2017, from FRED: https://fred.stlouisfed.org/series/DRSFRMACBS

Federal Student Aid Office. (2016, December 21). *2014–2015 Award year: Report and summary chart.* Retrieved July 23, 2017, from U.S. Department of Education: https://studentaid.ed.gov/sa/about/data-center/school/proprietary

Federal Student Aid Office. (n.d.). *Borrower defense to repayment.* Retrieved July 22, 2017, from U.S. Department of Education: https://studentaid.ed.gov/sa/repay-loans/forgiveness-cancellation/borrower-defense

Frankel, T. (1998). Definition of "fiduciary duties." In P. Newman (Ed.), *The new Palgrave dictionary of economics and the law* (Vol. 2, pp. 127–128). London, England: Palgrave Macmillan. doi:10.1007/978-1-349-14286-6

Freeman, R. E. (1984). *Strategic management: A stakeholder approach.* Boston, MA: Pitman.

Freeman, R. E., Harrison, J. S., Wicks, A. C., Parmar, B. L., & de Colle, S. (2010). *Stakeholder theory: The state of the art.* Boston, MA: Cambridge University Press. doi:10.1017/CBO9780511815768

Friedman, M. (1962). *Capitalism and freedom.* Chicago, IL: University of Chicago Press. doi:10.7208/chicago/9780226264189.001.0001

Kohn, D. L. (2010, May 13). *The Federal Reserve's policy actions during the financial crisis and lessons for the future: Remarks at Carlton University, Ottawa, Canada.* Retrieved July 22, 2017, from FRASER, Discover Economic History, Federal Reserve: https://fraser.stlouisfed.org/scribd/?item_id=10520&filepath=/files/docs/historical/kohn/kohn_20100513.pdf

Kolb, R. W., & Overdahl, J. A. (2010). *Financial derivatives: Pricing and risk management.* Hoboken, NJ: John Wiley & Sons, Inc. doi:10.1002/9781118266403

Lynch, M., Engle, J., & Cruz, J. L. (2010, November 22). *Subprime opportunity: The unfulfilled promise of for-profit colleges and universities.* Retrieved July 12, 2017, from The Education Trust: https://edtrust.org/resource/subprime-opportunity-the-unfulfilled-promise-of-for-profit-colleges-and-universities/

Mullainathan, S., Noth, M., & Schoar, A. (2011, April). *The market for financial advice: An audit study.* Retrieved August 6, 2017, from Department of Economics, Yale University: http://www.econ.yale.edu/~shiller/behfin/2011-04-11/Mullainathan.pdf

National Center for Education Statistics. (2015). *Digest of education statistics.* Retrieved July 15, 2017, from U.S. Department of Education: https://nces.ed.gov/pubs2016/2016014.pdf

National Center for Education Statistics. (2017, April). *The condition of education: Sources of financial aid.* Retrieved August 3, 2017, from U.S. Department of Education: https://nces.ed.gov/programs/coe/indicator_cuc.asp

National Center for Education Statistics. (2017, May). *The condition of education: Postsecondary institution expenses.* Retrieved July 21, 2017, from U.S. Department of Education: https://nces.ed.gov/programs/coe/indicator_cue.asp

National Center for Policy Analysis. (2015, May 11). *The 2008 housing crisis displaced more Americans than the 1930s dust bowl.* Retrieved July 25, 2017, from National Center for Policy Analysis: http://www.ncpa.org/sub/dpd/index.php?Article_ID=25643

National Student Loan Data System. (2016, September 26). *Official cohort default rate search for postsecondary schools fiscal years 2013, 2012, 2011.* Retrieved July 29, 2017, from National Student Loan Data System: https://nslds.ed.gov/nslds/nslds_SA/defaultmanagement/search_cohort_3yr_CY_20_13.cfm

Obama, B. (2012, April 27). *Executive Order — Establishing principles of excellence for educational institutions serving service members, veterans, spouses, and other family members.* Retrieved July 15, 2017, from Obama White House: https://obamawhitehouse.archives.gov/the-press-office/2012/04/27/executive-order-establishing-principles-excellence-educational-instituti

Rakoff, J. S. (2014, July 30). *Opinion and order case no. 1:12-cv-01422-JSR.* Retrieved July 12, 2017, from Document Cloud: https://assets.documentcloud.org/documents/2841697/Rakoff-Clean.pdf

Scharffs, B. G., & Welch, J. W. (2005). An analytic framework for understanding and evaluating the fiduciary duties of educators. *Brigham Young University Education and Law Journal, 2005*(2), 159–229. doi:10.2139/ssrn.2598765

Tanner, R. M. (2012). *APLU white paper on federal student aid policies.* Retrieved August 21, 2017, from Association of Public and Land-Grant Universities: http://www.aplu.org/library/federal-student-aid-access-and-completion/file

U.S. Congress. (2013, December 26). *Higher Education Act of 1965.* Retrieved August 4, 2017, from U.S. House of Representatives: http://legcounsel.house.gov/Comps/HEA65_CMD.pdf

U.S. Congress Office of Technology Assessment. (1984). *Effects of technology on financial services systems.* Washington, DC: U.S. Government Printing Office.

U.S. Department of Education. (2015, March 16). *Negotiated rulemaking 2013-2014— Gainful employment.* Retrieved July 23, 2017, from U.S. Department of Education: https://www2.ed.gov/policy/highered/reg/hearulemaking/2012/gainfulemployment.html

U.S. Department of Education. (2017, June 30). *DeVos presses pause on burdensome gainful employment regulations.* Retrieved November 3, 2017, from U.S. Department of Education: https://www.ed.gov/news/press-releases/devos-presses-pause-burdensome-gainful-employment-regulations

U.S. Department of Justice. (2015, November 16). *For-profit college company to pay $95.5 million to settle claims of illegal recruiting, consumer fraud, and other violations.* Retrieved November 3, 3017, from U.S. Department of Justice: https://www.justice.gov/opa/pr/profit-college-company-pay-955-million-settle-claims-illegal-recruiting-consumer-fraud-and

U.S. Department of Labor. (2016, April 8). *Federal Register, Vol. 81, No. 68, rules and regulations.* Retrieved July 30, 2017, from U.S. Department of Labor: http://webapps.dol.gov/FederalRegister/PdfDisplay.aspx?DocId=28806

U.S. Department of Labor. (2017, August 30). *Field Assistance Bulletin No. 2017-03.* Retrieved November 3, 2017, from U.S. Department of

Labor: https://www.dol.gov/agencies/ebsa/employers-and-advisers/guidance/field-assistance-bulletins/2017-03

U.S. Department of Labor. (n.d.). *Employee Retirement Income Security Act (ERISA)*. Retrieved July 29, 2017, from U.S. Department of Labor: https://www.dol.gov/general/topic/retirement/erisa#doltopics

U.S. Senate Committee on Health, Education, Labor, & Pensions. (2012). *For profit report: ITT Educational Services*. Retrieved July 11, 2017, from U.S. Senate Committee on Health, Education, Labor & Pensions: https://www.help.senate.gov/imo/media/for_profit_report/PartII/ITT.pdf

5   Bayer, Ethics, and the Anthrax Scare

Leveraging National Crisis for a Public Relations Bonanza

Hagai Gringarten

Introduction

On September 11, 2001, 19 terrorists associated with Osama bin Laden's al-Qaeda group hijacked four planes and carried out suicide attacks. Two planes crashed into the World Trade Center towers, one into the Pentagon in Washington, D.C., and the fourth plane crashed in rural Pennsylvania due to heroic behavior of passengers and crew. The terrorists' intended fourth target was the US Cap-

> **Check Your Understanding**
>
> *Anthrax*
>
> *Anthrax* is a serious infectious disease caused by bacteria known as Bacillus anthracis. Anthrax is rare in the USA and can be found naturally in nature and animals. It is readily found in soil and is responsible for causing disease in livestock. It is not contagious, like the cold or flu, but people can get sick with anthrax if they come in contact with infected animals or contaminated animal products.

itol. These terrorist acts killed more than 2,900 people and injured more than 6,000 people (History Channel, 2018; Hodge, 2002).

These coordinated terrorist attacks had a dramatic social-psychological impact on the US people that forever will be etched in memory and known simply as 9/11. It created an atmosphere of apprehension and uncertainty, and was one of the greatest crises in US history (Burke, 2005; The economic consequences of the new global terrorism, 2002).

About three weeks later on October 4, 2001, Florida health officials announced that Robert Stevens, a photo editor for American Media, Inc. had received a diagnosis of pulmonary anthrax. This extremely rare disease has a high mortality rate (Meyerhoff et al., 2004). This was the first such case in the USA in almost 25 years, and initially was attributed to natural sources. He died two days later on October 6, 2001, and almost immediately, the anthrax story became front-page news (Holmes, 2001).

Shortly thereafter, two Washington, D.C., postal workers died from inhalation-type anthrax. Other cases began to appear in New York, Connecticut, New Jersey, and Washington, D.C. Anthrax-tainted letters arrived at various government and media locations (such as the offices of Senators Tom Daschle and Patrick Leahy, and NBC anchor Tom Brokaw), causing great concern among postal employees, government officials, and media professionals.

Within two weeks, government officials realized these were multiple bioterrorism attacks. All Federal mail delivery in Washington, D.C., stopped, and mailrooms, congressional office buildings, and US Postal Service (USPS) closed and decontaminated its facilities for a period of several months at a cost of tens of millions of dollars. By the end of November 2001, anthrax-tainted letters stopped arriving at various locations, and the first bioterrorism attack on US soil in the twenty-first century seemed to have run its course (Center for Counterproliferation Research, National Defense University, 2002).

Government and US Public Response

Bioterrorism attacks were rare in the USA, and government readiness or lack thereof was based on rare historical accounts and modern risk assessments. In 1972, there was an effort to contaminate the water supply of several Midwestern cities. In 1984, salad bars in Oregon were contaminated with a form of salmonella, which resulted in 700 cases of food poisoning. The USA lacked experience in dealing with a large-scale psychological or physical bioterrorism (Hodge, 2002).

The effect of the first major bioterrorism attack on the USA in the twenty-first century was amplified by the September 11 attacks that occurred a few weeks earlier. The size, impact, and perspective of the two historical terrorist attacks on people in the USA were enormous in respect to monetary cost and psychological effect. Bioterrorism incidents pose more of a psychological threat than physical. While they are not very good at destruction, they do create public panic and loss of confidence in government (Moscrop, 2001).

In addition to the bioterrorism psychological effect, it was all learn-as-you-go for government, law, and health officials responding to the tragic events. Pulmonary anthrax was rare in the USA. This meant emergency room physicians lacked experience in diagnosing it accurately and in treating it properly, while government officials lacked experience in responding to such scenarios. Also, first responders initially lacked adequate resources and capabilities to handle such attacks. Health and Human Services (HHS) and Center for Disease Control (CDC) officials had difficulties providing information on how to identify and treat anthrax infected individuals (Wechsler, 2001).

The early cases were treated as isolated cases stemming from natural causes. Some were misdiagnosed. Initially, health officials failed to link the anthrax incidents, and it took about two weeks for a different picture to emerge. Investigators realized early on that someone was deliberately spreading anthrax spores. Given the proximity to the September 11 attacks, the early national consensus was that the anthrax attacks might be from a foreign source.

Laboratories across the nation were inundated with test requests, and the CDC reported more than 125,000 tests within weeks of the initial discovery. Initial responses were at times inconsistent or inaccurate with the information coming from multiple federal, state, and local sources. The initial lack of information from the US government, the great deal of speculation by the media, and the psychological effect of bioterrorism attacks and the unknown perpetrator all exacerbated public confusion and panic.

The learn-as-you-go was fast, and government officials communicated with employees and the public with transparency and timely messages. This helped alleviate public concerns and reduce anxiety and fear among the public, while state and federal agencies gained experience with the response to such a massive incident. Investigators determine that the letters also posed a grave threat to postal employees and to anyone who came into contact with them. Office buildings, mail-processing centers, and other locations were closed and evacuated so the process of evaluation and decontamination could begin. At the time, the only antimicrobial drug approved by the US FDA for use in treating an infection due to a biological agent used intentionally, was the drug ciprofloxacin hydrochloride. Bayer AG of Germany marketed it under the brand name Cipro. The FDA approved it in 1987, and in 2000, it approved that particular medicine that specified effectiveness in treating inhaled anthrax (Enserink, 2001; Meyerhoff et al., 2004; Wechsler, 2001).

Check Your Understanding

Cipro

Cipro is the Bayer AG brand name for the prescription antibiotic ciprofloxacin. In 2001, it was the only FDA-approved treatment for anthrax. Today, it is a big seller for the treatment of a broad range of serious infections

---

Check Your Understanding

US Food and Drug Administration (FDA)

FDA: The Food and Drug Administration is the oldest comprehensive consumer protection agency in the US federal government. The FDA is responsible for protecting the public health by ensuring the safety, efficacy, and security of human and veterinary drugs, biological products, and medical devices; and by ensuring the safety of our nation's food supply, cosmetics, and products that emit radiation.

With the increased media coverage of the situation, Cipro gained national and international prominence. The CDC rapidly deployed antibiotics to affected areas, and at the peak of the outbreak, more than 30,000 people were taking antibiotics. Anthrax is treatable if antibiotics are administered promptly and continued for 60 days with a treatment regimen of two pills a day. On October 10, 2001, the CDC requested Bayer AG to increase production of Cipro, while a "run on Cipro" was occurring by an uneasy and concerned public. By November 8, 2001, the CDC reported that about 32,000 people were prescribed antibiotics as a precaution, but only about 5,000 people actually needed it.

Bayer AG

Founded in 1863 by Friedrich Bayer and Johann Friedrich Weskott in Barmen, Germany, Bayer AG started as a manufacturer of synthetic dyestuffs. Its target market was the rapidly growing textile industry. After both founders died, around 1880, Bayer AG experienced an economic downturn because competitors were able to circumnavigate patents. Top management decided to diversify from the dyestuff industry and expand into chemicals and pharmaceuticals.

In 1897, Bayer invented what today people know as Aspirin and changed forever the market of fever and infection drugs. Launched into market in 1899, Bayer's timing could not have been more opportune. Around 1900, several serious influenza epidemics in Europe made Bayer a household name in Europe and North America. Following media frenzy and positive reviews as the "drug of the century," Bayer Aspirin gained tremendous brand equity and market share with the free and positive media publicity, and at minimal costs (Bayer, 2018; Jenneweim, Durand, & Gerybadze, 2010). A single brand can attain market value of more than the company's book value (Jenneweim et al., 2010); thus, the company "built on aspirin" continued to grow and became a global chemical and pharmaceutical powerhouse.

The company's fortunes changed dramatically when, in the summer of 2001, Bayer was forced to withdraw its cholesterol-lowering drugs, Baycol, in the USA, and Lipobay, in the UK, after 31 patients died. By September

---

Check Your Understanding

Bayer AG and Bayer Corporation

Bayer AG: Founded in Barmen, Germany, in 1863, by Friedrich Bayer and Johann Friedrich Weskott, Bayer AG (in German: *actiongesselschaft*, in English: *corporation*) is a German-based global pharmaceutical. Bayer AG is the manufacturer of Cipro. Headquartered in Leverkusen, Germany, it is the parent company of Bayer Corporation.

Bayer Corporation: headquartered in Pittsburgh, Pennsylvania, Bayer Corporation is the North American subsidiary of Bayer AG.

2001, share price of Bayer AG sank by 40%, and Bayer AG executives were contemplating selling the pharmaceutical division (Charatan, 2001; Jenneweim et al., 2010). A month later, the anthrax attacks changed the USA forever and in the process gave Bayer AG a lifeline.

Today, Bayer AG is a global "life science company" with core competencies in the areas of health care and agriculture, employing more than 99,000 people worldwide. The Bayer brand was recently valued at 6.3 billion Euros (Bayer, 2018).

US Government, Bayer AG, and Cipro: "In Cipro We Trust, But Not In Bayer"

Relations between the US government and Bayer AG started a decade before the anthrax attacks. During the Gulf war in 1991, the US Army needed Cipro for its soldiers, since it was the only FDA approved drug for inhalation anthrax. Bayer ultimately donated 10 million tablets (Holmes, 2001). It also worked with the US government on research, studies, and emergency scenarios, while it increased production of Cipro as a precaution. As the bioterrorism attacks unfolded in 2001, Bayer was slow to respond publicly, since executives did not want to give the impression that Bayer was trying to leverage a crisis. On October 15, 2001, 11 days after the first occurrence, Cipro gained national prominence when NBC anchor Tom Brokaw held to the camera a bottle of Cipro during his national nightly news segment and announced, "In Cipro we trust" (Herper, 2001). Bayer put its factory in Connecticut on a 24-hour-a-day, seven-days-a-week production schedule of Cipro. Timing could not have been better for Bayer, and Bayer's shares rose by almost 40% in the wake of the anthrax attacks.

With the US public in panic mode, and a major newscaster having visualized in their mind the only FDA approved anti-anthrax treatment, demand as well as anxiety skyrocketed. The same day, the government enquired with Bayer about supplying 100 million tablets (Holmes, 2001). Following the request, Bayer corporate communications organized a highly attended press conference. The single message was that Bayer would produce Cipro on a 24-hour-a day, seven-days-a-week schedule, and it would reopen another dedicated facility just for Cipro. The message was that Bayer always "fulfilled every order to date from the U.S. government with the requested delivery schedule, and we are prepared to work with the government to fulfill future orders" (Holmes, 2001, p. 6).

Bayer went to great lengths to convey that it would not take advantage of the bioterrorist attacks and would keep the same prices that were in place before the October attacks. Reassuring the US public of adequate supply, efficient distribution, and overall safety was key for Bayer. Top management wanted to avoid calls of "in Cipro we trust, but not in Bayer" (Fuhrmans & Winslow, 2001). Despite Bayer's initial public relations efforts, Senator Charles Schumer of New York (D-NY) and consumer lobby groups called for the government to override the company's patent so other manufacturers could assure supply of generic versions of Cipro at reasonable prices. Bayer's Cipro was protected for a period of 20 years by the Trade-Related Aspects of Intellectual Property Rights (TRIPS), but the agreement allows governments to override intellectual property rights during national health emergencies or unfair pricing (Fidler, 2002; *Lancet*, 2001). The Canadian government, under pressure from the Canadian generic-drug maker Apotex and public anxiety, went further. The government announced that it "will override Bayer's patent on Cipro and invite generic drug manufacturers to produce close to a million tablets" (Holmes, 2001, p. 9) because it wanted to build a stockpile of drugs adequate to treat 100,000 people (Harmon & Pearoct, 2001; cf., Pesik, Gorman, & Williams, 2002).

The drug industry accused the Canadian government and Apotex of "opportunistic behavior," since no anthrax case had appeared in Canada (Stewart, Denny, & Clark, 2001). The outcry did not hold back BristolMyers Squibb, Johnson & Johnson, GlaxoSmithKIine, Abbott, and other drug manufactures from offering to supply free medication to the government to treat anthrax, linking it to gaining formal FDA approval of anti-anthrax medicine (Charatan, 2001; Wechsler, 2001). This was a shrewd strategic move because it would allow them to gain entry and market share of a lucrative market, while improving their public image.

In addition, some accused Bayer of having created a monopoly for Cipro by signing an agreement in 1997 to pay Barr Laboratories an estimated $30 million a year to hold off production of generic Cipro, and paying Barr Laboratories and two other generic-drug makers a total of $200 million to abandon efforts to bring generic Cipro to market. The pressure mounted when it was revealed that 78 Indian-based pharmaceutical companies could produce generic Cipro for about 10 cents a tablet, as opposed to Bayer's $1.77 wholesale price before the September 11th attacks (Charatan, 2001; Herper, 2001; and Mokhiber & Weissman, 2001).

Bayer's Brand Crisis Management

With postal workers getting sick, the public realized that letters targeting politicians and media personalities are not the only ones affecting possible victims, but that anthrax could contaminate anyone who handles the mail. With high anxiety and an uncertain atmosphere, public outcry for overriding the Cipro patent increased greatly, and some suggested Bayer did not respond adequately to the crisis. Following this, the Canadian government bought one million tablets from the Canadian generic manufacturer Apotex. A *New York Times* article questioned Bayer's ability and readiness, and an op-ed in the *Los Angeles Times* called pharmaceutical companies "war profiteers." Some even called for Bayer to distribute Cipro for free (Holmes, 2001, p. 10; The Cipro circus, 2001).

The risk for pharmaceutical companies in general and Bayer in particular was high. Cipro represented $1.6 billion in worldwide sales a year. Patent overrides would open the door for low-cost generic drug manufacturers. This would lower drug prices and increase competition from companies that have a superior cost structure because they do not have to spend millions of dollars on research and development. The average cost of developing a new drug can be $500 million (The Cipro circus, 2001). Without the protection of intellectual property rights, pharmaceutical companies lack the incentive for innovation, and these moves would undermine research on new drugs.

After about two weeks of no decisive response to the crisis, Bayer's top German and US management team, working with Kekst & Company, a pre-eminent strategic communications firm, established and implemented a strategy to ensure safety of the US public, while protecting Bayer's brand image and market position. The objectives were to ensure ample supply of Cipro; work with the US government to build a stockpile of Cipro; assure the US public of its commitment; and reinforce Bayer's brand image as a caring, responsible, and patriotic company. The strategic communication plan consisted of several elements: establish proactive government relations efforts to facilitate a Cipro contract, communicate directly with the public through advertising, educate the media about Bayer's commitment, educate healthcare professionals on the appropriate use of Cipro, and develop communication channels for patients and consumers (Holmes, 2002).

Bayer's strategic approach went into motion within days. Bayer executives engaged in proactive government relations to secure a Cipro contract. Bayer global CEO Helge Wehmeier and the President of Bayer North America Wolfgang Plischke went to Washington, D.C., without an invitation, to meet with government officials and to show commitment, urgency, and efficiency. They met with the Director of Homeland Security Tom Ridge and members of the US Congress to provide reassurance of Bayer's commitment. They were in constant communication with US Health and Human Services (HHS) Secretary Tommy Thompson and other US government officials, assuring them and the public of Bayer's resilient commitment and production capabilities. Bayer executives made numerous television appearances, made daily phone calls to editors and reporters, and launched an internal campaign for "Bayer cares," distributing American pride buttons, US flags, and t-shirts to employees.

Bayer also donated two million tablets of Cipro to US health workers and first responders, and 200,000 tablets to the Canadian government (Fuhrmans & Winslow, 2001; Holmes, 2002). It followed with a media blitz of press releases, interviews by Bayer executives with major newspapers, and stories regarding Bayer's production efforts. This helped create the image Bayer wanted to convey of supply and safety for the US people. To reassure the US public, it placed full-page ads in major newspapers such as *The New York Times, Washington Post, Wall Street Journal, USA Today, Miami Herald, Palm Beach Post, the Financial Times*, and some local papers, at a cost of $3 million. The message was that "You can count on us" and that Bayer would supply enough Cipro, and do it in a timely manner and at a reasonable price (Fuhrmans & Winslow, 2001; Holmes, 2002). It also signed an agreement to supply the US government with 200 million Cipro tablets and significantly reduce the price from $1.77 before the anthrax attacks to 95 cents a tablet, which was equivalent to the generic Cipro price before the US anthrax outbreak (Cherney & Carlisle, 2001; Holmes, 2001, 2002).

The aggressive crisis brand management, which Kekst & Company directed, finally started to sway government and public opinion. After striking a deal with the US government, the Canadian government reinstated Bayer's Cipro patent, bought a million tablets of Bayer's Cipro and let Bayer warehouse the generic competition (The Cipro circus, 2001). As a result, media coverage was overwhelmingly positive in general, calling "big pharma" products "wondrous shields against the random horrors of terrorism" (Dickinson, 2001, p. 10). Editorials in the *Financial Times, Wall Street Journal, Investor's Business Daily,* and *The New York Times*, among others, praised "Bayer's patriotism, its ethics, and its commitment to doing the right thing" (Holmes, 2001), while *Forbes Magazine* stated "the U.S. may be best off sticking to the tried and true" (Herper, 2001).

Conclusion

The US anthrax outbreak of 2001 demonstrated the urgent need for safe and effective drugs to treat individuals exposed to biological agents used intentionally. In total, 43 confirmed anthrax cases were reported in Florida, Washington D.C., New York, and New Jersey; 22 people got sick, five people died, and 10,000 more people were considered at risk of possible exposure to anthrax (CDC, 2018). In the complex and ever-changing environment of the anthrax attacks and panic, Bayer AG had to navigate various marketing environment forces such as competitors, intermediaries, suppliers, regulatory agencies, and the public. By developing an effective marketing strategy, Bayer AG was able to be a good and ethical corporate citizen, placate the regulatory environment, impede entry for competitors, and enable the US government to provide the public with life-saving medicines.

The company that was built on Aspirin came back from the brink of economic disaster in 1900 with the brand known as the "drug of the century"–Bayer Aspirin. Almost 100 years to the day, Bayer AG came back from the brink of economic disaster with the Cipro brand based on timing, the right product, targeted strategies, public relations bonanza, and the strongest tagline in its branding history: "In Cipro we trust."

Check Your Understanding

National Pharmaceutical Stockpile (NPS)

National Pharmaceutical Stockpile: Bioterrorism defense program created by the Center for Diseases Control (CDC) to maintain a national repository of life-saving pharmaceuticals and medical supplies that can be delivered to communities in the event of a biological or chemical terrorist attack or an event involving mass casualties.

Discussion Questions

1   Imagine you work for US government during the anthrax crisis. Develop for your boss, both talking points for why and why not to override the Cipro patent.
2   Assume you are the vice President of Marketing at Bayer AG. Produce a memorandum for top management outlining critical issues facing Bayer AG and Bayer Corporation's marketing environment.
3   Produce a detailed recommended action plan to deal with Bayer Corporation and Bayer AG's marketing environment. Address differences and similarities between two entities.
4   Develop talking points for CEO to address media during the crisis.
5   What do you think of the tagline "In Cipro we trust" and the impact it had? Please explain and support your opinion.

To Cite This Chapter

Gringarten, H. (2018). Leveraging national crisis for a public relations bonanza: Bayer, ethics, and the anthrax scare. In H. Gringarten, & R. Fernández-Calienes (Eds.). *Ethical branding and marketing: Cases and lessons* (pp. 69–79). Routledge Management and Business Studies Series. London and New York: Routledge.

References

Bayer. (2018, July). *History and organization*. Retrieved from https://www. bayer.com/en/profile-and-organization.aspx
Burke, R. J. (2005). Effects of 9/11 on individuals and organizations: Down but not out! *Disaster Prevention and Management, 14*(5), 629–638. Retrieved from

http://proxy.stu.edu:2048/login?url=https://search.proquest.com/docview/214392723?accountid=14129

Center for Counterproliferation Research, National Defense University. (2002). *Anthrax in America: A chronology and analysis of the Fall 2001 attacks.* Washington, DC: Author. Retrieved from http://wmdcenter.ndu.edu/Portals/97/Documents/Publications/Articles/Anthrax-in-America.pdf

Centers for Disease Control [CDC]. (2018, July). *Anthrax.* Retrieved from https://www.cdc.gov/anthrax/resources/history/

Charatan, F. (2001). Bayer cuts price of ciprofloxacin after Bush threatens to buy generics. *BMJ: British Medical Journal, 323*(7320), 1023.

Cherney, E., & Carlisle, T. (2001, October 22). Apotex scores a victory with anthrax drug. *Wall Street Journal.* Retrieved from http://proxy.stu.edu:2048/login?url=https://search.proquest.com/docview/398763924?accountid=14129

The Cipro circus. (2001, October 25). *Wall Street Journal.* Retrieved from http://proxy.stu.edu:2048/login?url=https://search.proquest.com/docview/398943404?accountid=14129

Dickinson, J. G. (2001). Industry goes from villain to national asset. *Medical Marketing and Media, 36*(12), 10. Retrieved from http://proxy.stu.edu:2048/login?url=https://search.proquest.com/docview/228411521?accountid=14129

The economic consequences of the new global terrorism. (2002). *Economic Bulletin. Deutsches Institut Für Wirtschaftsforschung, Institut Für Konjunkturforschung, 39*(10), 327–332. doi:10.1007/s10160-002-0168-8

Enserink, M. (2001). Researchers question obsession with cipro. *Science, 294*(5543), 759–761. Retrieved from http://proxy.stu.edu:2048/login?url=https://search.proquest.com/docview/213601833?accountid=14129

Fidler, D. P. (2002). Bioterrorism, public health, and international law. *Chicago Journal of International Law, 3*(1), 7–26. Retrieved from http://proxy.stu.edu:2048/login?url=https://search.proquest.com/docview/237212498?accountid=14129

Fuhrmans, V., & Winslow, R. (2001, October 22). Bayer works to meet soaring Cipro demand as it starts campaign to keep patent in U.S. *The Wall Street Journal,* 1.

Harmon, A., & Pearoct, R. (2001, October 19). A nation challenged: Treatment; Canada overrides patent for Cipro to treat anthrax. *New York Times.* Retrieved from https://www.nytimes.com/2001/10/19/business/nation-challenged-treatment-canada-overrides-patent-for-cipro-treat-anthrax.html

Herper, M. (2001, October, 17) Cipro, Anthrax and the Perils of patents. Forbes. Retrieved July 19, 2018 from https://www.forbes.com/2001/10/17/1017cipro.html#163677ea7975

History Channel. (2018, July). *September 11 events.* Retrieved from https://www.history.com/topics/9-11-attacks

Hodge, J. G. (2002). Bioterrorism law and policy: Critical choices in public health. *The Journal of Law, Medicine & Ethics, 30*(2), 254–261. Retrieved from http://proxy.stu.edu:2048/login?url=https://search.proquest.com/docview/223499954?accountid=14129

Holmes, P. (2001, November 19). Bayer responds to Cipro crisis. Retrieved from https://www.holmesreport.com/latest/article/bayer-responds-to-cipro-crisis

Holmes, P. (2002, October 22). In Cipro we trust. Retrieved from https://www.holmesreport.com/latest/article/in-cipro-we-trust

Jenneweim, K., Durand, T., & Gerybadze, A. (2010). When brands complement patents in securing the returns from technological innovation: The case of bayer aspirin. *Management International, 14*(3), 73–85, 105–110. Retrieved from http://proxy.stu.edu:2048/login?url=https://search.proquest.com/docview/748835249?accountid=14129

Meyerhoff, A., Albrecht, R., Meyer, M. J., Dionne, P., Higgins, K., & Murphy, D. (2004, August 1). US Food and Drug Administration approval of Ciprofloxacin Hydrochloride for management of postexposure inhalational anthrax. *Clinical Infectious Diseases, 39*(3), 303–308. doi:10.1086/421491

Mokhiber, R., & Weissman, R. (2001, 12). Corporations behaving badly: The ten worst corporations of 2001. *Multinational Monitor, 22*, 8–19. Retrieved from http://proxy.stu.edu:2048/login?url=https://search.proquest.com/docview/208864135?accountid=14129

Moscrop, A. (2001). Mass hysteria is seen as main threat from bioweapons. *BMJ: British Medical Journal, 323*(7320), 1023.

Patent protection versus public health. (2001). *The Lancet, 358*(9293), 1563. Retrieved from http://proxy.stu.edu:2048/login?url=https://search.proquest.com/docview/198991593?accountid=14129

Pesik, N., Gorman, S., & Williams, W. D. (2002, March). The National Pharmaceutical Stockpile Program: An overview and perspective for the Pacific Islands. *Pacific Health Dialogue, 9*(1), 109–114. Retrieved from https://www.ncbi.nlm.nih.gov/pubmed/12737427

Stewart, H., Denny, C., & Clark, A. (2001, October 23). Bayer bows to pressure on anthrax antidote. *The Guardian.* Retrieved from https://www.theguardian.com/business/2001/oct/23/anthrax.businessofresearch

Wechsler, J. (2001). Bioterror response to alter pharmaceutical development and marketing. *Formulary, 36*(12), 867–868. Retrieved from http://proxy.stu.edu:2048/login?url=https://search.proquest.com/docview/229931184?accountid=14129

6   Is Academe Cheapened by Branding

Universities and Programs?

Larry Hubbell

Introduction

> **Check Your Understanding**
>
> *Guild*
>
> A *guild* is an organization, originated by merchants during the Middle Ages, that provided mutual support to its members.

In this chapter, I explore whether university officials should use branding to market universities and programs. Many academics are opposed to its use, arguing that branding and marketing in general are fundamentally antithetical to the values and norms that should guide a university. They liken the university to a relatively insular body – a "Republic of Scholars" – with its origins in the medieval guilds (Driori, Delmestri, & Oberg, 2016). Krause (1996) argues that the academic profession retains some guild-like characteristics. In such an organization, marketing and branding are not compatible. Indeed, Gibbs (2007) notes,

> ... when marketing – particularly advertising – is intended to persuade it may, under certain circumstances, work against the goals of independent, liberal, higher education by undermining critical thinking and autonomous actions. In these circumstances, its use is to counter the essence of autonomous education and ought to be avoided by universities on the grounds of moral duplicity.
>
> (pp. 3–4)

> **Check Your Understanding**
>
> *The Medieval Period*
>
> *The Medieval Period* occurred in Europe between the fifth and fifteenth centuries. It began with the fall of the Roman Empire and ended roughly with the Renaissance.

Others, especially those who manage the academic enterprise, dismiss such assertions contending that universities are not that different from corporations and thus could benefit from adopting capitalist principles and practices. (Indeed, there is a journal devoted to marketing higher education entitled the *Journal of Marketing for Higher Education*.) Among those principles is regarding the academic enterprise as a business – a business that employs marketing and branding to improve a university's competitive standing and ultimately increase revenue.

Indeed, in keeping with its business orientation, branding is pervasive in the university. For some, the issue of universities employing branding is a subject that university administrators resolved decades ago. For example, it is common for universities to employ branding by marketing their logo (Idris & Whitfield, 2014). Jillapalli and Jillapalli (2014) even suggest "certain professors can be branded and managed as brands" (p. 22). Taking the practice of branding one step further, the for-profit University of Phoenix even took the extraordinary step of spending $154 million to obtain the naming rights for the Arizona Cardinals' professional football stadium for 20 years (Weisbrod, Ballou, & Asch, 2008). However, broadly speaking, branding ultimately is the cultivation of a university's image (Aghaz, Hashemi, & Atashgah, 2015; Pampaloni, 2010). Regardless of what aspect of the educational experience a university brands, "a successful brand will involve a product with a recognizable identity and represent a particular set of values that is important to the consumer" (Thornton & Shannon, 2014, p. 162).

Specifically, in this chapter, I briefly discuss how universities were, and to a lesser extent are, relatively unique, compared with other institutions, as well as how universities are evolving. I also review how administrators reshaped the university as a business, and how marketing and branding have played a major role in that transformation. That development raises two interesting questions. Can the traditional ideals practiced in the university coexist with marketing techniques, specifically branding? Or does that create too much of a cultural disconnect?

The Origins and Unique Qualities of Universities

The modern US university owes its origins to Europe's medieval universities (cf., Daly, 1961). In his definitive book on the origins of universities, Hastings Rashdall (1936) wrote in *The Universities of Europe in the Middle Ages*,

> The institutions which the Middle Ages has bequeathed to us are of greater and more imperishable value even than its cathedrals. And the university is distinctly a medieval institution – as much so as constitutional kingships, or parliaments, or trials by jury.
>
> (p. 3)

Remarkably, although the modern university has evolved significantly, particularly in the past 20 years, the university still retains some qualities that it inherited from its ancient progenitors. However, the universities' hold on these practices is becoming increasingly tenuous, especially those institutions that face financial problems.

The University as Guild

A prominent feature of life during the medieval period was the guild. Even today, academic departments retain some guild-like characteristics.

> Guilds, also spelled gilds, an association of craftsmen or merchants, formed for mutual aid and protection and for the furtherance of their professional interests. Guilds flourished in Europe between the 11th and 16th centuries and formed an important part of the economic and social fabric in that era.
>
> (Britannica.com, 2010, n.p.)

Indeed, assistant professors, like their medieval apprentice counterparts, become full-fledged members of their department as the result of a vote. Accordingly, once an assistant professor has successfully completed her "apprenticeship," she receives tenure, which bestows upon the recipient something that is becoming increasingly rare in modern organizations – lifetime employment. Nevertheless,

> Life-time employment is not the expectation outside of academe. The idea of a job for life with one company is a thing of the past. It was a legacy of the 20th century, when large companies created by the Industrial Revolution brought armies of factory workers together.
>
> (Chow & Leung, 2016, p. 84)

In recent years, some cost-conscious universities have replaced tenure and lifetime employment with fixed term contracts. Nevertheless, even at institutions that retain tenure, it is weaker because of post-tenure review (Aper & Fry, 2003), making the practice that much more tenuous since in some circumstances professors can lose it.

Shared Governance

Check Your Understanding

Shared Governance

Shared governance is a long-held academic tradition in which a governing board, academic administrators, faculty, and sometimes staff govern a university jointly.

In the medieval period, faculty governance was a central principle of the university. Referring to the Bologna college, Rashdall (1936) noted that the rector (the US equivalent of the university president) was "elected annually by ballot"

(p. 201). Furthermore, "in important matters such as the alienation of property, the consent of the whole college is necessary" (p. 201).

The practice of faculty governance, especially in the USA, eventually morphed into shared governance, in which professors largely gave effective control over the university to full-time academic managers. In developing management structures that are more corporate-like, the university lost some of its distinctiveness.

> Guild control is thus diluted into what is called 'shared governance,' raising the issue of precisely which areas of higher education should be subject to professorial guild oversight. A strong case can be made for professorial control over issues of faculty recruitment and faculty evaluation, including promotion and dismissal. Currently, it is too often the case that the faculty role in these matters has been reduced to offering recommendations to the administration; by contrast, guild status would take the peer view to be authoritative.
>
> (Burstein, 2016, p. 36)

Shared governance, or some vestige of it, continues within US universities. In most cases, boards of trustees at US universities ultimately approve virtually all administrative decisions, including budget and personnel decisions, albeit through a process in which academic managers, often beholden to the boards, frame the decisions. Over the years, as academics lost substantial power, a university's board of trustees became virtually synonymous with a corporation's board of directors.

Sabbatical Leave

Contemplation was central in both Greek philosophy and the traditional university. Universities grant scholars the opportunity to engage in extended contemplation during sabbatical leaves. Scholars usually have the option to take a sabbatical leave every seventh year. Indeed, the word sabbatical "comes from the Greek word *sabatikos*, which means the day of rest that happens every seventh day" (Vocabulary.com, n.d., n.p.).

Sabbatical leave is a practice few institutions outside of academe provide, although General Mills, Microsoft, the Container Store, and American Express have made sabbaticals a component of their human resource strategy (Joseph & Kucera, 2004). Indeed, given our society's penchant for instrumental rationality, sabbaticals, even within academe, are becoming less common. In recent years, some universities have placed strictures on sabbaticals for maintaining "accountability." Indeed, Mamiseishvili and Miller (2010) note that scholars who have significant research records or those who have been successful in the past in obtaining grants are most likely to receive sabbaticals. In an increasing number of educational institutions, a scholar must justify his sabbatical by explaining in advance what will be accomplished during his or her leave (Mamiseishvili & Miller, 2010). In the contemporary university, faculty members, like employees in a corporation, are increasingly accountable, in contrast to the largely inner-directed academic of the past.

Mentoring Students

One of the most rewarding experiences that a faculty member engages in is mentoring. The concept of the mentor is a key aspect of Greek mythology. Before, academics began conceiving of students primarily as customers, they regarded them as mentees. The mentor–mentee relationship is one in which the mentor shares his or her knowledge and wisdom selflessly with the mentee. When this relationship occurs, it is academe at its best. According to Kram (1983), mentors when working with their mentees usually focus on some combination of psychosocial and career help. Yet, given the demands placed on professors, oftentimes mentorship becomes a lower level priority. Contemplation does not contribute to the bottom line.

> **Check Your Understanding**
>
> *Mentors*
>
> *Mentors* provide guidance to more junior organizational members in a variety of areas, including the unwritten rules of an organization, career assistance, and counseling.

How Its External Environment Has Reshaped the Modern University

The modern US university is a curious hybrid. It maintains some vestiges of its mostly medieval traditions while increasingly conforming to a highly capitalistic external environment. Capitalism influences universities in multiple ways. As a means of adapting to the demands of capitalism, universities have become more competitive with each other. That competition reflects, in part, their increased emphasis on revenue generation, a tendency to regard students as customers, and the transformation from being largely closed to largely open institutions. Indeed, given the demands of capitalism, the traditions inherited from the past appear to be increasingly antiquated in the twenty-first century university. Indeed, this increased focus on the external environment and the market enhances the appeal of branding within the university.

> **Check Your Understanding**
>
> *Open Institutions*
>
> Their external environment broadly affects *Open Institutions*. Leaders of those organizations frequently take cues from their environment to enhance their institution's survivability.

Competitiveness

The contemporary USA may be the most competitive society in the history of the world, and our universities increasingly mirror that reality. We compete for students. The university is no longer the isolated ivory tower, safe from competitive forces (Richardson, Nwankwo, & Richardson, 1995). Increased competition leads universities to conduct marketing campaigns complete with recognizable brands, which are a relatively new phenomenon (Dholakia & Acciardo, 2014, p. 146).

As a director of an institute at a private university, it is a rare meeting with my dean when the subject of how to increase revenue does not come up. We frequently discuss ways of exploring new markets, such as opening up a branch campus; offering new products, like academic certificates; providing additional services to students, like a program that links students with alumni; branding ourselves in such as a way that will make us more appealing to our current and potential student-customers; and, of course, besting the competition.

The university not only competes for students but also subjects its faculty members to the competitive standards they must meet if they are to receive tenure. The stakes are high. Within the past 30 years, there are fewer tenure and tenure track positions relative to the number of full- and part-time adjunct positions. If an assistant professor does not receive tenure, that person may be doomed to a precarious life as an adjunct, teaching at multiple institutions to make ends meet or leaving the profession altogether. At many schools, to fulfill one's research objectives, an assistant professor must not only publish but also publish in journals with a high impact. Academics also must be especially mindful of their teaching for not only they are subject to the occasional peer-review but also they receive reviews from consumer-oriented students. Competition with one's peers, although more concentrated among assistant professors, also affects tenured professors since merit pay became a staple at most universities beginning in the late 1980s (Blum, 1989).

Revenue Generation

The modern university has an insatiable appetite for more revenue. Most universities have adopted a "growth or perish paradigm." This "growth or perish paradigm" has been exacerbated in recent years, as online programs have proliferated. Universities primarily increase their revenues in the following ways:

- Universities initiate new programs by, for example, starting an online program, offering a new sought-after degree or starting a branch campus.
- They raise tuition. During the past 20 years, the average tuition and fees jumped 157% at private national universities, 194% for

out-of-state tuition at public national universities, and 237% for in-state tuition at public national universities (Mitchell, Leachman, & Masterson, 2016); meanwhile, during that same period, the Consumer Price Index increased only 52.5% (United States Department of Labor, Bureau of Labor Statistics, 2017).

- They try to persuade their state legislatures, if they are public institutions, to increase their funding, although between 2008 and 2016, state funding declined by an average of 18% to state institutions (Mitchell et al., 2016). For example, at the University of Colorado at Boulder, state appropriations constitute only 5% of that University's revenue (American Academy of Arts and Sciences, 2017).
- Universities seek external funding; however, "garnering these funds is very competitive and the use of these funds is highly restricted" (ibid.).
- They garner revenue from auxiliary services, such as food service and housing, except many of these operations are self-supporting and universities typically reinvest any surpluses in the operation (ibid.).
- They receive endowments. Although university endowments vary widely by institution – the top ten endowed universities controlled more than 33% of endowment funding in 2014 (National Center for Educational Statistics, 2016), and the endowed funds are typically highly restricted provided primarily for student financial aid, teaching, research and innovation, public service, and athletics (American Council on Education, 2017).

To ensure a university meets its revenue goals, it is essential that it develops a brand that successfully attracts students and donors, and in the case of public universities, appeals to a state legislature. Hundreds of quality universities exist in the USA. A successful branding strategy helps convince prospective students why they would want to go to a particular institution. Academic managers need to know their market niche and then develop a compelling brand that makes their institution seemingly irresistible.

Students as Customers

Today, the language of the market is common within educational institutions – institutions that were previously outside the market structure. As part of this larger trend, university administrators increasingly regard students as if they are customers. This "customerization" of students occurs not only because of increasing competition for tuition dollars but also because of the substantial investment universities are asking students to make in their education. With this increasing investment, students are only more likely to think of themselves as customers (Armstrong, 2010).

This change in consciousness is a development that many academics find disturbing, myself included. As an example, administrators place significant importance on student evaluations. Subpar student evaluations, whether deserved or not, can doom an academic who is coming up for tenure. Although many academics probably will not admit it, the importance they place on student evaluations also probably has had an enormous impact on the phenomenon of grade inflation.

Universities as Open Organizations

Especially in recent years, the US university evolved from a relatively closed organization to a highly open one. How do closed institutions differ from open institutions? "The closed-system models tend to focus on internal events when explaining organizational actions and behavior, while open system models focus on events occurring external to the organization that influences changes within the organization" (Allen & Sawhney, 2017, pp. 27–28). For centuries, the university was a relatively closed institution that underwent little change. The educational protocols of the fourteenth century also guided it during most of the twentieth century. It did not have to change because its environment was relatively stable and predictable. It was in the latter part of the twentieth century that the university changed dramatically.

What was a relatively stable environment became a highly competitive one. Capitalism caught up with the university and to a great degree enveloped it. Accordingly,

> The competitive process produces winners and losers. Some schools thrive and others falter – as in every other industry. Little recognized is that the higher education industry is very much in flux, with new schools emerging and existing schools closing, merging, and even switching ownership forms, as when a nonprofit college converts to a for-profit.
>
> (Weisbrod, 2008, p. 39)

To survive, most universities increasingly became open, sometimes radically open institutions, whose managers became much more aware of their external environments. What are the characteristics of an open organization?

> External influences can be experienced by organizations from the actions of the existing competitors, potential competitors, suppliers, customers and government. The influence of these external factors has been amplified in recent years due to a changing environment as reflected in growing globalization, increased diversity, rising ethical standards and rapid advances in technology accompanied by rising e-commerce.
>
> (ibid., p. 49)

In many cases, the universities that successfully made this transition to more of a market model were the ones that were able to retain some aspects of the medieval university, while at the same time also embracing a marketing strategy focused on branding.

> Market factors such as increased competition, economic pressures, and scrutiny by parents and students acting as 'consumers,' are putting increasing amounts of pressure on institutions of higher education to stand out and differentiate from competitors. To help combat the notion of higher education as a commodity, universities and colleges are developing expensive and sophisticated branding campaigns to engage their constituents.
>
> (Peruta, Ryan, & Engelsman, 2013, p. 11)

Those universities that adopted this strategy more than likely survived but also changed in the process. They became less distinctive. Like their counterparts in the private sector, successful universities usually developed a brand identity. They might be a university that touts the number of Nobel laureates employed there. Or on an epicurean note, they may emphasize the gourmet quality of their cafeteria food. Or they might choose to focus on their location, for example being situated in a so-called "urban laboratory." University administrators realize that

> Brand names are assets to any firm or organization. Colleges and universities, whether public, private nonprofit, or for-profit, are no different. Those that have national name recognition can attract a broader and more talented pool of applicants, more tuition revenue, and more donations.
>
> (Weisbrod, Ballou, & Asch, 2008, p. 175)

Conclusion

Are marketing and branding compatible with the traditional university culture? It is probably at best a marriage of convenience. On the one hand, the administrators tend to favor branding, thinking that it will help ensure the survival of the institutions they maintain. On the other hand, undoubtedly most academics are skeptical of branding, thinking it despoils the ethos of their institutions. They would prefer to continue the traditions the Medieval universities established. Although our current universities maintain some traditions from the Medieval Period, those traditions are weaker. The same principles that guide overtly market-oriented businesses now are common in the university, and branding is a central component of that business strategy.

I, for one, endorse the ongoing efforts to market and brand our universities, but I do not want the customer mentality also to invade the classroom. Our students are not customers, they are mentees. I am not sure whether it is possible to confine the marketing and branding function largely to services and amenities that universities provide students, like recreational centers, attractive dormitory rooms, and a competitive football team, while not impacting what transpires in the classroom. It may be difficult to conceive of students as customers outside of the classroom, but not within it. As one academic noted:

> I simply cannot see my relationship with students through the lens of customer relations. Great teaching touches minds, hearts, and souls... There are times I cannot be nice – I have to push hard. I have to challenge. I have to encourage students to do things they will not like. I have to mark a grade that is not what a student thought he or she earned. I can do so only in the context of a relationship built on trust and shared pursuit of knowledge and understanding, not in the context of students purchasing a product or service from me.
>
> (Tanner, 1999, p. 148)

Given the all-encompassing impact that capitalism has on our society, I am not sure that is a realistic expectation we can restrict partially the tentacles of capitalism as it envelops the university. However, at the very least, I would hope that academic administrators consider what they have given up to ensure their institution's survival. Perhaps, Thomas Kuhn provides a suitable explanation for the cultural clash that is ongoing. Driori et al. (2016) note the following:

> Like Kuhn's theory of paradigmatic changes, narratives that define the social role of the university emerge from a time and place-specific context, they rise to dominate the discourse, and then come to be overshadowed by a newly emerging narrative; rarely do they disappear completely, but rather they morph and change, get translated and sediment, and then co-exist.
>
> (p. 180)

It is extremely likely that universities will continue to place a significant emphasis on branding. Branding is here to stay. Nevertheless, I hope that in our desire to maintain the viability of our universities, we retain the characteristics that made them both great and unique.

Discussion Questions

1 In an effort to enhance their image, should a university brand individual professors?
2 Are university traditions handed down from the Medieval Period worth preserving?

3   Unlike many professions, tenured professors in most cases are guaranteed lifetime employment, given the financial difficulties that many universities face should educational institutions discontinue tenure?

4   Is it inevitable that students will increasingly view their interactions in the classroom as just another customer experience?

To Cite This Chapter

Hubbell, L. (2018). Is academe cheapened by branding universities and programs? In H. Gringarten, & R. Fernández-Calienes (Eds.). *Ethical branding and marketing: Cases and lessons* (pp. 80–91). Routledge Management and Business Studies Series. London and New York: Routledge.

References

Aghaz, A., Hashemi, A., & Atashgah, M. S. (2015). Factors contributing to university image: The postgraduate students' point of view. *Journal of Marketing for Higher Education, 25*(1), 104–126. doi:10.1080/08841241.2015.1031314

Allen, J. M., & Sawhney, R. (2017). *Administration and management in criminal justice: A service quality approach* (3rd ed.). Thousand Oaks, CA: Sage. Retrieved from http://www.sagepub.com/sites/default/files/upm-binaries/33001_2.pdf

American Academy of Arts and Sciences. (2017). Section 1: Current revenue sources for public research universities. Retrieved from http://www.amacad.org/content/publication/pubContent.aspx?d=22071

American Council on Education. (2017). Facts about college and university endowments. Retrieved from http://www.acenet.edu/news-room/Documents/Facts-About-College-and-University-Endowments.pdf

Aper, J. P., & Fry, J. E. (2003). Post-tenure review at graduate institutions in the United States. *Journal of Higher Education, 74*(3), 241–260. doi:10.1353/jhe.2003.0020

Armstrong, M. J. (2010, March 28). Students can behave too much like customers. *Chronicle of Higher Education*. Retrieved from https://www.chronicle.com/article/Students-Can-Behave-Too-Much/64840

Blum, D. E. (1989, October 18). Concept of merit pay for professors spreads as competition among institutions grows. *Chronicle of Higher Education, 36*(7), A1, A20.

Brittanica.com. (2010). Guild. Retrieved from http://www.brittanica.com/search?query=guild

Burstein, A. G. (2016, September–October). The AAUP and the idea of the university. *Academe, 102*(5), 23–26.

Chow, C., & Leung, C. (2016). *Reshaping universities for survival in the 21st century: New opportunities and paradigms.* Sharjah, United Arab Emirates: Bentham Science Publishers.

Daly, L. J. (1961). *The Medieval university 1200–1400.* New York, NY: Sheed and Ward.

Dholakia, R. R., & Acciardo, L. A. (2014). Branding a state university: Doing it right. *Journal of Marketing for Higher Education, 24*(1), 144–163. doi:10.1080/08841241.2014.916775

Driori, G. S., Delmestri, G., & Oberg, A. (2016). The iconography of universities as institutional narratives. *Higher Education, 71*, 163–180. doi:10.1007/s10734-015-9894-6

Gibbs, P. (2007). Does advertising pervert higher education? Is there a case for resistance? *Journal of Marketing for Higher Education, 17*(1), 3–11. doi:10.1300/J050v17n01_02

Idris, M. Z., & Whitfield, T. W. (2014). Swayed by the logo: Does university branding work? *Journal of Marketing for Higher Education, 24*(1), 41–58. doi:10.1080/08841241.2014.919979

Jillapalli, R. K., & Jillapalli, R. (2014). Do professors have customer-based brand equity? *Journal of Marketing for Higher Education, 24*(1), 22–40. doi:10.1080/ 08841241.2014.909556

Joseph, G. W., & Kucera, S. D. (2004, June–August). A comparative study of academic versus business sabbaticals. *Planning for Higher Education, 32*(4), 130–144.

Kram, K. E. (1983, December). Phases of the mentor relationship. *Academy of Management Journal, 26*(4), 600–625. doi:10.5465/255910

Krause, E. A. (1996). *Death of the guilds, professions, states, and the advance of capitalism, 1930 to the present.* New Haven, CT: Yale University Press.

Mamiseishvili, K., & Miller, M. T. (2010, January). Faculty sabbatical leaves: Evidence from NSOPF 1999 and 2004. *Journal of Faculty Development, 24*(1), 11–18.

Mitchell, M., Leachman, M., & Masterson, K. (2016). Funding down, tuition up: State cuts to higher education threaten quality and affordability at public colleges. *Center on Budget and Policy Priorities.* Retrieved from http://www.chpp.org/research/state-budget-and-tax/funding-down-tuition-up

National Center for Educational Statistics. (2016). *Fast facts.* Retrieved from http://www.nces.ed.gov/fastfacts/display.asp?id+73

Pampaloni, A. M. (2010). The influence of organizational image on college selection: What students seek in institutions of higher education. *Journal of Marketing for Higher Education, 20*(1), 19–48. doi:10.1080/08841241003788037

Peruta, A., Ryan, W., & Engelsman, R. (2013). Social media branding strategies for higher education: Comparing Facebook pages and web sites. *International Journal of Technology, Knowledge, and Society, 9*, 11–23.

Rashdall, H. (1936). *The universities of the middle ages, volume 1.* Oxford, UK: Oxford University Press.

Richardson, S., Nwankwo, S., & Richardson, B. (1995). Strategic issues for higher education strategists in the UK: A political contingency perspective. *International Journal of Public Sector Management, 8*(6), 7–16.

Tanner, C. A. (1999, April). Students as customers? *Journal of Nursing Education, 38*(4), 147–148.

Thornton, M., & Shannon, L. (2014). 'Selling the dream': Law school branding and the illusion of choice. In M. Thornton (Ed.), *Through a glass darkly* (pp. 157–176). Canberra, ACT: ANU Press.

United States Department of Labor, Bureau of Labor Statistics. (2017). CPI inflation calculator. Retrieved from http://www.bls.gov/data/inflation_calculator.htm

Vocabulary.com. (n.d.). Sabbatical. Retrieved from http://www.vocabulary.com/dictionary/sabbatical

Weisbrod, B. A., Ballou, J. P., & Asch, E. D. (2008). *Mission and money: Understanding the university.* Cambridge, UK: Cambridge University Press.

7 Ethical Branding, Homeowner Associations, and Judicial Review Using a Socially Responsible

Administrative Law "Hard-Look" Standard

Jeffrey Kleeger

Introduction

Pre-history city-fortresses protecting villages from invasion were the original Homeowner Associations (HOAs). Gates and walls secure a community. There is perceived value in a branded community that provides the goods and services it claims to offer (Crosby, 2010). This is the essence of ethical branding. Today gated communities, including high-rise condominiums and co-operatives legally organized as owner-associations,[1] are city-fortress-like to the extent they offer sanctuary and a sense of community, coupled with a comforting feeling of home, independence, safety, and provision of quality services (Fuselier, 2011). This modern HOA brand, offering maintenance and repair along with policing and other public goods, is a display of utopian fantasy that mystifies the practical reality of life in HOA-World, which may be less than ideal. While it is true, HOAs provide amenities at less cost by bulk-sharing and concentrated negotiating power to bid down prices, there are other, unadvertised costs in HOA-World such as the burden of living under a regime of restrictive rules and the inability of individuals to

---

Check Your Understanding

Administrative Law

Administrative Law: that body of law the fourth branch of government exercises combining executive, legislative, and judicial power to more efficiently manage public law interests. An example is the Environmental Protection

Agency enforcing rules it writes to protect the environment and adjudicating violations of same.

Judicial Review

Judicial Review: authority of courts to review executive and legislative actions. An example is the ruling in Citizens United v. Federal Elections Commission, 558 U.S. 310 (2010) holding legislative restrictions on political expenditures by private, non-profit associations violate freedom of speech rights.

adequately protect their private rights. Sometimes, HOAs, while blindly pursuing the holy grail of collective good, harm discrete, insular and otherwise vulnerable minorities by imposing fines to exact compliance. To avoid harm to hapless members, closer review of board action is necessary. This point is critical to fully comprehend the proprietary structure and administrative framework of HOAs, and resolve a deficiency of oversight using "Hard-Look" review.

The HOA Form

Ethics, sentiment, and social behavior drive consumer choice (Singh, Iglesias, & Batista-Foguet, 2012, p. 541). Membership in HOAs is voluntary, but the choice to join one is not, when a prospective member does not fully comprehend the practical significance of necessary fealty and homage due in a privatized, collective, residential association. If the marketed lifestyle is not genuine, (information is inaccurate), then prospective owner-members will make less-than-optimal choices, hoodwinked by deception. Life in HOA-World is ruled by a private governance regime operating with public power. That means the concentration of power can be substantial. Because there are minimal limitations to the exercise of such authority, there is potential for abuse. HOA executive boards are comprised of elected officers who are owners not necessarily trained in good governance. HOAs exercise a combination of executive, judicial, and legislative authority. One problem with this private governance form using public authority is the lack of checks and balances to constrain it. HOA boards are limited only by the corporate documents they themselves revise—but therein lies the dilemma— presently-in-use judicial review standards inadequately protect private rights. *This needs reform.*

Owners surrender personal sovereignty to a centralized,

Check Your Understanding

Private Governance

Private Governance: action by private associations taken with legally binding effect on persons. An example is when a private entity promulgates public-like policies to regulate the behavior of its members.

Private Law

Private Law: those fields of law concerning interactions between persons in which government plays no direct role. Examples include contract, property, and tort law actions where government is not typically a party and does not possess a vested interest in the outcome.

Privatization

Privatization: the transfer of ownership or management from government to a private entity. Such transfers may take the form of outright sale of assets or outsourcing of licensing and use rights. The purpose of such transfers is to enhance efficiency.

collective, private quasi-governmental authority that wields significant power. Part of that power is managerial and fiduciary, pertaining to maintenance contracts, service provision and so on that is largely ministerial and non-confrontational. This chapter does not concern the exercise of such authority. Instead, this chapter examines board actions that directly impact personal autonomy, private rights, and individual freedoms of member rights by regulating private behavior.

HOAs are a unique cultural community. They promote shared values, opinions, and beliefs. They are private, exclusionary social constructs promising collective good and personal autonomy (Fuselier, 2011), but those objectives may be mutually exclusive. While HOAs are creatures of private law, that does not mean the spillover effect of public functionality never justifies public law intrusion to ensure good governance and secure private rights. HOAs are private law entities that enhance property values. They combine security, amenities, and services, in an affordable, user-friendly package that is the HOA brand—but the brand is not ethical if the lifestyle is not genuine, with burdens on individual freedom that can make life miserable in HOA-World concealed from prospective owners before a purchase.

Ethical issues in consumption connect clean and green imagery with social responsibility (Singh et al., 2012, p. 541); but equally important is the corollary of good-faith marketing. Brands claiming to be ethical offer do-right, environmental-friendly products (Singh et al., 2012, p. 541); the important question to ask, however, is, are consumers receiving what they bargained-for? The literature describes social responsibility as a priority for business leaders. Some claim corporate social responsibility (CSR) is an excellent investment and is good business (Melo & Galan, 2011, p. 424). This is about adopting a recognized set of moral and ethical standards and promoting social good beyond the interest of the firm, conventional norms, and legal requirements (Melo & Galan, 2011, p. 425).

HOA branding can be consistent with CSR. HOAs provide clean, well-maintained common areas (landscaping, repairs, and maintenance), and a safe, secure, neighborly home setting. A problem with the HOA brand, however, arises when there is a lack of recourse for owners who discover the product they purchased does not meet their expectations. This chapter discusses how presently-in-use legal standards of review in the HOA context inadequately safeguard private rights when the expectation of expectations fails and how to remedy this problem.

Some theorists argue the HOA-World construct embodies private initiative, investment, law concepts, and characteristics that make it inappropriate to apply public law oversight (Reichman, 1976, p. 256). However, the argument that HOAs are wholly private because they are organized privately is inapposite. While HOAs are indeed privately organized legal entities, they behave as if they were a local government providing public services, representing constituents, formulating rules, regulating conduct, adjudicating offenses, and punishing transgressions. Because HOAs exercise a combination of legislative, executive, and judicial authority, they are administrative agency-like and as such are capable of substantially impacting the lives of private citizens. It is, therefore, necessary to better supervise their activities—to secure individual protections. Without sufficient oversight, personal liberty is at risk. Better protection of freedoms require enhanced judicial review standards.

Corporate Social Responsibility and Ethical Branding

CSR is an attribute, product feature, and reason to purchase a brand. Consumers base purchase decisions on their perception of a product's use-value (Smith, 2008). If HOA branding is unethical, consumers may make choices under false pretenses, bad-faith dealing, or deceptive trade practices. Aside from the possibility of criminal prosecution, unethical branding may lead to a damaged business reputation and, in the case of HOAs, diminishing returns on property resales. To avoid that from happening, branding requires compliance with minimal standards of good ethical conduct. For HOA-World, the best defense against allegations of unethical branding is to ensure the ethically branded lifestyle that was promised in fact materializes.

The social contract of business theory holds corporations duty-bound to those they serve to perform their moral-ethical obligation and do right. Business and society are partners and enjoy mutual, reciprocal rights and obligations (Melo & Galan, 2011, p. 426). Theorists urge adoption of a strategic CSR to achieve optimal benefit from minimal investment (Melo & Galan, 2011, p. 426). In HOA-World, governing board police power may burden private rights to promote public good. Under such circumstances, it is incumbent upon regulatory oversight structures to ensure compliance with law. Monitoring HOA board action as if boards were a government entity, and holding them appropriately accountable, would accomplish that objective. After all, HOAs are private governance forms that display public, government-like characteristics, provide public services, operate under bureaucratic rulemaking, and exercise state police power with broad enforcement authority. The problem with this union of public–private elements, in the absence of separation of powers constraints, is potential for abuse. Under these circumstances, it is difficult to reconcile the inapplicability of state action doctrine limitations on private governance forms (Reichman, 1976). The thesis of this chapter is a more rigorous judicial review of HOA actions better protects private rights.

Brand value can be a performance estimator and core component of corporate reputation (Melo & Galan, 2011, p. 427, citing Fan, 2005). Trust is its base. A partner must feel confident that her counterpart is reliable and will comport with integrity (Singh et al., 2012, p. 543). Trust is an asset that gradually develops with nurturing over time, but is capable of quick destruction by misstep, neglect, or oversight. The study of ethics in business measures conduct on conventionally accepted standards of what is proper, in contrast to what is not (Singh et al., 2012, p. 542). An ethical brand promotes collective good functioning with attributes of honesty, integrity, diversity, responsibility, quality, respect, and accountability (Singh et al., 2012, p. 542). Entities actively engaged in CSR, consistent with the urging of Fan (2005), integrate innovation with ethics and good social behavior. Efficiency is good, ethics is better, and ethically infused efficiency is best. A system of private provision of public services allows associates to directly influence the character of their neighborhood and control costs (Nelson, 1999, p. 829). The effort to brand products as ethical requires integrating honesty, integrity, respect, and accountability with equity.

To the extent life in HOA-World represents culture, lifestyle, and the promise of the good life—with happiness or misery in the balance—it is a brand the literature understands as a name, term, sign, symbol, design, or any combination of the same reflecting values, beliefs, and sentiments (Fan, 2005, p. 342) about what is important. While ethical branding is a marketing tool that respectfully seizes upon emotions, feelings, and images to identify and differentiate goods and services in the minds of consumers in a specifically filtered way to persuade them to want and get a certain product, it is ethical only if it adheres to certain acceptable requirements. Branding is a reflected image of a product. *Ethical* branding is the extent to which a brand-creator follows moral and social rules to self-regulate and comply with ethical, moral, and socially acceptable messaging and targeting. This is the meaning of ethical branding.

Commercial actors self-regulate (Fan, 2005) to avoid punishment in the form of boycotts by dissatisfied customers or liability for the harm they may cause. A problem with collective, privatized economic, political, and social organization is the isolation paradox it produces and the possibility of detachment resulting from closing off a community from the outside world (Doucet & Smit, 2016). However, isolationism is not practical in modern economic networks and the rule of reason acknowledges no person is an island unto herself—rather, each is an integral part of the whole (Donne, 1624). The negative spillover of privatization functioning as fragmentation to produce spatial inequality (Doucet & Smit, 2016, p. 653) is curable by introducing positive, nurturing community-sensibility in a family-friendly HOA. But is this promise real? A brand is the public face of a company (Fan, 2005) that embodies a lifestyle offering truth and value (Smith, 2008). The key necessary component to ethical branding is it be genuine and benefit the consumer who holds a legitimate expectation the product she invests in will satisfy her expectations.

How HOA Governance Relates to Ethical Branding

The modern rise in HOA popularity makes analyzing it in terms of ethical branding relevant. HOAs manage 25 million housing units, serve 60 million residents, comprising about 20% of the nation's population (Pollack, 2013, p. 841). While that number is not as impressive as the 50% prediction of the 1970s (Reichman, 1976, note 8 at p. 256), HOAs clearly touch a significant component of the population. The number of HOAs has increased by 2,500% between 1970 and 2003 (Weiser & Wang, 2006, p. 2), and the trend continues. HOAs are doing something right in terms of marketing and must be offering a sufficient degree of, or at least perception of, competitive value to customers to remain so popular.

HOAs seek to improve members' quality of life. A cost in doing so is risk of harm to personal autonomy. Yet, individuals associate to realize collective good. Privatization achieves positive results but also is capable of damaging personal autonomy. The privatization of social forms can lead to the privatization of government forms. The literature is replete with discussions of extreme case studies where HOAs act aggressively and harm individuals in ways that burden private rights in the name of promoting collective good. The problem with this is the collective good is sometimes a thinly veiled pretext to justify abuse or the rule in question may be under-inclusive, selective, overbroad, or vague. In any event, HOAs harm individual rights by restricting freedoms unnecessarily. This chapter considers how implementing a hard-look administrative law judicial review standard can address and eliminate this problem.

A case study involving a woman and her battle to keep her cats in her home (the Nahrstedt case study appearing below) demonstrates how judicial review standards now in use fail to protect individual rights. Presently-in-use judicial review falls short of minimally desired results. Opportunity costs arising from submission to a collective will burden individual liberties and erode freedoms. Benefits that accrue to the collective good in the course of regulating private rights are justifiable in some cases, but not all. Judicial review standards need to be more searching to adequately protect private rights.

Corporate branding builds on the identity of a company forcing it to be accountable for its actions. In this way, entities avoid the promise–performance gap (van de Ven, 2008, p. 346) by which a firm might fail to achieve its branded outcomes because its promises are empty. In HOA-World, this can happen when governing boards act unreasonably under the circumstances. An example of this is a rule that imposes costly burdens in exchange for questionably beneficial results or a case where a minimally beneficial collective good creates a substantial risk of harm to personal freedom to implement (Bollinger, 2008, p. 271). Following a cost-benefit analysis, such a course is not logical. Ethics are context-based. The Nahrstedt case study proves this by demonstrating how the legal system is complicit in the privatization of social functions when it tolerates damage to personal autonomy in upholding an unreasonable HOA decision (Fuselier, 2011; Levi, 2009). While there are instances where courts reject HOA rules in favor of personal autonomy, those cases are rare.[2] The pet restriction in that case, while not unconscionable, was damaging.

Conventional wisdom holds good governance responds to stakeholder needs (Frankental, 2001, p. 18), with management accountable for its acts and decisions. Companies can take inventory of environmental, reputational, and business-probity issues in decision-making (Frankental, 2001, p. 19) considering financial impacts and sociological implications of their choices (Frankental, 2001). Companies adopting CSR aspire to achieve social and environmental gain remain open to public scrutiny, comply with law, and serve the public ethically (Frankental, 2001). Yet, because participants in a highly competitive commercial environment set the bar of attributes ever higher, it is increasingly difficult to claim a unique position in real estate sales marketing based on CSR (van de Ven, 2008, p. 346, citing Schlegelmilch & Pollach, 2005, p. 273). This presents a competitive advantage challenge for entities hoping to differentiate on offerings.

Some theorists argue the branded lifestyle is not a positive development suggesting privatization and exclusivity are dominant characteristics, while citizenship and community are subordinate. This conclusion is accurate when gated communities remove public space and corrode core constitutional values such as the right to travel, express speech, and uphold universal access to public space (Siegel, 2009, pp. 809–810). An added concern is whether governing boards adhere to good ethical behavior (Siegel, 2009, p. 812) such as by imposing externalities on those outside the gates because enhancing security within creates a risk of harm without.

The modern interest in gating began with financial motivation. Developers who are the brand-creators sought competitive advantage marketing gain in selling the idea of a desirable, friendly, and safe community labeled "home." The marketing-mix differentiates *this* community from all others making *it* appear more safe, affordable, satisfying, and therefore, more valuable than alternatives. The arrangement of physical open and built spaces, and associated lifestyle imagery, is the dream-world developers sell. The literature on successful marketing includes advice on using creative communication strategies to promote products reinforcing symbolic positive ideas in the minds of consumers (Parsons, 2007, pp. 267, 270); for example, capitalizing on childhood nostalgia. The traditional approach is to cast the available product in as positive a light as possible to enhance brand value. Companies can legitimately paint a rosy picture of what they offer but may not use deceptive trade-practices to promote their product. The subtle almost unobserved characteristic of branding is creating, shaping, and communicating a consumer's identification with a product (Parsons, 2007, p. 270) producing in the context of HOAs a sense of belonging – a spirit of community – or brand-value. Examining branding in the context of HOAs is relevant to the meaning of ethical branding because what the bill of sale describes is product imaging, and if what is described is dishonest, inaccurate, or fake then the branding is not ethical. Persuasive messages radiate logos through branding to generate an information-filled idea *logically* describing product value, ethos by focusing on the *credibility* of the source, and pathos in disseminating *emotionally charged messaging* (Parsons, 2007, p. 271). Socially responsible strategies for ethical marketing require combining ethical, legal, and moral communications and actions (Parsons, 2007, p. 271). In this regard, the inapplicability of state action doctrine to HOAs means regulating them is more difficult and that places individuals at greater risk of harm from abuse by governing authority.[3] This is an example of unethical branding.

The ability of individuals to assert claims against private HOA regimes is quite limited (Siegel, 2009, n.23). State action theory is not typically applicable to HOAs but making it so would provide more effective regulation of HOA acts and offer a better response to erosion of the public sphere by expansion of unregulated privatized governance than the presently in vogue laissez-faire attitude can ever hope to achieve (Siegel, 1998). CSR combats this poor result encouraging entities to demonstrate their sincerity about their impact on society in general and individuals in particular. The strategy of building a virtuous brand focuses on protecting corporate reputation (van de Ven, 2008, p. 346). Focus should also be on doing good. The Five Pillars of Ethics is a reminder and provides useful guidance in helping shield an entity from challenges. It holds one should (1) do no harm, (2) aspire to do good, (3) communicate truth, (4) respect confidentiality, and (5) act fairly (Parsons, 2007, pp. 273–274). These characteristics exemplify ethical branding. When a governing board adheres to principles of good governance, it will accomplish good for its members. Although public law constitutional restrictions apply to state government actors, such application does not guarantee public law restrictions on private law regimes that behave as if they were public – even if it is appropriate that they apply (Siegel, 2009, pp. 812–813).

Private law regimes using public law authority fall under the ambit of heightened judicial review if they create risk of harm to private rights. Ethical branding and CSR, coupled with enhanced judicial review standards, may remedy risk of harm to personal autonomy. The absence of oversight, coupled with tolerance of the same by authorities amounts to an abdication of regulatory responsibility. Heightened self-regulation will not completely banish unethical branding from the marketing landscape. If courts would implement a practice of raising the rigor of judicial review and lowering the degree of deference they grant to board decisions, then better, more equitable results may follow, reducing the risk of harm to persons and brand. CSR is necessary because it impacts corporate performance (Melo & Galan, 2011, p. 423). HOAs are corporate-like entities. Developers produce an imagined lifestyle-image to sell product and quickly exit the community replacing itself once it completes its project[4] with a governing board of owner-members.

Members purchase a lifestyle image they wish to live when they buy a membership. In making such a purchase, the consumer must believe an available image is desirable, and the associated cost is justifiable. It would be a clear-cut case of fraud or deceptive marketing if the product for sale did not possess the attributes described in the marketing materials. In exchange for benefits promised, prospective members willingly submit to the authority of a collective will. They enter into an agreement with certain expectations. Residents accept restrictions on freedom in exchange for rule of law. This is an expression of the social contract. Boards inherit control of member behavior through covenants and restrictions. This is why courts must review HOA actions from an administrative law approach. The only viable solution to resolve overbearing privatized authority is the effective regulation of hard-look review.

Data Collection for This Project

This study examines HOA member versus board disputes. The population settled-upon resulted from multiple searches of legal databases identifying cases of restrictions on private rights by collectively imposed rules. While it is possible there could be selection bias due to nuances in keyword terms, focusing on the four most densely populated jurisdictions in the USA broadened the diversity of case returns to minimize any such risk. Data collection using keywords such as fines solicited returns to test the hypothesis of the need to modify judicial review standards. Queries focused on HOA acts impacting individuals by limiting personal autonomy shed light on the problematic. One such search returned 8,000 cases. Others returned tens of thousands. While the study sought to avoid discarding relevant data, limiting the focus to burdens on private rights effectively narrowed returns. In selecting appropriate cases, care went to identifying dependent and independent variables. The dependent variable is risk of harm to personal autonomy. Independent variables broadly include jurisdiction, judicial review standards, and type of harm suffered. The data analysis leads to negation of the null hypothesis supporting the conclusion of need to enhance judicial review to better-protect personal autonomy. The data reveal risk of unethical branding in cases where the image people desire is inconsistent with the product. In such cases, Caveat Emptor does the buyer no good. HOA governance under present standards of review is just too powerful and that leads to injustice. The Nahrstedt case study below illustrates dysfunctionality and risk of harm to civil liberties in contested economic and social relations. The only viable solution is enhancing judicial review. The inescapable conclusion is administrative law hard-look review better protects individual rights than the minimally rigorous business judgment and reasonableness standards. Table 7.1 (below) describes cases in the study. Cases from Texas are absent because the law in this area is predominately statutory-based (Figure 7.1).

This chapter concludes by finding judicial review using any variation of California's reasonableness, New York's business judgment, or Florida's hybrid blend of the two inadequately protects individual rights. The case law identified a naturally uniform, interconnected whole favoring boards in disputes with owners. For example, California endorses a reasonableness test adopting elements of Florida law and largely rejects New York's more relaxed approach; New York employs a minimally rigorous business judgment rule but adopts aspects of California and Florida's reasonableness mix; Florida innovatively blends elements of the other two approaches. Texas's statutory focus sets it apart. Upon collection of data, the question arose: What is the relevance of these legal standards to ethical branding? Because presently-in-use review standards ineffectively protect private rights, a less deferential approach of review is necessary to approximate ethical precepts.

Table 7.1 State Court Cases by Litigated Issue: California, Florida, and New York

Issue	Fees & Fines (%)	Enforcement (%)	Owner Rights (%)	Board Power (%)	Restrictions (%)
California	10—12	10—32	2—14	6—33	10—32
Florida	35—42	13—42	4—29	6—33	17—55
New York	38—46	8—26	8—57	6—33	4—13
Totals	83—47	31—18	14—8	18—10	31—18

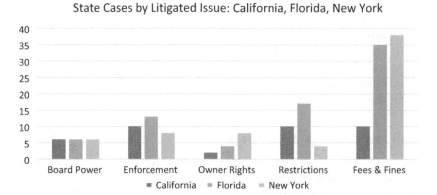

Figure 7.1 State cases by litigated issue: California, Florida, New York.

A system that prioritizes HOA actions demoralizes individuals dissuading them from asserting their rights. As a result, boards conduct themselves more aggressively to exact compliance. Such excessive board action symbolizes variance between expectations and reality in branding. Sharp distinctions between the imagery in marketing materials and facts are unethical. This study acknowledges litigation is fraught with unknowns including cost, measure of injury, probability of success, and commitment of time; and such factors militate against successful challenges to HOA actions (Weiser & Wang, 2006). Hard-look review could remedy this imbalance by reversing the tendency to favor boards over individuals.

Judicial Standards

Courts presently review HOA action with deference. Florida focuses on fact-based circumstances, holding boards responsible to demonstrate a challenged decision reasonably relates to a lawful purpose (Hidden Harbor Estates, Inc., v. Norman, 1975). That approach is more protective of individual interests, compared to other jurisdictions. New York is less protective. More recently, Florida has blended the business judgment and reasonableness standards holding board action lawful if within the scope of authority, not arbitrary, capricious, or in bad faith (Nichols, 2012) as it applies in Lamden v. La Jolla Shores Clubdominium Homeowners Association (1999). The court in Hidden Harbor Estates, Inc. v. Basso (1981) used a slightly higher standard requiring the board demonstrate its decision reasonably relates to its purpose. In Papalexiou v. Tower West Condominium (1979), citing Hidden Harbor Estates, Inc. v. Norman (1975), the court applied a reasonableness standard then accepted the less burdensome business judgment showing of lack of fraud in declining to issue a ruling. In Hollywood Towers Condominium Association, Inc. v. Hampton (2010), the court adopted the enhanced business judgment standard of Lamden (1999), finding board action valid if not arbitrary, capricious, or in bad faith – meaning it was ethical. In the Matter of Levandusky (1990), the court initially declared the lower court ruling arbitrary and capricious then withdrew the decision declining to rule based on business judgment precepts. These litigation results clearly demonstrate judicial review in its present form offers inadequate legal protection for private rights.

Null Hypothesis & Limitations

The null hypothesis stating private rights are not at risk in HOA decision-making is in error. HOAs offer security, reduce nuisances, and provide beneficial public services (Wiseman, 2012, pp. 2067, 2072). Still, rules restricting personal behavior are overbroad and excessive in some instances.[5] The null hypothesis that owners live safe, secure, and free from risk of abuse of authority with respect to their rights under HOA regimes exercising privatized public authority is questionable given evidence pointing to contrary results. Weiser and Wang (2006) explain how judicial deference to HOA actions leads to less litigation because boards win disputes at higher rates but what that result in fact reveals is that individuals are powerless to resist overbearing board action effectively.

Given that there are several standards of judicial review in use, what standard is most appropriate? Courts implement diverse applications of two highly deferential standards that inadequately restrict HOAs. Courts avoid use of the State action doctrine. Privatized governance is not subject to public law constraints. For example, the State cannot enforce a statute prohibiting a person from displaying a political endorsement in her private yard because that would interfere with freedom of speech; but HOAs use courts, an arm of the State, to enforce such restrictions. The State action doctrine is generally inapplicable to private entities, meaning constitutionally mandated restrictions do not limit their authority. Under public law, when State-authorized actions harm persons, the injured have recourse; under private law, there is no equivalent remedy, which is inequitable. To resolve this defect of oversight in governance, courts must recognize private law regimes functioning under public law auspices are sufficiently public-like to justify subjecting them to administrative law limitations. Reichman (1976, p. 306) argued in favor of maintaining clear division between public law restraints and residential private government enforcement activities, until the need for public law regulation was clear. That time is now. Public-like governance requires public-like oversight. The need for enhanced regulation arises because judicial review standards inadequately protect individual, private rights.

This study is imperfect because random generation of search terms and reliance on models from cases in the data set cannot fully account for factors such as asymmetric stakes, known and unknown information about the relative strength of a case, evidentiary considerations, bias, party irrationality, probability of remedy, motivation of parties, and costs – all factors influencing disposition – which cannot be controlled-for (Weiser et al., 2006, p. 10). Notwithstanding these limitations, the study is useful because it identifies the need for enhanced standards of review. This chapter reaches the conclusion that presently-in-use judicial review inadequately protects private rights. Hard-look review would resolve this deficiency making boards better guardians of private rights.

How Ethical Branding Informs Legal Analysis

The conclusion that private governance inadequately safeguards private rights runs counter to the branding promise. Ethical branding fails when the collective unfairly, excessively, and unnecessarily imposes its will on private interests to promote an arguably insignificant common good end. Courts fail individuals when judicial review inadequately protects liberty. Courts cannot resolve this problem if they defer blindly to board decisions. Excessive deference harms private rights. For example, the Inwood (1987) court affirmed board action directed against members by treating lien rights as equivalent to covenant and servitude rights allowing foreclosure of ownership because of past due fees, despite homestead protection (Fuselier, 2011, p. 28, pp. 808–809; Shoked, 2011, pp. 762–763). Similarly, as Boudreaux (2009, pp. 506–507) observes, Nahrstedt v. Lakeside Village Condominium Association (1994) wrongly places the burden on individuals to prove a challenged rule is reasonable based on holistic collective interest, rather than atomistic personal circumstance. Under this construct, the equities are not in balance. Regulators must justify liberty-limiting rules consistent with tenets of ethical branding. Some theorists disavow the Nahrstedt holding arguing circumstances do matter. The element of exigency justifying use of State police power is normally lacking in the HOA context, but issues of conflict due to regulating private behavior are present in privatized regimes. As Boudreaux (2009, p. 481) points out, HOAs are State actors in all but name and constitutional restrictions that ordinarily limit the scope and breadth of State action are relevant. The Slaughterhouse Cases (1873) reinforce this point. In 1860s New Orleans, lack of sanitary requirements for slaughterhouse operations produced a public health crisis. The remedy was to create a private association to regulate operations concentrating power to enforce compliance with rules promoting public health and safety. The association required enforcement of strict sanitary standards that were burdensome to businesses but necessary to protect the public. It is sometimes necessary to limit private liberties to promote the common good.

Dysfunctionality in Private HOA Governance

HOAs are creatures of statute that arise by the filing of association documents with the State. Associations consist of the personalities of their members who revise self-governance rules to regulate the culture of communal social life to fit a certain lifestyle. Covenant violations are subject to fines and court orders to enforce compliance. The rule of law within the walls restricts land use and demands the sacrifice of autonomy favoring the collective will. Members may challenge actions that do not reasonably relate to accepted collective objectives, that exceed lawful authority, or that are excessive and seek reversal (Boudreaux, 2009, p. 482). State legislative authority produces a framework for HOAs to establish tenancies and regulate ownership. The governing board must promote a safe, stable, and pleasant community and is guardian of the collective good. In exchange, the board executes its obligations responsibly, meaning it is honest, faithful, and fair. The capacity of board officers to act faithfully in exercising their official duties depends on their level of knowledge, skills, training, and individual will. Judicial review of board action may be the only means available to ensure good governance. At the same time, members pay a price for private governance in dues and limits on personal freedom (Nelson, 1999, p. 835; Shoked, 2011, p. 764). The distinction between public and private governance is unclear in this context because HOAs conduct themselves as if they were a public entity providing traditionally public functions (Wiseman, 2012, p. 2075), when in fact no public law restricts their exercise of public power.

Privatization is correlated with cost-effective provision of goods and services, yet an unintended consequence is harm to private rights because HOAs are not accountable, and supervisory oversight is often deficient. This is capable of correction because the State is possessed of authority to regulate HOAs and may invalidate acts that violate law; but States refrain from taking such action because HOAs are private associations, free to be more flexible and efficient compared to public government. This is their competitive advantage. HOAs function and operate as municipalities do, yet because private rights are vulnerable under presently-in-use standards of judicial review, it is entirely reasonable to conclude public law-limiting constitutional requirements are necessary (Fuselier, 2011, p. 822). To better protect private rights, decision-makers must ethically leverage competitive advantage resources and apply them to eliminate obstacles to achieving goals, while avoiding unnecessary sacrifice of private rights.

A neighborhood's character is the branded image it presents. Its brand stimulates emotional and intellectual conceptions of community, individual, and place. The social bond between land and community is what it means to be human (Shoked, 2011, p. 771; Stern, 2014, p. 145). This touches on social understandings of communal life. Exclusion is a negative act that encourages separateness and destroys belonging and sociality (Lai, 2016, p. 378; Levi, 2009, pp. 638–639). Public governance uses zoning to impose a collective will on individuals (Nelson, 1999, p. 839). Private governance uses judicial covenant enforcement to achieve the same (Kress, 1995, p. 838). Public and private governance are similar, utilize corresponding sources of authority, and collaterally limit private rights. As a result, there is no reason to tolerate inconsistent review of acts of similarly situated regimes. In fact, condoning such inconsistency after acknowledging its irrationality, wrongly perpetuates a dysfunctional, ethically questionable, intentional disparity. That is not a socially responsible result.

Creating Functionality in Private Governance Out of Chaos

At the first level of engagement, developer-written rules are servitudes that run with the land. Enforcement occurs by notice to non-compliant members to cease violations (Wiseman, 2012, p. 2077). HOA regimes are land tenure systems that recognize owners take an interest in what neighbors do. Purposeful design promotes informal conflict resolution (Nelson, 1999, p. 840). It is necessary to acknowledge that in society conflicts of interest arise. While the imagined community is an abstract, invented idea based on beliefs about what residents perceive is good, moral, and just – which is the essence of ethical branding, HOAs are physically constituted tangible structures of housing product that private citizens control. The HOA board is a vestibule of authority that holds mirror-image concentrations of conflicting elements and manages them. These include dichotomous elements such as control–delegation, public–private, and inclusion–exclusion. Members agree to observe rules about land use to promote public good in a social construct. Boards control the community and enforce compliance to promote collective good. Conflict arises when there is a difference of opinion about what course is proper. It is fair to say law is complicit in the privatization of the State when it favors private collective will over individual rights. Courts are particularly complicit when they defer to board decisions with minimal review leaving individuals powerless to resist a centralized concentration of privatized power that amounts to an abdication of judicial review and a diminution of private rights.

HOAs emerge victorious from litigation with members because courts defer to board action. The traditional approach to judicial review of HOA actions has been to prioritize the privatized legal status of such entities, celebrating their efficiencies of scale, and minimizing the resulting risk of harm to persons. The sociological and jurisprudential facts are that residents and outsiders must interact, gates are porous, and associations that guard against external-to-community social relations may cause harm. HOAs impose externalities on non-members enhancing safety within while creating increased risk of harm without, thereby reallocating risk to the disadvantage of outsiders (Levi, 2009, pp. 644–645). These factors signify that HOAs operate with minimal accountability raising doubts about the ethics of their branding.

Courts hesitate to interfere with HOA actions that reflect a reasonable, honest exercise of judgment. In practice, the corporate expertise necessary to justify the high degree of deference they enjoy is often lacking. Frequently, board members possess minimal, if any professional training in governance (Pollack, 2013, p. 849). If the results of judicial review are to be meaningful, the standard of review in place must also be. Instead, many courts apply a reasonableness analysis mixed with elements of corporate business judgment dilutive of sufficient rigor (Nichols, 2012). There must not be too great a degree of deference for HOA decisions if review is to be truly meaningful. Meanwhile, judicial review cannot be meaningful under presently-in-use standards if courts persist in asking only whether a decision bears any rational relationship to the entity's purpose. That threshold is too easy to satisfy and inadequately protects private rights.

It is instructive to compare standards of judicial review along with a bit of their historical application. Administrative law rules were once extremely deferential to the presumed expertise of officials. The initially minimal arbitrary and capricious standard evolved toward a more robust "hard-look" inquiry into particularized facts and circumstances of unique cases in terms of information-gathering and decision-making to enhance rigor and ensure more accountable, comprehensive results. Why should HOAs escape that prescription? The hard-look standard requires decision-makers create a well-developed record outlining a reasoned analysis of all possible alternatives to explain the rationale for decisions reached (Garry, 2006). With less deference, and a record clearly documenting decision-making steps, courts can engage in more meaningful review of actions. Courts need to rule on whether the scope of authority is proper, action was reasonable, and review of unique facts and circumstances sufficiently comprehensive. The hard-look standard provides better protection for private rights than alternative methods. Such review is consistent with ethical branding because it encourages HOAs to match the actual association lifestyle with the imagery it promised prospective purchasers in marketing materials. Ethical branding requires product advertising be honest and truthful.

Hard-look review is more demanding than the reasonableness or business judgment approaches. It requires boards take additional procedural steps to create a substantive record reflecting meaningful fact-finding and comprehensive study prior to reaching decision. Hard-look review requires documenting reasonableness and is therefore more likely to produce better-quality, informed choices and results. The more fully developed record that follows from using hard-look review would provide courts with a meaningful record to review. The hard-look standard requires actors provide detailed explanations of the rationale for decision-making, that decision-makers specify policy premises and offer factual support to demonstrate full consideration of all relevant factors was integral to the decision-making process (Garry, 2006, p. 156, n.40). Taking a hard-look means reviewing courts will demand boards explain the basis for decisions; consult with, inform, and obtain feedback from members; examine all objections and relevant factors, and consider available alternatives with better effect (Garry, 2006, p. 154, n.19). Hard-look review is a more exacting standard that requires articulation of the basis for decisions. In a nutshell, hard-look produces better, more ethical decision-making and more potently safeguards private rights.

108   *Jeffrey Kleeger*

An Instructive Case Study—Nahrstedt v. Lakeside Village

Condominium Association

Introduction, Background, and Problem

Nahrstedt is a California Supreme Court case that denied a woman the right to keep her three cats in her home. The HOA imposed an absolute ban on pets ostensibly to protect the health and safety of the community and Mrs. Nahrstedt challenged the prohibition. She argued it was unreasonable – explaining that her cats remained inside her unit at all times, made no noise or odor, and created no nuisance offensive to others. Applying the rule against her, she claimed, was an unreasonable limitation of her rights at the hands of her overbearing neighbors who could enforce unjustifiable rules against her without being subject to independent review or challenge (Arabian, 1995, pp. 2, 30). The problem this presents is it tolerates majoritarian domination at the cost of personal autonomy rights.

Why Nahrstedt is Important

Mrs. Nahrstedt purchased a unit in Lakeside Village, a common interest community, with ownership subject to covenants, conditions, and restrictions (CC&Rs), set forth in the developer's declaration (Arabian, 1995, p. 2). The community maintained a pet restriction prohibiting animals in units. Upon learning of the cats, the board demanded their removal and threatened fines for non-compliance. Mrs. Nahrstedt denied having prior knowledge of the restriction when she purchased her unit and claimed the restriction was unreasonable because her pets created no harm (Arabian, 1995, p. 3, citing Nahrstedt, pp. 1278–1279). Mrs. Nahrstedt sought to eliminate the restriction (Arabian, 1995, p. 3, citing Nahrstedt, p. 1279) claiming her set of circumstances did not correspond to proper imposition of the rule. The board claimed the rule in fact furthered the collective interest by promoting health, happiness, and peace of mind for all residents in the community consistent with the product or brand (of privatized governance) they purchased. The lower court upheld the rule, it was reversed on appeal on reasonableness, and the State supreme court accepted review to consider "on what basis might an owner prevent enforcement of a recorded restriction?" (Arabian, 1995, p. 4, citing Nahrstedt, pp. 1278–1279). The Supreme Court ultimately denied Mrs. Nahrstedt the right to keep her cats holding CC&Rs presumptively valid and therefore not subject to challenge based on personal considerations (Arabian, 1995, p. 4, Nahrstedt, generally). The majority reasoned anyone purchasing a unit in an association does so with knowledge of HOA enforcement authority and recognizes implicitly such enforcement is necessary to the effective functionality of the common unity (Arabian, 1995, pp. 6–7, citing Nahrstedt, p. 1282). Of course, this entire argument collapses when branding is unethical (the advertised branded image is not real).

Judge Arabian (1995) explained in dissent that the majority favored enforceability of use restrictions considering them the equivalent of equitable servitudes binding against all members without requiring explicit notice. Thus, a restrictive recording in public records is constructive notice. As far as the majority was concerned, (Arabian, 1995, p. 7, citing Nahrstedt, pp. 1286–1287), deference applied broadly enhances stability and comports with the expectation of expectations. The court burdened the individual to establish reasonableness and rejected challenges of rules despite possible violations of public policy or harm disproportionate to their benefit (Arabian, 1995, p. 8). The majority criticized the lower court for making a case-by-case reasonableness inquiry concluding the standard for determining reasonableness should reference the community as a whole. The court held that as long as a restriction is applicable uniformly against all residents, is not arbitrary, and does not violate a fundamental public policy or impose burdens on the use of affected property in ways that substantially outweigh the identified benefit the restriction seeks to promote, it is lawful (Arabian, 1995). The majority, according to Arabian (1995), found courts must enforce such restrictions. Arabian (1995) took exception to the majority's conclusion arguing the rule was unreasonable in light of the practical reality of the modern role pets have come to play in people's lives (1995, p. 9). He explained an absolute prohibition on pets that create no nuisance is prima facie unreasonable because it creates a significant burden on individuals without corresponding benefit to the community. Arabian (1995, p. 10) also observed that boards hold far too much authority to intrude into the everyday lives of private individuals in HOAs, are too unaccountable for their actions, and are capable of significantly threatening individual rights because of the excessive deference courts afford them.

Aim, Objective, and Approach

Nahrstedt (1994) elucidates the need to better protect individual rights in the context of HOAs. Arabian (1995) critiqued the reasonableness test in Hidden Harbor Estates v. Norman (1975), where a restriction prohibited alcohol in common areas to promote the health, happiness, and enjoyment of life for all residents in the community. Arabian (1995, p. 12) observed Norman (1975) implies HOAs must assume responsibility for establishing the reasonableness of a restriction. He (Arabian, 1995) also critiqued Hidden Harbor Estates v. Basso (1981), where the court found no wrongdoing when an owner drilled a well without permission because the reviewing court concluded that when a board has discretionary decision-making authority, its decision must demonstrate a reasonable relationship between its action and fulfillment of legitimate community objectives. In Basso (1981), the court held the board failed to demonstrate approval of the permit would create risk of harm to the community. Thus, reasonableness is necessary before rights may be restricted; but the standard still fails to adequately protect individuals because boards can define reasonableness and the validity of such a declaration is not reviewable.

Arabian (1995, pp. 15–16) also critiqued the business judgment approach equating HOA boards with corporate boards finding insufficient equivalency because HOA boards are not equally accountable to constituents; and concluded the business judgment approach offers less protection to individuals than reasonableness because it *requires* a finding of board malfeasance such as fraud, self-dealing, or other unconscionable conduct *before* a court will entertain a challenge to HOA action. This analytical pathway benefits HOAs, explains Arabian (1995), shielding them from challenges and inadequately protects persons as it condones deference without any indication of fraud, dishonesty, or incompetence. The result is to unfairly place the burden of proof on the individual. The business judgment rule is therefore equally, if not more so than the reasonableness standard, inadequate to protect individual liberties.

Arabian (1995, p. 18) suggests a possible solution to the problem in establishing a bill of owner-member rights. While statutory protections could better protect individuals from overreaching governing boards, a better-still approach may be to enhance the standard of judicial review by minimizing judicial deference. This chapter concludes with the suggestion that the better alternative solution would be to force HOAs to follow a more comprehensive decision-making process. Implementing hard-look judicial review would enhance private rights and secure ethical branding in the context of privatized public governance.

Conclusion

Hard-look review would promote ethical branding and CSR by holding governing boards accountable for their actions. Private HOAs are an effective alternative to local government (Nelson, 1999, p. 861) because they provide what local government cannot – lower crime rates, stable property values, flexibility, efficiency, and sense of community (Doucet & Smit, 2016). While HOAs offer collective good, private harm can be quite damaging, so efforts to avoid it are necessary. Presently-in-use standards of judicial review of HOA actions fail to adequately protect individual rights. The most effective, efficient solution to this problem is to enhance the rigor of judicial review courts apply. The proposed hard-look review would accomplish this objective minimizing deference by institutionalizing comprehensive record-building and review.

While this recommendation might impose burdens on HOA boards and courts in the short-term requiring more effort to construct adequate records for review, the long-run benefits of better decision-making that safeguards personal liberty and fulfills the promise of ethical branding, justify such up-front costs.

Discussion Questions

1   Do you believe HOAs practice ethical branding when enforcing rules to promote the collective good to the detriment of individual private rights? Explain your reasoning using an example from the chapter.
2   Do you believe presently-in-use judicial standards of review sufficiently protect individual private rights? If so, defend your position. If not, what alternative solution would you offer? Explain your reason.
3   Do you believe Mrs. Nahrstedt should have been permitted to keep her cats? Do you believe the governing board had a justifiable argument for enforcing its pet restriction? Do HOAs exercise too much power over the lives of individuals? Explain your reasoning.
4   Describe three instances of ethical branding. How do your examples fit within the definition provided in the chapter?
5   Describe three instances of unethical branding. How do your examples fit within the definition provided in the chapter?

To Cite This Chapter

Kleeger, J. (2019). Ethical branding, homeowner associations, and judicial review: Using a socially responsible administrative law "hard-look" standard. In H. Gringarten, & R. Fernández-Calienes (Eds.). *Ethical branding and marketing: Cases and lessons* (pp. 92–114). Routledge Management and Business Studies Series. London and New York: Routledge.

Notes

1 Siegel (2009, p. 805, n.1) distinguishes territorial from nonterritorial community associations explaining cooperatives and condominiums are non-territorial because they do not manage land, only units and common space. That distinction does not impact the analysis in this chapter. Here, all common interest communities function as a single housing choice – that of privatized collective self-governance.
2 For example, a non-resident owner gave unit access to her elderly mother who failed to supervise her teenaged grandchildren when they used the tennis court in the community. The HOA fined the owner for unsupervised amenity usage by non-residents. In rejecting the HOA penalty as an abuse of authority, the court explained boards must act within the scope of their authority and action taken must reflect reasoned judgment. The court

concluded distinguishing resident from non-resident owners was unlawful discrimination (Weiser, 2006, citing Major v. Miraverde, 1992). This is significant because entity bad behavior in the form of social irresponsibility coupled with inequitable application of rules devalues the HOA brand. To the extent the imagery of a family-friendly lifestyle is flawed in a branded community, the marketing of lifestyle as family-friendly is inaccurate. Branding is unethical when promise and fact are inconsistent or diverge.

3 Siegel (2009, n.22) explains how The Civil Rights Cases (1883) held 14th Amendment protections apply only to State action. By that measure, discriminatory, wrongful private conduct is not actionable under federal law. Yet, the Court, beginning in the 1930s, began to distinguish between public and private conduct, and under certain circumstances characterized acts of private parties as equivalent to State action – hence the doctrine's name. Examples of conduct amounting to State action include Georgia v. McCollum, 505 U.S. 42, 54 (1992) where the Court recognized State action in use of peremptory challenge rights in a criminal case; Lugar v. Edmondson Oil Co., 457 U.S. 922, 942 (1982) in a creditor-obtained prejudgment writ of attachment of debtor's property; Burton v. Wilmington Parking Authority, 365 U.S. 715, 725 (1961) in racially discriminatory conduct of a privately owned restaurant leasing space from a government agency; Shelley, 334 U.S. 1, 18 in judicial enforcement of a private restrictive covenant; Marsh v. Alabama, 326 U.S. 501, 505 (1946) in the operation of a company town functioning as if it were a municipality; and Smith v. Allwright, 321 U.S. 649, 663 (1944) in the context of political party primary elections.

4 The State grants authority to Developers to initiate a project. Once a developer sells 75% of planned units, governance devolves to members (Hannaman, 2008).

5 For example, a man was jailed for failing to sod his lawn and a woman fined for displaying a "Support Our Troops" sign on her yard honoring her husband deployed in military combat overseas (Boudreaux, 2009, p. 479).

References

Arabian, A. (1995). Condos, cats, and CC&Rs: Invasion of the Castle common. *Pepperdine Law Review, 23*(1), 1–30.

Bollinger, J. M. (2008, Spring). Homeowners' associations and the use of property planning tools: When does the right to exclude go too far? *Temple Law Review, 81*(1), 269–302.

Boudreaux, P. (2009, December). Homes, rights, and private communities. *University of Florida Journal of Law & Public Policy, 20*(3), 479–536.

Civil Rights Cases, 109 U.S. 3 (1883).

Crosby, L. A. (2010, Winter). A different tale of two cities: Learn to understand the bases of brand community. *Marketing Management, 19*(4), 12–13.

Donne, J. (1624). *Meditation 17, deviations upon emergent occasions.* Retrieved from http://www.poemhunter.com/poem/no-man-is-an-island

Doucet, B., & Smit, E. (2016, December). Building an urban 'renaissance': Fragmented services and the production of inequality in Greater Downtown Detroit. *Journal of Housing and the Built Environment, 31*(4), 635–657. doi:10.1007/s10901-015-9483-0

Fan, Y. (2005). Ethical branding and corporate reputation. *Corporate Communications, 10*(4), 341–350. doi:10.1108/13563280510630133

Frankental, P. (2001). Corporate social responsibility – a PR invention? *Corporate Communications, 6*(1), 18–23.

Fuselier, B. M. (2011). Home sweet homestead? Not if you are subject to a mandatory homeowner's association. *St. Mary's Law Journal, 42*(3), 793–836.

Garry, P. M. (2006, Fall). Judicial review and the hard-look doctrine. *Nevada Law Journal, 7*(1), 151–170.

Hannaman, E. R. (2002, March 19; 2008). *State and municipal perspectives— Homeowners associations*, presented to Rutgers University Center for Government Services, 231–241, 1–7. Retrieved from http://pvtgov.org/pvtgov/downloads/hannaman-NJ.pdf, StarMan Publishing

Hidden Harbor Estates, Inc. v. Norman, 309 So. 2d 180 (Fla. 4th Dist. Ct. App. 1975).

Hidden Harbor Estates, Inc. v. Basso, 393 So. 2d 637 (Fla. 4th Dist. Ct. App. 1981).

Hollywood Towers Condominium Association, Inc. v. Hampton, No. 4D09-383 (Fla. 4th Dist. Ct. App. 2010).

Inwood North Homeowners' Association v. Harris, 736 S.W.2d 632 (Tex. 1987).

Kress, C. B. (1995, February). Beyond Nahrstedt: Reviewing restrictions governing life in a property owner association. *University of California Los Angeles Law Review, 42*(3), 837–884.

Lai, L. W. C. (2016). Stone walls do not a prison make, nor iron bars a cage": The institutional and communitarian possibilities of "gated communities." *Land Use Policy, 54*, 378–385.

Lamden v. La Jolla Shores Clubdominium Homeowners Association, 980 P.2d 940 (Cal. 1999).

Levi, R. (2009, Summer). Gated communities in law's gaze: Material forms and the production of a social body in legal adjudication. *Law & Social Inquiry, 34*(3), 635–670.

Major v. Miraverde Homeowners Association, 7 Cal.App.4th 618, 9 Cal. Rptr. 2d 237 (1992).

Marsh v. Alabama, 326 U.S. 501 (1946).

Matter of Levandusky v. One Fifth Avenue Apartment Corp., 75 N.Y.2d 530 (N.Y. 1990).

Melo, T., & Galan, J. I. (2011, April). Effects of corporate social responsibility on brand value. *Journal of Brand Management, 18*(6), 423–437. doi:10.1057/bm.2010.54

Nahrstedt v. Lakeside Village Condominium Association, 11 Cal. Rptr. 2d 299. (Ct. App. 1992), rev'd Nahrstedt v. Lakeside Village Condominium Association, 878 P.2d 1275 (Cal. 1994).

Nelson, R. H. (1999, Summer). Privatizing the neighborhood: A proposal to replace zoning with private collective property rights to existing neighborhoods. *George Mason Law Review, 7*(4), 827–880.

Nichols, M. (2012, February 29). Reasonableness standard versus business-judgment rule. *American Bar association, section of litigation.* Retrieved from http://apps.americanbar.org/litigation/committees/businesstorts/articles/winter2012-reasonableness-standard-business-judgment-rule.html

Papalexiou v. Tower West Condominium, 401 A.2d 280 (N.J. Super. Ct. Ch. Div. 1979).

Parsons, P. J. (2007). Integrating ethics with strategy: Analyzing disease-branding. *Corporate Communications, 12*(3), 267–279. doi:10.1108/13563280710776860

Pollack, M. C. (2013, Spring). Judicial deference and institutional character: Homeowners associations and the puzzle of private governance. *University of Cincinnati Law Review, 81*(3), 839–896.

Reichman, U. (1976, Winter). Residential private governments: An introductory survey. *The University of Chicago Law Review, 43*(2), 253–306.

Schlegelmilch, B. B., & Pollach, I. (2005, April). The perils and opportunities of communicating corporate ethics. *Journal of Marketing Management, 21*(3–4), 267–290.

Shelley v. Kraemer, 334 U.S. 1 (1948).

Shoked, N. (2011, Summer). The community aspect of private ownership. *Florida State University Law Review, 38*(4), 759–826.

Siegel, S. (1998, Spring). The constitution and private government: Towards the recognition of constitutional rights in private residential communities fifty years after Marsh v. Alabama. *William & Mary Bill of Rights Journal, 6*(2), 461, 546–563.

Siegel, S. (2009, Winter). The public interest and private gated communities: A comprehensive approach to public policy that would discourage the establishment of new gated communities and encourage the removal of gates from existing private communities. *Loyola Law Review, 55*(4), 805–838.

Singh, J. J., Iglesias, O., & Batista-Foguet, J. M. (2012, December). Does having an ethical brand matter? The influence of consumer perceived ethicality on trust, affect and loyalty. *Journal of Business Ethics, 111*(4), 541–549. doi:10.1007/s10551-012-1216-7

Slaughterhouse Cases. See The Slaughterhouse Cases (below).

The Slaughterhouse Cases, 83 U.S. 36 (1873).

Smith, J. W. (2008, January–February). Selling doing good: It takes more than social responsibility to sell a product or service. *Marketing Management, 17*(1), 56.

Stern, S. (2014). Takings, community, and value: Reforming takings law to fairly compensate common interest communities. *Journal of Law & Policy, 23*(1), 141–202.

van de Ven, B. (2008, October). An ethical framework for the marketing of Corporate Social Responsibility. *Journal of Business Ethics, 82*(2), 339–352. doi:10.1007/s10551-008-9890-1

Weiser, J., & Wang, Z. (2006, June 25). Judicial review standards & litigation frequency: An empirical study of Homeowners Association decisions and the business judgment rule. Retrieved from SSRN: https://papers.ssrn.com/sol3/papers.cfm?abstract_id=914100

Wiseman, H. J. (2012). Rethinking the renter/owner divide in private governance. *Utah Law Review, 12*(4), 2067–2126.

8 Ethical Branding Best Practices

A Study of Fabindia in the Context of Social Business

Dinesh Kumar and Punam Gupta

Introduction

A brand is a method of differentiating the products of a business with respect to other companies and brands (adapted from American Marketing Association, 1960). It creates emotional bonds with customers, turning brands into icons. Very often, brands go beyond products of a company but begin to represent the firm.

Branding is an important function in marketing that gives an identity to products and companies. It involves building organizational relationships with all stakeholders, including customers. Branding is a well-known construct that is a common area of study in marketing. It is less common to find study and reporting, however, on ethical branding. At one level, it relates to moral principles and following a generally considered right behavior in branding decisions. That is, a brand not only is an economic, marketing, or financial construct but also holds value by moral considerations. Kapferer (2010) has listed several brand requirements. Among them is being ethical and ecology-conscious: "The brand must adopt ethical principles and demonstrate that consumption is not a synonym for inefficient waste, pollution and exploitation – themes to which society is becoming increasingly sensitive" (p. 92).

But ethical branding is an abstract concept. What morals or moral values is a brand supposed to follow? Is it ethical, for instance, if a company seeks to reduce consumer costs by sourcing products from poor countries – where labor rates are low – but may seem as exploiting the poor? Customers love the low prices, and the company breaks no laws. So, where should the moral compass point? Hence, it is difficult to find an agreement on what exactly is ethical branding.

Ethical Branding

From a moral point of view, branding may be ethical if it does not do things people commonly accept as bad. These include targeting vulnerable groups including children, selling harmful products such as alcohol and cigarettes to youngsters, over-promising or exaggerating benefits, exploiting workers, indulging in false and misleading advertising, promoting

> ## Check Your Understanding
>
> ### Ethical Approach
>
> *Ethical branding* calls for an ethical approach right from the time when brands are conceived.
>
> *Ethical approach* has to be built into brands right from supply chains to distribution to image building. It goes against traditional brand building that has the basic purpose of creating needs while *appearing* to be prim and proper.

conspicuous consumption, and so on. The assumption is that ethical branding can promote sales of a product by building a positive image of the brand in the mind of the customer. In reality, however, companies that do indulge in unethical activities do not lose goodwill and continue to do good business simply because they are able to offer lower prices than the competition.

Ethical branding, thus, has to be more than merely doing the right things. It also means changing the company and its objectives so that the companies not only *are seen* as ethical but also *are* ethical in their approach and operations. We argue for a complete reorientation of business toward a *social business*. The thinking toward social business has resulted from two developments: first, the need of companies to reduce their dependence on saturated urban markets, and second, for environmental sustainability. The very orientation of business has to change – from mere pursuit of profit making to more social and environmental purposes. It goes much beyond corporate social responsibility and calls for a radical change in the approach of business. Bower, Leonard, and Paine (2011) point out in their book, *Capitalism at Risk: Rethinking the Role of Business*, business has twin roles of innovator and activist and must follow strategies that transform communities.

A *fourth sector* is emerging, one that goes beyond the traditional understanding of business.

> Over the past few decades, the boundaries between the public (government), private (business), and social (non-profit) sectors have been blurring as many pioneering organizations have been blending social and environmental aims with business approaches.
>
> (Fourth Sector, 2017, n.p.)

Sabeti (2011) calls it the "for-benefit corporation" (p. 99). A new sector of the economy is emerging, consisting of companies that reconcile business and societal objectives. Porter and Kramer (2002) write, "We are learning that the most effective way to address many of the world's most pressing problems is to mobilize the corporate sector where both companies and society can benefit" (p. 58).

Thus, while profit generation and maximization are legitimate objectives of companies, economic, social, and environmental betterment also must accompany them. The existing model of capitalism thus needs to become a more "humane capitalism." Research reports increasingly point out that we are at the limits of sustainability – the planet cannot sustain the excessive consumption and waste that the economic system entails. In this context, integrating social objectives in business is the way forward.

Social Business

A social business is different from a "normal" business. A traditional company makes products, sells them, and thereby earns profit – which it then distributes to shareholders. At the other end of the spectrum are non-governmental organizations (NGOs), which meet social objectives but do not necessarily seek profits. They have to depend on donations and other fund-raising activities to survive. An NGO without funds quickly becomes unsustainable, as it is unable to meet its costs and expenses. A social business, however, meets some social objectives but also seeks profits, which it reinvests for the development of society or in the business itself.

A social business is one in which a business recovers all the costs and reinvests the surpluses generated (Yunus & Weber, 2007). Figure 8.1 shows the positioning of a social business. It is different from other forms of business in that it combines both financial *and* social profit maximization so the businesses are sustaining and profitable operations. The social business re-invests profits; hence, the promoters do not make profits for themselves. The social business thus is like a regular business, which sells products and services but does not pay dividends to promoters. Social businesses call for using managerial skills creatively

> ### Check Your Understanding
>
> #### Social Business
>
> Milton Friedman wrote, "the sole purpose of a business is to generate profits for its shareholders." This is also the principle on which capitalism works. But *social business* tries to modify this basic tenet. The first principle of business is to do good for all stakeholders including society, while profits are secondary.

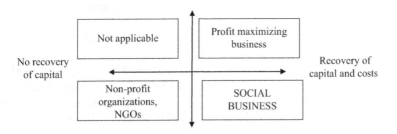

Figure 8.1 Nature of social business (Yunus & Weber, 2007).

Check Your Understanding

Corporate Social Responsibility

UNIDO defines *corporate social responsibility* as a concept in which companies "integrate social and environmental concerns in their business operations." Ethical branding builds on this concept but places social concerns as prime movers of business.

to solve social problems. A social business thus meets three objectives: first, it seeks to alleviate social problems; second, it recovers its costs and makes profits; and third, it reinvests the profits in the business, rather than paying them to shareholders.

People often see social business as corporate social responsibility (CSR). A social business actually goes beyond traditional CSR, which simply implies using a part of profits for doing good in society. While some companies have started schools and environmental initiatives, many others simply donate money to NGOs with the aim of obtaining an image of doing something socially useful. This is because companies find it easy simply to give away the money than to really do something about a social cause. But, a social business has social objectives in its DNA: that is the reason for its existence.

Yunus and Weber (2007) write that social business aims for the "maximization of profit and doing good to people and the world" (p. 243). They explain that such businesses must have social objectives as their core purpose and ambition:

- move to open innovation, drawing on the "wisdom of the crowd" to develop completely new solutions for age-old rural problems;
- must be embedded in a larger innovation ecosystem of other players that include technology providers, funders, capacity builders, partners, and supply chain players;
- develop collaborative and creative approaches in the area of distribution in remote areas;
- build cross-sector partnerships with not only NGOs but also governments, customers, and academic partners;
- integrate both environmental sustainability and a triple bottom line perspective into the objectives of the company, as opposed to the earlier approach of companies trying to build models to serve the poor; and
- create livelihoods and alleviate poverty in remote areas.

Building a social business is difficult to achieve. Making money is, after all, a driving force for business. But, when we were researching initiatives for our book, *Rural Marketing* (2017), we found several companies that have been able to establish sustainable social businesses across the world. They have been able to address some rural problem while establishing commercially viable operations.

Alibaba, for instance, was successful in creating production hubs, called *taobao* villages in China, and upgraded thousands of poor people to become producers. As volumes increased, logistics and other services developed around these village clusters. The initiative has been responsible for a large number of people getting out of poverty (*The Guardian*, 2014). In India, the e-choupal initiative of ITC Ltd. invested in an IT infrastructure so villagers could get information relevant to their crops, a platform for selling their produce, as well as a one-stop e-commerce site for getting products from ITC and other manufacturers. The e-choupal effectively worked around the restrictive laws that plague Indian agriculture (Goyal, 2010).

Essilor made available reading glasses to poor populations in villages that lacked the resources to pay for an eye test or spectacles. It is expanding the program to many countries apart from India (Inclusive Business Action Network, 2015). In Peru, Café Feminino provides help to women coffee growers and gets them a fair price for their produce (Café Feminino Foundation, 2017). In India, Jain Irrigation helps farmers increase their income through micro-irrigation and offers a buy back for their produce (Haanaes, David, Jurgens, & Rangan, 2013). In France, Renault Mobiliz has set up "solidarity garages" that repair the cars of poor customers at a nominal cost. Its website says people on low incomes can buy a car or can have someone repair it at a Renault Socially Responsible Garage. Renault Mobiliz also has an investment firm, Mobiliz Invest, which provides financing for businesses that offer innovative mobility solutions for socio-economically disadvantaged people (Renault, 2017). In India, Fabindia has brought weavers and artisans in touch with markets, increasing their earnings in the process (Ramachandran, Pant, & Pani, 2011).

Grameen Bank in Bangladesh is a classic example of a social business. It gave micro loans to poor people outside the banking system so that they could start small businesses and become independent (Grameen Bank, 2017). It was instrumental in introducing mobile phones in villages through Grameen Phone. In a joint venture with Danone, it provides an affordable source of nutrition through *shoktidoi*, a tasty yogurt to meet the nutritional needs of children. The product was first distributed in rural areas by shokti ladies, who sold the product on commission basis (Yunus & Weber, 2007). Grameen Bank and Muhammad Yunus received the Nobel Peace Prize in 2006 (The Nobel Peace Prize, 2006).

These are a few examples of companies that have built social businesses, but there are many more such initiatives across the world.

The common element in these initiatives is that the companies built businesses that not only helped the disadvantaged section of societies in some way but also were able to achieve profits. Each of these companies solved an outstanding problem of villages, and built products and services around those.

The Case of Fabindia

Fabindia Overseas Private Limited (Fabindia) retails handloom and handicraft products, furniture, cosmetics, apparel, and various other items. What is special about Fabindia is that it sources all products from BoP producers who live in villages. The company engages with village communities and artisans across the country, providing them designs and knowhow to make quality goods that urban markets accepted and for exports, supports them, and buys their produce from them at remunerative prices. In doing so, it provides poor people access to markets that would be impossible for them otherwise. It helps rural communities and empowers them.

Fabindia combines marketing and distribution with empowering artisans at the same time. The company today not only has supply chains to source quality products from villages but also strengthens the artisan community by linking artists to the market and even running a school in Bali, Rajasthan.

The story of Fabindia is an interesting one. Its founder, John Bissell, had noticed that the producers of traditional handicrafts of India were poor while the products they produced sold at high prices in foreign markets. Bissell set up Fabindia in New Delhi with the objective of helping the producers with a system of "inclusive capitalism," that is, of selling the handicrafts at a profit but also ensuring "a fair, equitable, and helpful relationship with our producers, and the maintenance of quality" (Fabindia, 2017, n.p.).

Fabindia began exports of handloom home furnishings sourced from villages. It opened its first retail store in New Delhi in 1976, which became very popular, and sales began increasing. Today, the company provides marketing support to more than 55,000 rural producers while creating rural employment opportunities. It also preserves the tradition of India's rich handicrafts. *The Economic Times* (Malviya, 2016) reported that Fabindia Overseas has become the largest retail apparel brand in the country, ahead of global brands operating in the country.

"At Fabindia we celebrate India, and endeavour to bring all that we love about India to customers around the world" (Fabindia, 2017, n.p.), declares its vision statement. To do this, the company endeavors to make traditional products that delight customers, and to "harness the transformative power of a well-run business committed to profitable growth" (Fabindia, 2017, n.p.). However, the company is a social business in that it takes up the twofold task of marketing products while supporting village-level producers. Its website says that it is committed to provide products that delight them and to protect the environment.

Fabindia provides marketing inputs to the craftspeople of India. Earlier, the craftspeople had no access to markets or designs. They produced whatever they could and tried to sell directly to customers or suffered

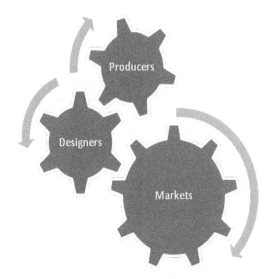

Figure 8.2 The Fabindia business model combines three essential business operations.

exploitation by intermediaries. Fabindia broke that chain and linked the craftspeople to designers and buyers, thereby providing a direct link with the market (see Figure 8.2). As John Bissell had envisaged, the company adopted indigenous skills and designs suitable for the market, providing those inputs for production, and by regular supervision ensured it met production commitments.

The company guides artisans to produce contemporary designs that find favor with urban consumers even while using their indigenous techniques. It guides producers by providing contemporary designs, maintaining quality control, and even providing access to raw materials and helping out in production techniques. Its business model consists of training artisans and upgrading them. It combines three business operations – buyers who can estimate demand requirements, designers who develop contemporary designs, and the producer, who earlier was separated from the marketing and design process. Designers too had received training, as they could not work with local handlooms. The company created a team of "domain specialists," who worked with designers, providing them with both production assistance as well as design and guidance about the "look" of the product.

The company's product line consists textiles, embroidery, and home products, all made by hand by village-level workers. It has slowly expanded its range: it now sells organic food products, personal care products, ready-to-wear garments and accessories, furniture, lighting, stationery, tableware, cane baskets, and handcrafted items. Its range of organic foods includes grains, pulses, spices, various kinds of teas, honey, and fruit preserves. One also can find soaps, shampoos, and other cosmetics on Fabindia shelves. All the products come from the village communities, which traditionally have supplied furnishing and apparel to the company over the years, showing how deep the relationship is between Fabindia and its village communities. The company has expanded its engagement with farmers and woodwork workers within these communities.

Fabindia also set up a craft workers welfare association, which created the Craftmark to distinguish its products from machine-made garments available widely in the country. The "Craftmark" logo and certification guarantees products as genuine Indian handloom products. This helped Fabindia to establish its brand: *The Economic Times* (Raghavan, 2015) wrote that Fabindia is popular among mall owners as its stores result in better footfalls.

We can sum up the model of Fabindia as making profits with equitable distribution. The business model combines two opposing objectives: profitable growth and meeting social goals. In the words of William Bissell, Managing Director of Fabindia since 1999, "In addition to making profits, our aims are constant development of new hand-woven products, a fair, equitable, and helpful relationship with our producers, and the maintenance of quality on which our reputation rests" (Menon, 2009, n.p.).

To encourage self-sufficiency of village artisans, Fabindia has set up Supplier Region Companies (SRCs), which are community-owned enterprises that have common facilities, train workers, and implement standards. SRCs manage the production and quality control issues while Fabindia focuses on marketing and distribution. The SRCs distribute production requirements to its members and deliver the produce to Fabindia for distribution and marketing.

To strengthen the community, Fabindia started a school in the village of Bali, Rajasthan, in 1992. The idea was to empower young people in rural Rajasthan through a model school. Literacy rates have been traditionally low in the state, especially among women. The school adopts creative approaches to education to bring out each child's inherent talent and include environmental education in a local context.

Conclusion

Our study shows how companies, and especially Fabindia, are able to build sustainable social businesses when social betterment exists in their DNA. This is becoming increasingly important, as the world cannot continue to survive if we ignore environmental and social concerns. Nor can companies expand if they continue to ignore the majority of the population that is poor and disadvantaged. Businesses have recognized this and hence have taken to CSR activities. However, this chapter shows that throwing money at CSR activities is not as effective as changing the very orientation of companies toward social causes. Earning profits is not a bad thing, but companies may well face a backlash if companies do not invest profits in solving social problems.

Ironically, it means going back to Gandhian economics. In the words of Mahatma Gandhi:

> Recall the face of the poorest and the weakest man whom you may have seen, and ask yourself, if the step you contemplate is going to be of any use to him. Will he gain anything by it? Will it restore him to a control over his own life and destiny? In other words, will it lead to swaraj for the hungry and spiritually starving millions?
>
> (Johnson, 2006)

Discussion Questions

1 Ethical branding is more about building an image – it means building an ethical approach in a brand's DNA. Discuss this statement in light of the Fabindia approach.
2 A social business attempts to maximize social profits. In what ways does Fabindia maximize both financial and social profits?
3 How does ethical branding correlate with building social business? Discuss the common elements in light of the Fabindia case study. What else can companies do to promote ethical branding?

To Cite This Chapter

Kumar, D., & Gupta, P. (2018). Ethical branding best practices: A study of Fabindia in the context of social business. In H. Gringarten, & R. Fernández-Calienes (Eds.). *Ethical branding and marketing: Cases and lessons* (pp. 115–124). Routledge Management and Business Studies Series. London and New York: Routledge.

References

Alibaba delivers benefits of a new digital economy to remotest China. (2014, August 25). *The Guardian*. Available at http://www.theguardian.com/technology/2014/aug/ 25/china-taobao-ecommerce-alibaba-rural-china. Accessed 29 October 2017.

American Marketing Association. (1960). *Marketing definitions: A glossary of marketing terms*. Chicago, IL: Author.

Bower, J. L., Leonard, H. B., & Paine, L. S. (2011). *Capitalism at risk: Rethinking the role of business*. Boston, MA: Harvard Business Review Press.

Café Feminino Foundation. (2017). Our story. http://www.coffeecan.org/about-us

Fabindia. (.   npany. Available at https://www.fabindia.com/
pages/abc   aspx. Accessed 29 October 2017.
Fourth Sect   e fourth sector. https://www.fourthsector.net/
learn. Ac   17.
Goyal, A. (.   ct access to farmers, and rural market performance   ican Economic Journal: Applied Econom-
ics, 2(3),   doi:10.1257/app   3.22
Grameen E   (2017).   About   http://www.grameen-info.org/about-us/.
Accessed   October 2017.
Haanaes, K   David, M. Jorgen, I. S.   angan, S. (2013, March). Making sus-
tainability profitable. Harvard Business Review, 91(3), 110–115.
Inclusive Business Action Network. (2015). http://www.inclusivebusinesshub.
org/micro-site/inclusive-business-action-network/
Johnson, R. L. (Ed.). (2006). *Gandhi's experiments with truth: Essential writings by and about Mahatma Gandhi.* Lanham, MD: Lexington Books.
Kapferer, J.-N. (2010). *The new strategic brand management: Creating and sustaining brand equity long term* (4th ed.). London, England: Kogan Page.
Kumar, D., & Gupta, P. (2017). *Rural marketing: Challenges and opportunities.* New Delhi, India: Sage.
Malviya, S. (2016, January 19). Fabindia crosses Rs 1,000 crore in sales; becomes largest retail apparel brand in the country. *The Economic Times.* Available at https://economictimes.indiatimes.com/industry/services/retail/fabindia-crosses-rs-1000-crore-in-sales-becomes-largest-retail-apparel-brand-in-the-country/articleshow/50632859.cms. Accessed 29 October 2017.
Menon, B. D. (2009, September 17). With plans just Fab. *The Hindu Business Line.* Available at http://www.thehindubusinessline.com/todays-paper/tp-brandline/with-plans-just-fab/article1083885.ece. Accessed 29 October 2017.
The Nobel Peace Prize 2006. (2017). https://www.nobelprize.org/nobel_prizes/peace/ laureates/2006/
Porter, M. E., & Kramer, M. R. (2002, December). The competitive advantage of corporate philanthropy. *Harvard Business Review, 80*(12), 56–68.
Raghavan, P. (2015, August 27). Why local brands like FabIndia and Metro are being pursued more by shopping malls. *The Economic Times.* Available at https://economictimes.indiatimes.com/industry/services/retail/why-local-brands-like-fabindia-and-metro-are-being-pursued-more-by-shopping-malls/articleshow/48689948.cms. Accessed 29 October 2017.
Ramachandran, J., Pant, A., & Pani, S. K. (2011, October). Building the BoP producer ecosystem: The evolving engagement of Fabindia with Indian handloom artisans. *Journal of Product Innovation Management, 29*(1), 33–51.
Renault, M. (2017). Renault mobiliz socially responsible garages. Available at https://group.renault.com/en/commitments/mobility-2/mobiliz-program/renault-mobiliz-socially-responsible-garages/. Accessed 29 October 2017.
Sabeti, H. (2011, November). The for-benefit enterprise. *Harvard Business Review, 89*(11), 98–104.
Yunus, M., & Weber, K. (2007). *Creating a world without poverty: Social business and the future of capitalism.* New York, NY: Public Affairs.

9 Happy Brands and Ethical Implications

Wonkyong Beth Lee and
Timothy Dewhirst

Introduction

The attribution of human qualities to brands, through means such as personification or anthropomorphism, has become commonplace (Aaker, 1997). Much like people, brands may link to qualities such as success, sophistication, ruggedness, and happiness. Indeed, several brands have integrated happiness into their positioning or differentiation strategies, for example, McDonald's "Happy Meal," Coca-Cola's "Open Happiness," and Disney's "The Happiest Place on Earth." Accounting for consumers' insatiable desire for happiness, marketing communication linking brands with happiness has become ubiquitous.

It is easy to see why marketers commonly associate brands with happiness. Happiness is a desirable attribute and marketers seek to provide consumers with satisfying and pleasurable experiences. If brands can facilitate customers feeling "happy," "joyful," or "affectionate," consumers are likely to express stronger attitudinal (commitment) and behavioral (purchase) loyalty (Chaudhuri & Holbrook, 2001). Satisfied consumers are commonly happy consumers who generate significant revenues for companies through consumer retention (Paliwal & Indu, 2013).

Brands integrate happiness into their branding strategies by seemingly cultivating happiness among consumers (Isen, Labroo, & Durlach, 2004; Mogilner & Aaker, 2009). While happiness often equals joy, pleasure, and satisfying experiences, brands associated with happiness also may suggest enhancements to consumer well-being and welfare. Nevertheless, happiness appears particularly applicable to hedonic rather than utilitarian consumption, and products pertaining to hedonic consumption may not ultimately be beneficial or healthy to consumers. In this chapter, we explore such dilemmas relating to "happy" branding strategies and provide case examples, including those pertaining to the marketing of McDonald's "Happy Meal" and Newport cigarettes, which has the longstanding tagline "Alive with Pleasure!" "Happy" branding strategies raise a number of ethical concerns, especially those meant to appeal to children as a target market or those pertaining to addictive and harmful behavior.

There are several key ethical considerations concerning marketing communication that associates brands with happiness. With the advertising of "happy brands," emphasis is often on short-term gratification (i.e., immediate pleasure from consumption) and overlooks the consequences of repeated and persistent consumption (e.g., highly processed food, alcohol, and smoking). The association of happiness with brands is commonly for products that are not healthful, yet are appealing to youth and children. More generally, advertising regularly infers that happiness comes from consumption and the acquisition of goods, which is especially problematic if children develop such attitudes and beliefs at early ages. Accordingly, marketers and other stakeholders, including policy-makers, need to consider the minimum age that may be appropriate for targeting purposes.

What is Happiness?

> **Check Your Understanding**
>
> *Happiness*
>
> *Happiness:* Human qualities, such as cheerful, honest, charming, and successful are associated with a particular brand.

Philosophers have a longstanding interest in happiness. In particular, the hedonist philosophy of Aristippus of Cyrene theorized that happiness was the sum of material pleasures, and the meaning of life was the maximization of delight (Fromm, 1976; Layard, 2005). This hedonistic perspective of happiness was particularly influential in the eighteenth and nineteenth centuries and continues in contemporary consumer culture with the belief of "having more" is "being more" (Fromm, 1976). According to Merriam-Webster's Collegiate Dictionary (2009), happiness is "a state of well-being and contentment; a pleasurable or satisfying experience" (n.p.). Despite considerable attention among psychologists and consumer researchers, happiness is problematic to observe and a difficult construct to define (Mogilner, Aaker, & Kamvar, 2012; Robbins, Francis, & Edwards, 2010).

Psychologists commonly define happiness as a human personality trait (i.e., something that is comparable, measurable, and predictable across contexts) (Diener, 1984; Diener, Suh, Lucas, & Smith, 1999; Eysenck, 1983; Gilbert, 2006; Layard, 2005). For example, happiness is stable extraversion and the ability to have pleasant interactions and easy sociability (Eysenck, 1983). A necessary component of defining happiness is the presence of good social relationships (Diener & Seligman, 2002). Data support that happiness accompanies stable extraversion (Robbins et al., 2010). Various individuals experience happiness as a trait in the same way (Layard, 2005; Myers & Diener, 1995).

Other psychologists use *subjective well-being* as a construct to describe happiness (Diener et al., 1999), which reflects happiness as a non-physical state that we cannot measure objectively. Subjective well-being is "the degree to which an individual judges the overall quality of his/her own life-as-a-whole favorably" (Veenhoven, 2001, p. 4). Myers and Diener (1995) discovered that frequent positive affect, infrequent negative affect, and a global sense of satisfaction with life equates with high subjective well-being.

Regarding subjective well-being, Gilbert (2006) describes that happiness means distinct things to different individuals, and given everyone has unique lives, we should create a unique view of happiness. For example, happiness is a feeling of excitement to some people, yet a feeling of calmness to others (Mogilner et al., 2012). Happiness is not set, and it systematically changes over an individual's life span (Mogilner, Kamvar, & Aaker, 2011). Although not everyone defines happiness in the same way, some similarities within a given culture or age group exist. To illustrate, younger people tend to find greater happiness in extraordinary experiences, whereas older people usually find greater happiness in ordinary events (Mogilner & Norton, 2015).

What Makes People Happy?

This longstanding question has attracted the attention of many researchers. In particular, psychologists have identified several predictors of happiness: extraversion, assertiveness, cooperativeness, high self-esteem, the ability to savor positive events, satisfying and close relationships, and an engagement in leisure activities (Argyle & Lu, 1990a, 1990b; Bryant, 1989, 2003; Bryant, Smart, & King, 2005; Layard, 2005; Lu & Argyle, 1991, 1992, 1994; Tugade & Fredrickson, 2007).

What about the role of money? Does money buy happiness? In a seminal paper from 1974 by economist, Richard Easterlin, he observed that wealth increases, in several countries in the years after World War II, did not associate with increases in average happiness. This observation became Esterlin's paradox (Stevenson & Wolfers, 2008). Although income may increase in a given country, disparity is likely to persist – there are still many people who become richer and poorer – and relative income, on balance, likely remains the same (Argyle, 1999; Diener, Lucas, & Napa Scollon, 2006; Easterlin, 1995; Frey & Stutzer, 2002). Nevertheless, other scholars have started critiquing and reassessing the Easterlin paradox. Stevenson and Wolfers (2008) have shown a positive relation between income and happiness with more comprehensive data: the richer in a given country are more satisfied with their lives than the poorer, and this pattern is consistent in most countries around the world. Based on a United Nations–sponsored report, Norway, Denmark, Iceland, Switzerland, and Finland are the "happiest" countries in the world (Rahim, 2017). Interestingly, Scandinavian countries, which generally have wealth, but high taxes and lessened economic and social disparity among citizens, are typically the happiest (whereas the United States, despite its considerable wealth, ranked fourteenth in 2016).

Nobel Prize winner Daniel Kahneman has raised an interesting argument regarding the money and happiness relation. Kahneman and Deaton (2010) found that possessing a higher income increases a person's life evaluation. More specifically, earning beyond $75,000 in the USA does not enhance experienced happiness, but it continues to raise an individual's life satisfaction. Some researchers argue that where or how we spend money is more important to happiness than how much money someone earns. Prosocial spending on friends, family, or those who are close to you relates to happiness; the more people give to others, the happier they are likely to become (Mogilner & Norton, 2015).

Committed time also affects happiness: Spending time with significant others and socializing relates to a higher level of happiness in contrast to commuting and working, which result in lower levels of happiness (Mogilner, 2010). Expanding on this idea of time versus happiness, Mogilner and Norton (2015) conducted a study to see the ways in which people should use their time and money to enact maximum happiness, and results showed that happiness is less contingent on the amount of time and money at hand and more so dependent on how individuals choose to spend them.

Check Your Understanding

Brand Personality

Brand Personality: Human qualities, such as cheerful, honest, charming, and successful, are associated with a particular brand.

Much of the reviewed literature pertaining to happiness focuses on individual differences, but the possibility of public policy interventions to account for shared social problems suggests a need to consider the subject on a more collective level. According to philosopher, Jeremy Bentham, "The greatest happiness of the greatest number is the foundation of morals and legislation" (cited in Fitzhenry, 1993, p. 192).

Happiness in Consumption Contexts

Although consumers may aim to increase their happiness levels through consumption, research has shown increases in consumption do not necessarily increase happiness (Belk, 1985; Diener & Biswas-Diener, 2002; Easterlin, 1995; Kasser & Ryan, 1993, 1996; Richins, 1994; Richins & Dawson, 1992). For example, those more agreeable with statements such as "Some of the most important achievements in life include acquiring material possessions" and "Buying things gives me a lot of pleasure," tend to be less satisfied with life (Richins & Dawson, 1992). Moreover, materialism links positively to different psychological problems such as depression, paranoia, and narcissism (Kasser & Ryan, 1993).

According to Van Boven and Gilovich (2003), there are two types of consumption and their relations with happiness: (1) *experiential purchases* that people make with the primary intention of acquiring a life experience such as travel, attending a concert, and going out to a restaurant; and (2) *material purchases* that people make with the primary intention of acquiring a material possession such as a laptop, car, and clothing. Research has shown that experiential purchases, compared to material purchases, make people happier (Carter & Gilovich, 2010, 2012; Van Boven & Gilovich, 2003).

There are several possible reasons for why experiential purchases make people happier and are more gratifying than material purchases. First, experiential purchases boost social relations more easily and effectively than material goods. Positive, meaningful social relationships contribute to people's happiness (Diener & Seligman, 2002, 2004; Myers, 2000). We tend to engage in experiential purchases with others: We typically go on vacation with family and go to concerts with friends. We may potentially enjoy material purchases with others, but we often do so by ourselves (Gilovich, Kumar, & Jampol, 2014). Consequently, experiential purchases that more deeply connect us to others tend to contribute more happiness to people compared to material purchases. Second, experiential purchases, compared to material purchases, relate more closely to the self (Carter & Gilovich, 2012; Gilovich et al., 2014). For example, when people describe a purchase experientially, rather than materially, they are likely to think that the qualities of the purchase overlap with their lives and identities (Carter & Gilovich, 2012). Third, experiential purchases evoke fewer social comparisons than material purchases and consequently make people more satisfied with their purchases. While we try keeping up with the Joneses, comparing what we have to what others have, we may experience less satisfaction and happiness (Frank, 1999; Schwarz & Strack, 1999; Suls, 2003). However, because we cannot easily compare our own experience purchases with those from others – relative to material goods – we may engage less in social comparisons (Carter & Gilovich, 2010; Van Boven, 2005).

Brands and Happiness

Despite consumers obtaining more satisfaction from experiential purchases than material purchases (Gilovich et al., 2015), brands still attract consumers and are ultimately a definitive expression of materialism (Holt, 1995; Kozinets & Handelman, 2004; Schmitt et al., 2014). A brand's traditional functions include an identification role that helps consumers link a name or image to the product (Elliott & Wattanasuwan, 1998), being an object of desire (Belk, Ger, & Askegaard, 2003), and serving as friends, partners, and other relationship roles (Aggarwal, 2004; Fournier, 1998; Fournier & Alvarez, 2012). An additional emerging

Check Your Understanding

Vulnerable Consumers

Vulnerable Consumers: Those who may not fully understand the implications of marketing messages due to their level of cognitive development such as children.

function of brands is to provide consumer experiences. Schmitt (1999) proposes an integration of the numerous ways in which consumers may experience brands. Brand experiences are consumers' subjective responses (sensations, feelings, cognitions, and behaviors) when consumers search for, shop for, and consume brands. When consumers have stronger and more intense experiences with a brand, consumers' satisfactions are higher. Brand experiences can influence consumers' satisfaction and loyalty directly and indirectly (Brakus, Schmitt, & Zarantonello, 2009).

Although consumers find more happiness from experiential purchases than material purchases, brands – the epitome of materialism – may play an important role in a consumer's well-being. Schmitt et al. (2014) argue that brands can create and evoke experiences among consumers. For example, consumers experience strong and meaningful relationships with brands and become emotionally attached to them as they do with their significant others (Fournier, 1998; Thomson, MacInnis, & Park, 2005). When a brand transgresses a consumer, however, the broken relationship can take a toll on the brand (Thomson et al., 2012) as well as consumers (Thomson, Whelan, & Johnson, 2012). Such illustrations indicate that consumers can experience through brands. In addition, when consumers have strong and favorable brand experiences, brands can influence consumers' well-being and can make consumers happy (Bettingen & Luedicke, 2009; Schmitt, 2014).

For the most part, the aforementioned functions of brands are positive for consumer well-being, but brands also have been central to criticism and moral questions (Handelman, 1999; Holt, 2002; Klein, 1999; Kozinets & Handelman, 2004). Such studies point to branding as potentially promoting over-consumption and resulting in the damage of human and environmental resources as well as a diminished quality of human relationships and overall well-being (Csikszentmihalyi, 1999). In particular, we now move our attention to ethical issues surrounding "happiness" brands when vulnerable consumers serve as target markets (i.e., children) and hedonic consumption that relates to addictive and harmful behavior (i.e., cigarette smoking).

Cases of Happy Branding

Happy and Fun in Food Marketing Targeting Children

The food industry is a major contributor to the problem of childhood obesity given their substantial promotion of food that is high in sugar, salt, and fat without substantial nutritional value (Elliott, 2008; Kant & Graubard, 2004). Overall, children are often a target of high levels of food marketing (Elliott, 2008) and, in particular, food-related media messages targeting children has been dominant historically in television advertising (Chamberlain, Wang, & Robinson, 2006; Gantz, Schwartz, Angelini, & Rideout, 2007). Not surprisingly, the more children see television advertising, the greater their preference is for unhealthy foods (Institute of Medicine, 2006). In the Canadian province of Quebec, where advertising targeting children less than 13 years of age is not allowable – including fast-food advertising – fast-food consumption has notably declined (Dhar & Baylis, 2011).

To complement television advertising, the fast-food industry has commonly used toy premiums – providing toys with the purchase of meals – to target children (Scholsser, 2001). Utilizing cross-promotions, toy premiums link with the entertainment industry including feature characters from popular children's movies or television programs (Hobin, Hammond, Daniel, Hanning, & Manske, 2012). In 2006, the fast-food industry spent nearly $330 million in the USA on toy premiums with children's meals, and such meals were the top-selling fast-food item to children (Federal Trade Commission, 2008). Toy premiums clearly influence children's food choices (Hobin et al., 2012; Institute of Medicine, 2006).

A well-known example of toy premiums is McDonald's Happy Meal. Bob Bernstein, founder and CEO of Bernstein-Rein, a marketing and communications firm, coined the name "Happy Meal" in 1977 (Lawrence Journal-World, 2004).

Although Bernstein might have not predicted the power of "happiness" in branding when he came up with the name, happy and fun are particularly appealing when targeting children. Research has shown that appeals to fun – in addition to taste and the use of other persuasive techniques (e.g., promotional characters) – increase children's recall, liking of advertising, purchase-requests, and food preferences (Cairns, Angus, Hastings, & Caraher, 2013; Hastings, McDermott, Angus, Stead, & Thomson, 2006). Fun is a popular theme in food marketing targeting children and refers to non-verbal displays of happiness (e.g., smiling or playing) or verbal use of "fun," "happiness," or "pleasure" (Hebden, King, & Kelly, 2011). Several content analyses have shown that fun or happiness is the most frequent emotional appeal in food marketing targeting children (Folta, Goldberg, Economos, Bell, & Meltzer, 2006; Kunkel & Gantz, 1992; Warren, Wicks, Wicks, Fosu, & Chung, 2007). Fun is a common theme in many different countries when targeting children on television (e.g., the USA, Australia, Canada, UK, Turkey, Switzerland, and Bulgaria) (Jenkin, Madhvani, Signal, & Bowers, 2014).

A critical lens on targeting children, however, warns that children can be vulnerable consumers, who are "those who may not fully understand the implications of marketing messages" (Rittenburg & Parthasarathy,

1997, p. 52) due to their level of cognitive development. Children may not have sufficient cognitive abilities and defensive mechanisms to understand fully the persuasive or possibly manipulative intent of marketing messages (e.g., McAlister & Cornwell, 2009; Pechmann, Levine, Loughlin, & Leslie, 2005). Themes of fun and happiness in marketing communication often suggest to children that the product may make you happy (i.e., mood alteration), and this kind of emotional appeal can provide a strong positive association with food brands while deemphasizing and distracting from information relating to the product (Wicks, Warren, Fosu, & Wicks, 2009).

Attracting children with McDonald's as a happy brand appears to be a principle strategic initiative for the company. The US-based McDonald's website provides some basic information about Happy Meal options with a tagline of "Make 'em smile with a HAPPY MEAL®" (https://www.mcdonalds.com/us/en-us/full-menu/happy-meal.html). The company's separate website of Happy Meals (www.happymeal. com) exclusively covers various incentives of Happy Meals. The website obviously targets children by containing games, activities, and information about toys accompanying Happy Meals. This kind of "advergames" is widespread on websites targeting children; interactive games include brand messages that are colorful and fun. While playing games and engaging in activities on the website, children become more aware of brands, and marketers encourage children to visit their websites repeatedly (Moore, 2004).

In addition to the various games and activities, Happy Meal's mascot, "Happy," has a predominant presence on the Happy Meal website. In 2014, McDonald's added a Happy Meal Ambassador, "Happy," in the USA. In a press release, Julie Wenger, senior director of US marketing for McDonald's, states: "At McDonald's, we're always looking to bring fun and happiness to families" (McDonald's, 2014). Marketing communication of its "happy" brand is pervasive in McDonald's websites in various countries. The McDonald's website for Singapore, for example, states that "Happiness Starts Here."

Interestingly, McDonald's Happy Meal once had a longstanding co-branding partnership with Disney, in which its Disneyland theme park has a tagline of "The Happiest Place on Earth." In 2006, however, the Happy Meal partnership with Disney ceased after ten years of cross-promotion. McDonald's Happy Meals had provided children with little figurines of Disney's Nemo, Mr. Incredible, and so on. According to Steve Jobs, who was Disney's largest shareholder and Pixar Animation Studios chief, acknowledged that there is value in fast-food tie-ins, "but there are also some concerns, as our society becomes more conscious of some of the implications of fast food" (Abramowit, 2006).

Over the years, McDonald's Happy Meals have evolved in which they now provide healthier food options such as apple slices or milk (instead of Coke, even though McDonald's and Coke are additional brands with a longstanding strategic partnership and inextricably linked) (see Gelles, 2014). Nevertheless, McDonald's use of "happy" branding targeting children raises ethical issues: As the mood alteration literature has shown (e.g., Wicks et al., 2009), children may rely on McDonald's to make them happy, and encourage food choices that contribute to the obesity epidemic and link with health risks.

Pleasure and Satisfaction in Tobacco Marketing Targeting Youth

Tobacco serves as a principal example of an inherently harmful product (Dewhirst, Lee, Fong, & Ling, 2016; Rittenburg & Parthasarathy, 1997). The harm coming from tobacco use in the USA as well as globally is astounding. In the USA, cigarette smoking is attributable to an estimated 443,000 premature deaths annually, which represents approximately one of every five deaths domestically (U.S. Department of Health and Human Services, 2012). Globally, experts anticipate tobacco use as a cause of more than eight million deaths per year by 2030 (World Health Organization, 2008).

The tobacco industry's consumer research and marketing planning documents have well documented that smoking initiation typically occurs during adolescence. Additionally, reviews of internal tobacco industry documents, which became public from litigation, reveal that cigarette brands have been successfully targeting youth, including the classification of "starter" or "new smoker" consumers (e.g., Cummings, Morley, Horan, Steger, & Leavell, 2002; Dewhirst & Sparks, 2003; National Cancer Institute, 2008; Perry, 1999). In particular, Newport, a mentholated cigarette brand from the Lorillard tobacco company, is particularly appealing to youth and those initiating smoking (Hersey et al. 2006; Pollay et al., 1996).

For Newport, test marketing began in 1956, and 1957 represents the brand's formal introduction. Newport has been a brand celebrated from the onset as a "fun cigarette" (Yellen, 1964, p. 01124261). According to Lorillard documentation, Newport "was advertised as such and obtained a youthful group as well as an inmature [sic] group of smokers. Newport was marketed successfully according to plan" (Yellen, 1964, p. 01124261).

In 1972, the company moved the Newport advertising account from Grey Advertising to the Will Graham Company, which quickly elevated "Alive with Pleasure" from minor ad copy status to its longtime use as a bold tagline for the brand. Newport cigarette advertising "emphasized couples or small groups having highly pleasurable experiences depicted against a bright kelly green background with the Newport name in dayglow orange" (Jarrett, 1993, p. 91915559).

For the creative strategy of Newport, the target market has been "all smokers, and young adults entering the market, with specific emphasis placed against competitive menthol smokers" (Lorillard, 1973, p. 04231759). By the late 1970s, market research for Lorillard Tobacco revealed that,

> The success of Newport has been fantastic during the past few years. Our profile locally shows this brand being purchased by black people (all ages), young adults (usually college age), but the base of our business is the high school student.
>
> (Achey, 1978, p. 03537131)

Newport has been a common "starter" brand for those beginning to smoke, typically between the age of 10 and 17, with half of study respondents starting between 10 and 13 years old (Shoi Balaban Dickinson Research, 1981). When respondents – young adults ages 18–24 – generally described Newport advertising, they understood

> the people shown in the ads as happy, or 'having fun' and healthy. They said the people shown were 'into the outdoors' and often reiterated they did not think people such as those shown in the ads would be smokers.
>
> (Shoi Balaban Dickinson Research, 1981, p. 84411683)

In separate and earlier research, respondents who were entirely US smokers of the Newport brand, described a Newport advertisement featuring a couple as

> depicting people who are young, happy, and in love. It was said that this ad 'showed' that smoking Newport is being younger and active. The headline 'Alive with pleasure!' was thought to relate to the picture both in terms of the people shown and the situation.
>
> (Shoi Balaban Dickinson Research, 1976, p. 84187589–84187590)

An additional ad, depicting those playing tug of war, was "said to show people in a situation where they 'are having fun.' It was also described as 'outdoorsy,' as 'alive,' and 'happy'" (Shoi Balaban Dickinson Research, 1976, p. 84187594).

Among menthol cigarette smokers, interviews concerning their perceptions of outdoor billboard advertising found the "Alive with Pleasure" marketing communication focusing on "pleasurable," which also was similar with "enjoyable" (Communicus, 1978, p. 84175897). Focus group research, with attention to the image associations of Newport, has found that the

> brand has a personality – a friend, approachable, always there for them. We know that Newport smokers' perceptions of other

Newport smokers, that they know and those they envision the
Brand to attract, mirror their perception of themselves – youthful,
outgoing, active, happy, warm, friendly, modern, extroverted.

(Lorillard, 1993, p. 93285629)

While pleasure and fun have been longstanding themes in Newport cigarette advertising, the "Alive with Pleasure" tagline also points to being
vibrant, energetic, active, and infers healthiness. Current advertising
uses the tagline "Newport pleasure!"

The models in Newport advertisements are typically youthful and
carefree with emphasis on sociability (i.e., multiple people in the promo-
tions, with romantic couples or a small group of friends – involving both
men and women – usually in the ads). The common themes in Newport
cigarette advertising reflect the aforementioned underpinnings of happiness: satisfying relationships, engagement in leisure activities, cooperativeness, and extraversion.

Discussion and Conclusions

Happiness commonly links to consumer well-being, yet it appears con-
tradictory to associate health and welfare with highly processed food
and smoking. In this chapter, we have focused on two prominent case
examples – McDonald's and Newport – but the applicability of happiness branding for youth-appealing and unhealthy or harmful products
appears more widespread. Double Happiness, for example, is a leading
cigarette brand in China. Additionally, "happy hour" is a common marketing term consumers hear when venues such as restaurants and bars
offer discounted alcoholic beverages during a defined time period (e.g.,
4 p.m.–6 p.m.), although such promotional initiatives may prompt binge
drinking and overconsumption. Coca-Cola is a brand commonly linking
to happiness despite the product's youthful appeal and scrutiny for contributing to the problem of childhood obesity. Moreover, Mondelēz International (formerly known as Kraft Foods), self-described as a "global
snacking powerhouse" that offers "well-being snacks," has introduced a
"Bring on the Joy" campaign for its nutritionally questionable portfolio
of products that includes leading brands of gum, crackers, cookies, and
chocolate bars.

As associating human personalities and emotions with qualities attributed to particular products and brands becomes commonplace, the
blurring of people and goods within such symbolic structures might be
merely amusing to some and unquestioned among others given its prevailing normalcy. While it may seem playful or trivial that brands link to
happiness, it is a theme that marketers often use when appealing to children and youth as well as for unhealthy or harmful products, thus raising ethical questions. Target marketing of children and teens – as well as

the marketing of "unsafe" or "harmful" products – is principal ethical issues (e.g., Murphy, Laczniak, Bowie, & Klein, 2005; Rittenburg & Parthasarathy, 1997). In closing, while consumers consider happiness as positive terms and outcomes, there is a darker side for consideration.

Discussion Questions

1   Bo Derek, a US model and actress, has said, "Whoever said money can't buy happiness simply didn't know where to go shopping." To what extent do you agree or disagree with this statement? Provide reasons why you are taking this position.
2   Marketers often use emotional appeals relating to happiness, pleasure, and fun targeting children and youth. Is this ethical?
3   Should free toy premiums be allowable for promoting unhealthy food offerings?
4   Is it appropriate for marketers to associate happiness with unhealthy or harmful products?

To Cite This Chapter

Lee, W. B., & Dewhirst, T. (2018). Happy brands and ethical implications. In H. Gringarten, & R. Fernández-Calienes (Eds.). *Ethical branding and marketing: Cases and lessons* (pp. 125–142). Routledge Management and Business Studies Series. London and New York: Routledge.

References

Aaker, J. L. (1997). Dimensions of brand personality. *Journal of Marketing Research, 34*(3), 347–356. doi:10.2307/3151897
Abramowit, R. (2006, May 08). Disney loses its appetite for Happy Meal tie-ins. *The Los Angeles Times*. Retrieved from http://articles.latimes.com/2006/may/08/entertainment/et-mcdonalds8
Achey, T. L. (1978, August 30). Product information. Letter from T. L. Achey to C. Judge. Lorillard Tobacco Company. Trial Exhibit 10,195, *State of Minnesota and Blue Cross and Blue Shield of Minnesota v. Philip Morris, Inc., et al.* Bates No. 03537131 [TINY 0003062].
Aggarwal, P. (2004). The effects of brand relationship norms on consumer attitudes and behavior. *Journal of Consumer Research, 31*(1), 87–101. doi:10.1086/383426
Argyle, M. (1999). Causes and correlates of happiness. In D. Kahneman, E. Diener, & N. Schwartz (Eds.), *Well-being: The foundations of hedonic psychology* (pp. 353–373). New York, NY: Russell Sage. Retrieved from http://www.jstor.org/stable/10.7758/9781610443258.22
Argyle, M., & Lu, L. (1990a). The happiness of extraverts. *Personality and Individual Differences, 11*, 1011–1017. doi:10.1016/0191-8869(90)90128-E
Argyle, M., & Lu, L. (1990b). Happiness and social skills. *Personality and Individual Differences, 11*, 1255–1261. doi:10.1016/0191-8869(90)90152-H

Belk, R. (1985). Materialism: Trait aspects of living in the material world. *Journal of Consumer Research, 12*(3), 265–280. doi:10.1086/208515

Belk, R. W., Ger, G., & Askegaard, S. (2003). The fire of desire: A multisited inquiry into consumer passion. *Journal of Consumer Research, 30*(3), 326–351.

Bettingen, J. F., & Luedicke, M. K. (2009). Can brands make us happy? A research framework for the study of brands and their effects on happiness. In A. L. McGill & S. Shavitt (Eds.), *Advances in Consumer Research, 36* (pp. 308–318). Duluth, MN: Association for Consumer Research.

Brakus, J., Schmitt, B., & Zarantonello, L. (2009). Brand experience: What is it? How is it measured? Does it affect loyalty? *Journal of Marketing, 73*(3), 52–68. doi:10.1509/jmkg.73.3.52

Bryant, F. B. (1989). A four-factor model of perceived control: Avoiding, coping, obtaining, and savoring. *Journal of Personality, 57,* 773–797. doi:10.1111/j.1467-6494.1989.tb00494.x

Bryant, F. B. (2003). Savoring Beliefs Inventory (SBI): A scale for measuring beliefs about savoring. *Journal of Mental Health, 12,* 175–196. doi:10.1080/0963823031000103489

Bryant, F. B., Smart, C. M., & King, S. P. (2005). Using the past to enhance the present: Boosting happiness through positive reminiscence. *Journal of Happiness Studies, 6,* 227–260. doi:10.1007/s10902-005-3889-4

Cairns, G., Angus, K., Hastings, G., & Caraher, M. (2013). Systematic reviews of the evidence on the nature, extent and effects of food marketing to children. A retrospective summary. *Appetite, 62,* 209–215. doi:10.1016/j.appet.2012.04.017

Carter, T., & Gilovich, T. (2010). The relative relativity of material and experiential purchases. *Journal of Personality and Social Psychology, 98*(1), 146–159. doi:10.1037/a0017145

Carter, T., & Gilovich, T. (2012). I am what I do, not what I have: The differential centrality of experiential and material purchases to the self. *Journal of Personality and Social Psychology, 102*(6), 1304–1317. doi:10.1037/a0027407

Chamberlain, L., Wang, Y., & Robinson, T. (2006). Does children's screen time predict requests for advertised products? Cross-sectional and prospective analyses. *Archives of Pediatrics and Adolescent Medicine, 160,* 363–368. doi:10.1001/archpedi.160.4.363

Chaudhuri, A., & Holbrook, M. (2001). The chain of effects from brand trust and brand affect to brand performance: The role of brand loyalty. *Journal of Marketing, 65*(2) 81–93. doi:10.1509/jmkg.65.2.81.18255

Communicus, Inc. (1978, June). An evaluation of three Newport outdoor ads. Advertising and packaging research conducted for Lorillard. Bates No. 84175893-84175943.

Csikszentmihalyi, M. (1999). Implications of a systems perspective for the study of creativity. In R. Sternberg (Ed.), *Handbook of creativity* (pp. 313–338). Cambridge, UK: Cambridge University Press.

Cummings, K. M., Morley, C. P., Horan, J. K., Steger, C., & Leavell, N-R. (2002). Marketing to America's youth: Evidence from corporate documents. *Tobacco Control, 11,* i5–i17. doi:10.1136/tc.11.suppl_1.i5

Dewhirst, T., Lee, W. B., Fong, G. T., & Ling, P. M. (2016). Exporting an inherently harmful product: The marketing of Virginia Slims cigarettes in the United States, Japan, and Korea. *Journal of Business Ethics, 139*(1), 161–181. doi:10.1007/s10551-015-2648-7

Dewhirst, T., & Sparks, R. (2003). Intertextuality, tobacco sponsorship of sports, and adolescent male smoking culture: A selective review of tobacco industry documents. *Journal of Sport and Social Issues, 27*(4), 372–398. doi:10.1177/0193732503258585

Dhar, T., & Baylis, K. (2011, October). Fast-food consumption and the ban on advertising targeting children: The Quebec experience. *Journal of Marketing Research, 48*, 799–813. doi:10.1509/jmkr.48.5.799

Diener, E. (1984). Subjective well-being. *Psychological Bulletin, 95*(3), 542–575. doi:10.1037/0033-2909.95.3.542

Diener, E., & Biswas-Diener, R. (2002). Will money increase subjective well-being? A literature review and guide to needed research. *Social Indicators Research, 57*, 119–169. doi:10.1007/978-90-481-2350-6_6

Diener, E., Lucas, R., & Scollon, C. (2006). Beyond the hedonic treadmill: Revising the adaptation theory of well-being. *American Psychologist, 61*, 305–314. doi:10.1007/978-90-481-2350-6_5

Diener, E., & Seligman, M. (2002). Very happy people. *American Psychological Society, 13*, 81–84. doi:10.1111/1467-9280.00415

Diener, E., & Seligman, M. (2004). Beyond money: Toward an economy of well-being. *Psychological Science in the Public Interest, 5*(1), 1–31. doi:10.1111/j.0963-7214.2004.00501001.x

Diener, E., Suh, E. M., Lucas, R. E., & Smith, H. L. (1999). Subjective well-being: Three decades of progress. *Psychological Bulletin, 125*, 276–302. doi:10.1037/0033-2909.125.2.276

Easterlin, R. (1995). Will raising the incomes of all increase the happiness of all? *Journal of Economic Behavior & Organization, 27*(1), 35–47. doi:10.1016/0167-2681(95)00003-B

Elliott, C. (2008). Assessing "fun foods": Nutritional content and analysis of super- market foods targeted at children. *Obesity Reviews, 9*(4), 368–377. doi:10.1111/j.1467-789X.2007.00418.x

Elliott, R., & Wattanasuwan, K. (1998). Brands as symbolic resources for the construction of identity. *International Journal of Advertising, 17*, 131–144. doi:10.1080/02650487.1998.11104712

Eysenck, H. J. (1983). *I do: Your guide to a happy marriage.* London, England: Century.

Federal Trade Commission. (2008, July). *Marketing food to children and adolescents: A review of industry expenditures, activities and self-regulation.* Retrieved from http://www.ftc.gov/os/2008/07/P064504foodmktingreport.pdf

Fitzhenry, R. I. (Ed.). (1993). *The Fitzhenry & Whiteside book of quotations* (40th anniversary ed.). Markham, ON, Canada: Fitzhenry & Whiteside.

Folta, S. C., Goldberg, J. P., Economos, C., Bell, R., & Meltzer, R. (2006). Food advertising targeted at school-age children: A content analysis. *Journal of Nutrition Education and Behavior, 38*, 244–248. doi:10.1016/j.jneb.2006.04.146

Fournier, S. (1998). Consumers and their brands: Developing relationship theory in consumer research. *Journal of Consumer Research, 24*(4), 343–353. doi:10.1086/209515

Fournier, S., & Alvarez, C. (2012). Brands as relationship partners: Warmth, competence, and in-between. *Journal of Consumer Psychology, 22*(2), 177–185. doi:10.1016/j.jcps.2011.10.003

Frank, R. (1999). *Luxury fever: Money and happiness in an era of excess.* Princeton, NJ: Princeton University Press.

Frey, B. S., & Stutzer, A. (2005). Happiness research: State and prospects. *Review of Social Economy, 63*(2), 207–213. doi:10.1080/00346760500130366

Fromm, E. (1976). *To have or to be.* New York, NY: Harper & Row Publisher.

Gantz, W., Schwartz, N., Angelini, J. R., & Rideout, V. (2007, March). *Food for thought: Television food advertising to children in the United States.* Retrieved from http://www.kff.org/entmedia/upload/7618.pdf

Gelles, D. (2014, May 15). Coke and McDonald's, growing together since 1955. *The New York Times.*

Gilbert, D. T. (2006). *Stumbling on happiness.* New York, NY: Knopf.

Gilovich, T., Kumar, A., & Jampol, L. (2015). A wonderful life: Experiential consumption and the pursuit of happiness. *Journal of Consumer Psychology, 25*(1), 152–165. doi:10.1016/j.jcps.2014.08.004

Handelman, J. (1999). Culture jamming: Expanding the application of critical research project. In E. J. Arnould & L. M. Scott (Eds.), *Advances in Consumer Research, 26* (pp. 399–404). Provo, UT: Association for Consumer Research.

Hastings, G., McDermott, L., Angus, K., Stead, M., & Thomson, S. (2006). *The Extent, nature and effects of food promotion to children: A review of the evidence.* Technical Paper prepared for the World Health Organization. Geneva, Switzerland: WHO. Retrieved from http://whqlibdoc.who.int/publications/2007/9789241595247_eng.pdf

Hebden, L., King, L., Chau, J., & Kelly, B. (2011). Food advertising on children's popular subscription television channels in Australia. *Australian and New Zealand Journal of Public Health, 35*(2), 127–130. doi:10.1111/j.1753-6405.2011.00610.x

Hersey, J. C., et al. (2006). Are menthol cigarettes a starter product for youth? *Nicotine and Tobacco Research, 8*(3), 403–413. doi:10.1080/14622200600670389

Hobin, E., Hammond, D., Daniel, S., Hanning, R., & Manske, S. (2012). The Happy Meal® effect: The impact of toy premiums on healthy eating among children in Ontario, Canada. *Canadian Journal of Public Health, 103*(4), 244–248. doi:10.17269/cjph.103.3181

Holt, D. (1995). How consumers consume: A typology of consumption. *Journal of Consumer Research, 22*(1), 1–16. doi:10.1086/209431

Holt, D. (2002). Why do brands cause trouble? A dialectical theory of consumer culture and branding. *Journal of Consumer Research, 29*(1), 70–90. doi:10.1086/339922

Institute of Medicine. (2006). *Food marketing to children and youth: Threat or opportunity?* Washington, DC: The National Academies Press. Retrieved from doi:10.17226/11514

Isen, A. M., Labroo, A. A., & Durlach, P. (2004). An influence of product and brand name on positive affect: Implicit and explicit measures. *Motivation and Emotion, 28*(1), 43–63. doi:10.1023/B:MOEM.0000027277.98917.9a

Jarrett, J. (1993). The Lorillard Informer. Lorillard internal newsletter. Bates No. 91915552-91915589.

Jenkin, G., Madhvani, N., Signal, L., & Bowers, S. (2014). A systematic review of persuasive marketing techniques to promote food to children on television. *Obesity Reviews, 15,* 281–293.

Kahneman, D., & Deaton, A. (2010). High income improves evaluation of life but not emotional well-being. *Proceedings of the National Academy of Sciences, 107*(38), 16489–16493. doi:10.1073/pnas.1011492107

Kant, A., & Graubard, B. (2004). Eating out in America, 1987–2000: Trends and nutritional correlates. *Preventive Medicine, 38*(2), 243–249. doi:10.1016/j.ypmed.2003.10.004

Kasser, T., & Ryan, R. M. (1993). A dark side of the American dream: Correlates of financial success as a central life aspiration. *Journal of Personality and Social Psychology, 65*, 410–422. doi:10.1037/0022-3514.65.2.410

Kasser, T., & Ryan, R. M. (1996). Further examining the American dream: Differential correlates of intrinsic and extrinsic goals. *Personality and Social Psychology Bulletin, 22*, 280–287. doi:10.1177/0146167296223006

Klein, N. (1999). *No logo*. Toronto, ON, Canada: Random House of Canada.

Kozinets, R. V., & Handelman, J. M. (2004). Adversaries of consumption: Consumer movements, activism, and ideology. *Journal of Consumer Research, 31*(3), 691–704. doi:10.1086/425104

Kunkel, D., & Gantz, W. (1992). Children's television advertising in the multichannel environment. *Journal of Communication, 42*(3), 134–152. doi:10.1111/j.1460-2466.1992.tb00803.x

Lawrence Journal-World. (2004, August 14). K.C. marketer behind Happy Meals' success. *Associated Press*. Retrieved from http://www2.ljworld.com/news/2004/aug/14/ kc_marketer_behind/

Layard, R. (2005). *Happiness: Lessons from a new science*. New York, NY: Penguin.

Lorillard. (1973). Newport creative strategy. Bates No. 04231759.

Lorillard. (1993, October). Newport exploratory research. Bates No. 93285629-93285631.

Lu, L., & Argyle, M. (1992). Receiving and giving support: Effects on relationships and well-being. *Counselling Psychology Quarterly, 5*, 123–133. doi:10.1080/09515079208254456

Lu, L., & Argyle, M. (1994). Leisure satisfaction and happiness: A function of leisure activity. *Kaohsiung Journal of Medical Sciences, 10*, 89–96.

McAlister, A. R., & Cornwell, T. B. (2009). Preschool children's persuasion knowledge: The contribution of theory of mind. *Journal of Public Policy & Marketing, 28*(2), 175–185. doi:10.1509/jppm.28.2.175

McDonald's. (2014, May 19). *McDonald's USA introduces new low fat yogurt side and happy meal ambassador*. Retrieved from http://news.mcdonalds.com/US/releases/McDonald-s-USA-Introduces-New-Low-Fat-Yogurt-Side

Merriam-Webster's Collegiate Dictionary. (2009). Springfield, MA: Merriam-Webster.

Mogilner, C. (2010). The pursuit of happiness: Time, money, and social connection. *Association for Psychological Science, 21*(9), 1348–1354. doi:10.1177/0956797610380696

Mogilner, C., & Aaker, J. (2009). The 'time vs. money effect': Shifting product attitudes and decisions through personal connection. *Journal of Consumer Research, 36*, 277–291. doi:10.1086/597161

Mogilner, C., Aaker, J., & Kamvar, S. (2012). How happiness affects choice. *Journal of Consumer Research, 39*, 429–443. doi:10.1086/663774

Mogilner, C., Kamvar, S., & Aaker, J. (2011). The shifting meaning of happiness. *Social Psychological and Personality Science, 2*(4), 395–402. doi:10.1177/1948550610393987

Mogilner, C., & Norton, M. (2015). Time, money, and happiness. *Science Direct, 10*, 12–16. doi:10.1016/j.copsyc.2015.10.018

Moore, E. S. (2004). Children and the changing world of advertising. *Journal of Business Ethics, 52*, 161–167. doi:10.1023/B:BUSI.0000035907.66617.f5

Murphy, P. E., Laczniak, G. R., Bowie, N. E., & Klein, T. A. (2005). *Ethical marketing*. Upper Saddle River, NJ: Pearson Prentice Hall.

Myers, D. (2000). The funds, friends, and faith of happy people. *American Psychologist, 55*(1), 56–67. doi:10.1037/0003-066X.55.1.56

Myers, D., & Diener, E. (1995). Who is happy? *Psychological Science, 6*(1), 10–19. doi:10.1111/j.1467-9280.1995.tb00298.x

National Cancer Institute. (2008). *The role of the media in promoting and reducing tobacco use*. Tobacco Control Monograph No. 19. Bethesda, MD: US Department of Health and Human Services, National Institutes of Health, National Cancer Institute.

Paliwal, R., & Indu. (2013). The role of consumer happiness in relationship marketing. *Global Journal of Management and Business Studies, 3*(4), 407–412.

Pechmann, C., Levine, L., Loughlin, S., & Leslie, F. (2005). Impulsive and self-conscious: Adolescents' vulnerability to advertising and promotion. *Journal of Public Policy and Marketing, 24*(2), 202–221. doi:10.1509/jppm.2005.24.2.202

Perry, C. L. (1999). The tobacco industry and underage youth smoking. *Archives of Pediatrics and Adolescent Medicine, 153*, 935–941. doi:10.1001/archpedi.153.9.935

Pollay, R. W., Siddarth, S., Siegel, M., Haddix, A., Merritt, R. K., Giovino, G. A., & Eriksen, M. P. (1996). The last straw? Cigarette advertising and realized market shares among youths and adults, 1979–1993. *Journal of Marketing, 60*, 1–16. doi:10.2307/1251927

Rahim, Z. (2017, March 20). This is the happiest country in the world. *Time*, available online at http://time.com/4706411/country-happiest-united-nations-sustainable-development/

Richins, M. (1994). Special possessions and the expression of material values. *Journal of Consumer Research, 21*, 522–533. doi:10.1086/209415

Richins, M., & Dawson, S. (1992). A consumer values orientation for materialism and its measurement: Measure development and validation. *Journal of Consumer Research, 19*, 303–316. doi:10.1086/209304

Rittenburg, T. L., & Parthasarathy, M. (1997). Ethical implications of target market selection. *Journal of Macromarketing, 17*(2), 49–64. doi:10.1177/027614679701700205

Robbins, M., Francis, L., & Edwards, B. (2010). Happiness as stable extraversion: Internal consistency reliability and construct validity of the Oxford Happiness Questionnaire among undergraduate students. *Current Psychology, 29*, 89–94. doi:10.1007/s12144-010-9076-8

Schmitt, B. H. (1999). *Experiential marketing*. New York, NY: The Free Press.

Schmitt, B. H., Brakus, J., & Zarantonello, L. (2015). The current state and future of brand experience. *Journal of Brand Management, 21*(9), 727–733. doi:10.1057/bm.2014.34

Scholsser, E. (2001). *Fast food nation: The dark side of the all-American meal*. New York, NY: HarperCollins.

Schwarz, N., & Strack, F. (1999). Reports of subjective well-being: Judgmental processes and their methodological implications. In D. Kahneman, E. Diener, & N. Schwarz (Eds.), *Well-being: The foundations of hedonic psychology* (pp. 61–84). New York, NY: Russell Sage Foundation.

Shoi Balaban Dickinson Research, Inc. (1976, February/March). An exploratory study: Newport smokers and their reactions to some proposed changes in advertising. Consumer research conducted for Lorillard. Bates No. 84187570-84187611.

Shoi Balaban Dickinson Research, Inc. (1981, October). An exploratory study for Newport: Smoking and purchase behavior of young adults. Consumer research conducted for Lorillard. Bates No. 84411662-84411689.

Stevenson, B., & Wolfers, J. (2008). Economic growth and subjective well-being: Reassessing the Easterlin paradox. *Brookings Papers on Economic Activity, 1*, 1–87. doi:10.3386/w14282

Thomson, M., MacInnis, D. J., & Park, C. W. (2005). The ties that bind: Measuring the strength of consumers' emotional attachments to brands. *Journal of Consumer Psychology, 15*(1), 77–91. doi:10.1207/s15327663jcp1501_10

Thomson, M., Whelan, J., & Johnson, A. (2012). Why brands should fear fearful consumers: How attachment style predicts retaliation. *Journal of Consumer Psychology, 22*(2), 289–298. doi:10.1016/j.jcps.2012.05.007

Tugade, M., & Fredrickson, B. (2007). Regulation of positive emotions: Emotion regulation strategies that promote resilience. *Journal of Happiness Studies, 8*, 311–333. doi:10.1007/s10902-006-9015-4

U.S. Department of Health and Human Services. (2012). *Preventing tobacco use among youth and young adults: A report of the Surgeon General*. Atlanta, GA: U.S. Department of Health and Human Services, Centers for Disease Control and Prevention, National Center for Chronic Disease Prevention and Health Promotion, Office on Smoking and Health.

Van Boven, L. (2005). Experientialism, materialism, and the pursuit of happiness. *Review of General Psychology, 9*(2), 132–142. doi:10.1037/1089-2680.9.2.132

Van Boven, L., & Gilovich, T. (2003). Do or to have? That is the question. *Journal of Personality and Social Psychology, 85*(6), 1193–1202. doi:10.1037/0022-3514.85.6.1193

Veenhoven, R. (2001). Are the Russians as unhappy as they say they are? Comparability of self-reports across nations. *Journal of Happiness Studies, 2*, 111–136. doi:10.1023/A:1011587828593

Warren, R., Wicks, J., Wicks, R., Fosu, I., & Chung, D. (2007). Food and beverage advertising to children on us television: Did national food advertisers respond? *Journalism and Mass Communication Quarterly, 84*, 795–810. doi:10.1177/107769900708400409

Wicks, J., Warren, R., Fosu, I., & Wicks, R. (2009). Dual-modality disclaimers, emotional appeals, and production techniques in food advertising airing during programs rated for children: Is there good balance? *Journal of Advertising, 38*(4), 93–105. doi:10.2753/JOA0091-3367380407

World Health Organization. (2008). *Mpower: A policy package to reverse the tobacco epidemic*. Geneva, Switzerland: World Health Organization.

Yellen, M. (1964, September 15). Lorillard sales position. Memo to M.J. Cramer, President, Chief Executive Officer, Lorillard. Bates No. 01124257-01124265.

10 Slavery, Chocolate, and Artificial Intelligence

Brands Ethical Dilemmas in a Modern World

Nellie Munin

Introduction

Although officially slavery ended in the nineteenth century, and international legal agreement currently prohibits it, the world still struggles with the need to solve employment (mainly, but not only, by MNEs) in exploiting conditions, taking place particularly in "Third World" countries, perceived as modern slavery.

MNEs and other employers, accused of such exploitations, argue that had they not employed them, these employees would have no way to earn their living at all, and that what seems as exploiting employment terms in a Western context is reasonable in local terms. MNEs invest in campaigns aiming at depicting them as positive contributors to less and least developed countries.

While this discourse continues, on the other end of the global scale – the modern Western world – intensive research on and development of artificial intelligence takes place. Robots designed to replace human beings in many professional functions threaten to increase unemployment rates, making many current occupations irrelevant. Countries aware of this threat, for example, Finland, already have started an experiment of giving their citizen a monthly low "salary," or rather maintenance allowance, regardless their employment (Finland trials basic income for unemployed, 2017). In a world where robots perform most labor, Western countries' citizens soon may find they are not immune to a reality similar to that "Third World" citizens' experience: Might most of us be unemployed, or have to compromise lower terms of employment than robots, just to stay employed? Will we have to learn to make a living with much lower salaries or maintenance allowances? Would we be forced to agree installation in our bodies of artificial devices that would turn us more efficient workers? Eventually, if robots develop higher intelligence than us, would most of the human population globally face a risk of turning into such robots' "slaves"?

After reviewing the current situation and the conflicting narratives explaining it, this chapter will examine whether ethical dilemmas connected to the activities of MNEs in the "Third World" (which most of

Western society conveniently overlooks, preferring to believe their campaigns and consume their products) may meet the Western sophisticated society down the road, as modernization progresses. It will examine further whether the current "Third World" exploiting reality may serve as a good laboratory for the development of ethical rules that may be valid to restrain and regulate the development and use of such robots, to prevent human slavery in the robots' era.

Modern Slavery

"Slavery" is usually associated, in our minds, with pictures from previous centuries, in which people were abducted from their home countries and transferred in inhumane conditions, by slave ships, to other continents, where they were sold as slaves, thus losing their independence completely and becoming the property of their owners, or people who colonialists dominated in their countries of origin, forcing them by violent means to become their slaves.

International agreement, embodied into many declarations and conventions, ratified by the majority of states globally (e.g., ILO, 1930, 1957, 1999; and UN, 1989, Arts. 35 and 36),[1] currently prohibits slavery and servitude.

Article 4 of the United Nations' (UN) Universal Declaration on Human Rights (UN, 1948) provides:

> No one shall be held in slavery or servitude; slavery and the slave trade shall be prohibited in all their forms.

Article 4 of the European Convention on Human Rights (1953) provides:

Check Your Understanding

Slavery

Slavery: the treatment of individuals as property of other individuals, who can own, buy, and sell them and enjoy their work without paying them remuneration. Slaves are unable to withdraw unilaterally from such arrangements, that law may back (de jure), or that may exist de facto. A person can become enslaved from the time of his or her birth, capture, or purchase. Slavery existed even before written history. In recent centuries, it has been gradually outlawed globally. The last country that outlawed slavery was Mauritania, in 2007.

No one shall be held in slavery or servitude.

No one shall be required to perform forced or compulsory labour.

Both these broad prohibitions do not define "slavery." Article 1 of the Slavery Convention (UN, 1926) defines slavery narrowly as "the status or condition of a person over whom any or all of the powers attaching to the right of ownership are exercised."

The US Department of State (US, 2017) associates modern slavery with trafficking in persons and human trafficking,[2] used as "umbrella terms for the act of recruiting, harboring, transporting, providing, or obtaining a person for compelled labor or commercial sex acts through the use of force, fraud, or coercion."

The US Federal Victims of Trafficking and Violence Protection Act (US, 2000) and the UN Protocol to Prevent, Suppress, and Punish Trafficking in Persons, especially Women and Children (2000) use additional terms, including "involuntary servitude," "slavery," or "practices similar to slavery," "debt bondage," and "forced labor."

Broadly defined, Thomson Reuters estimates this global industry at some US$150 billion per year (How can data help bankrupt the billion-dollar slavery industry, 2017).

The Global Slavery Index (2017) estimates that in 2016, 45.8 million people, including children, in 167 countries, are "subject to some form of modern slavery." According to this assessment, the countries with the highest estimated prevalence of modern slavery by the *proportion of their population* are North Korea, Uzbekistan, Cambodia, India, and Qatar, while the countries with the highest *absolute numbers* of people in modern slavery are India, China, Pakistan, Bangladesh, and Uzbekistan.

In sum, modern slavery may take advantage of vulnerable places and people, involve criminal acts, force, and debt bondage to obtain extreme exploitation in the employment and living conditions of men, women, and children who find themselves unable to change their situation, either physically or for other reasons. While most of slavery legal prohibitions presuppose forced work, some of these cases may simply result from a lack of other work choices that drives people to work voluntarily in exploiting terms. Moreover, while some of these workers, or slaves, or both, end up in criminal industries such as the commercial sex industry, others engage in manufacturing common commercial products that most of us consume on daily bases.

Hosting States' Dilemma

Indeed, several poor countries "provide the low-cost labour that produces consumer goods for markets in Western Europe, Japan, North America and Australia." Most of these countries try to somehow combat this phenomenon or at least provide some service to its victims (Global Slavery Index, 2017).[3] Nevertheless, the devastating number of victims reflects this treatment's relative insufficiency, or inefficiency, or both (e.g., Jansson, 2014).

The reason may be the dilemma countries hosting industries relying on modern slavery face: Insisting adherence to common standards of employment (as well as environmental and other standards) may deter MNEs from investing in them, thus prevent the creation of desperately necessary jobs. MNEs may subject their investment in a country to government's consent to settle for low environmental standards, labor standards etc. Governments' surrendering to such demands, undermining their sovereign power to a certain extent (Woods, 2000, p. 3), occurs particularly – but not only – in relatively economically weak countries.

Possibly, a well-coordinated global effort may solve this dilemma, creating a strong bargaining position to the governments involved in negotiating new terms of operation with MNEs. Unfortunately, governments seem to face a "prisoner's dilemma" in the global competition over MNEs, thus avoiding, or watering down, such initiatives.

Multi-National Enterprises

MNEs become major players in a global economy. International trade liberalization improves their access to cheap inputs, such as labor and raw materials, facilitating distributed production, and the operation of supply chains. Globalization enhances MNEs' access to tax havens and to regimes offering favorable rules on intellectual property. MNEs exhaust comparative advantages accruing from rapidly changing circumstances, for example, governments' decisions, consumers' preferences, and new technologies (Trebilcock & Howse, 2005, pp. 441, 443).

Consequently, many accuse them of encouraging a standards race to the bottom, for example, by operating sweatshops where workers work in exploiting conditions in terms of hours, space, salaries, etc. Such sweatshops are an issue for global social debate (e.g., International Labor Rights Forum, 2013).[4] The hosting countries of such sweatshops often prevent the intervention of labor unions and NGOs to change this reality, to prevent MNEs withdrawal from their market that might increase unemployment and deter potential investors.

According to the Fair Labor Association (2017), at least 18 countries are operating sweatshops, including Bangladesh, Costa Rica, El Salvador, China, the Dominican Republic, India, Vietnam, Honduras, Indonesia, Armenia, Brazil, Haiti, Taiwan, the Ivory Coast, Nicaragua, Mexico, the USA, and its territories.

Check Your Understanding

Multinational Enterprises (MNEs)

Multinational Enterprises (MNEs): Officially: corporate organizations owning or controlling production of goods or services in more than one country. In essence, this term usually refers to strong, rich corporations (such as Nike, McDonald's, Microsoft, and Procter and Gamble), acting in many countries, enjoying considerable global political and economic power and influence that they use to promote their vested interests. MNEs often receive criticism for lacking ethical standards, and for evading ethical laws and leveraging their own business agenda with capital. Some also have become associated with tax avoidance activities.

Exploiting patterns of employment are common in industries such as clothing, shoes, plastic, electronics (Qiu & Lin, 2017), agriculture (e.g., cotton and cannabis), foods, and even in the chocolate industry.

In Western Africa, one of the major resources of cocoa beans from which chocolate is produced, supplying cocoa to international giants such as Hershey's, Mars, and Nestlé, cocoa farmers earn less than $2 per day, an income below the poverty line. Thus, they often resort to the use of child labor to keep their prices competitive.

> The children of Western Africa are surrounded by intense poverty, and most begin working at a young age to help support their families. Some children end up on the cocoa farms because they need work and traffickers tell them that the job pays well. Other children are "sold" to traffickers or farm owners by their own relatives, who are unaware of the dangerous work environment and the lack of any provisions for an education. Often, traffickers abduct the young children from small villages in neighboring African countries, such as Burkina Faso and Mali, two of the poorest countries in the world. Once they have been taken to the cocoa farms, the children may not see their families for years, if ever.
>
> Most of the children laboring on cocoa farms are between the ages of 12 and 16, but reporters have found children as young as 5.
> (Food Empowerment Project, 2017)

These children work for many hours, using chainsaws to clear the forest and heavy dangerous knives to cut the cocoa pods from high trees they must climb, and then carry 100 pounds pods sacks. The children are under-fed and live in bad conditions (ibid.). In this example, unlike the former one, chocolate producers mentioned may not directly run these ventures, but yet consciously enjoy the cheap raw materials (cocoa powder and butter) so produced. Some chocolate firms prefer to brand themselves as "ethical chocolate companies," proud of using cocoa from other, more ethical resources (e.g., Slave Free Chocolate website, 2017).

Global Commodity Chains, MNEs, and States

MNEs focus on economic choices (unlike states, focusing on political choices) (Veseth, n.d., p. 1). Globalization facilitates these choices, breaking down barriers separating "nation states, cultures, labor markets or national economies" (ibid, p. 12). To handle issues, globalization may affect, such as human rights, intellectual property rights, and the environment, states must coordinate their policies. That erodes their sovereign power (Woods, 2000, pp. 3, 10).

Governments' abstention from regulation or enforcement may obtain the same effect as effective deregulation to lower standards, to attract MNEs.

Global Commodity Chains (GCCs) provide one example. These are "complex webs of global business that link independent businesses into a coordinated production and distribution process...GCCs gain and exercise power through their ability to mobilize and coordinate global market forces" (ibid., p. 12) including labor. An Oxfam report reflects how such GCCs encourage the exploitation of workers. Based on workers' experiences in 12 countries,[5] the report describes how tariff reductions over the last decades encouraged the establishment of Export Processing Zones (EPZ) enjoying tax holidays and incentives for investment, in particular in developing countries (Oxfam, 2004; Women, 2004). Large global retail companies, such as *El Corte Inglés* controlling 90% of Spanish department stores, or Wal-Mart, particularly in the garment and food industries, take advantage of these zones, controlling local producers through "real time" means of global communication to achieve short-lead time at the expense of the latter, who respond by imposing the costs on their workforce. The substantial reduction of transport costs, emanating from globalization and technological innovations, facilitates these practices. Governments of the countries where laborers suffer from these practices abstain intervention to protect workers, settling to sustain economic activity and jobs MNEs create.

MNEs Affecting the Global Arena and Standards

In recent decades, MNEs gradually shifted from viewing their political environment as given to acting as political players, involved in bargaining with their host countries and with international organizations responsible for shaping the regulatory environment (Dahan, Doh, & Guay, 2006, pp. 1574, 1578–1595). Political economy is "concerned with the distribution of two scarce resources, money and authority" (ibid, p. 1578). Enhanced interaction with other players in the global arena – i.e., governments, international organizations, and NGOs – helps MNEs affect global political economy.

MNEs promote their interests in the global arena in different ways, including the use of strong *lobbyists*; initiation, or participation in existing, *policy networks*; assuming "soft power" by "spreading ideas, shaping cognitive frames through discursive strategies and symbolic actions, and participating in the promotion of certain social norms and values" (Anderson, 2005, p. 27).

MNEs collaborate with partners supporting the same ideas to *build coalitions* (Dahan et al., 2006, p. 1576). *Possessing resources that other seek* (individually or with other members of their coalition) may serve as another potential source of pressure, to affect policy decisions (ibid., p. 1586).

Unlike governments, MNEs are not committed to voters. However, where public opinion may bear economic implications, affecting consumers' choice, it may affect MNEs' behavior. To obtain *positive public opinion*, MNEs brand themselves as non-discriminating against workers.

In order to *gain positive public opinion*, MNEs publish on their Internet websites data reflecting their non-discriminating approach toward their workers; participate in international forums discussing ethical issues; and symbolically fund global activities supporting the improvement of labor conditions and rights (Munin, 2013).

MNEs may confront issues involving political (national or international) pressure to determine standards by opting for voluntary *codes of conduct* they[6] or others[7] initiate. Publishing their commitment to such codes may spare others' anticipation that they join codes of conduct globally phrased, for instance by international organizations, which may impose on them stricter terms of behavior.

MNEs will naturally choose the most comfortable arena (national, regional, or multilateral) to maximize their success chances.

Simultaneously, they would prefer low publicity of the preferred status they may obtain by any of these methods, to minimize competition (Dahan et al., 2006, p. 1584).

Arguments Supporting MNEs' Position

MNEs deny the direct link between their global activity and the "race to the bottom" in certain countries, using, among others, the following arguments:

- The choice of their investment locations does not depend on low wages and taxes as much as it depends the requirements of knowledge-intensive production (Woods, 2000, p. 5), or on the relations between productivity and labor-cost (depending on many factors, including, e.g., labor availability, infrastructure, health care, public investment in education and training) (Trebilcock & Howse, 2005, p. 560). Domestic regulation restricts the free market, increases the production and costs, thus enhancing poverty. Surprisingly, developing countries find this argument very convincing, thus opposing to any attempt at the WTO to link market access with labor standards (ibid., p. 451). The wage gap between developed and developing countries may merely reflect differences in the cost of living, rather than necessarily reflecting MNEs' non-compliance with labor standards, as employers in developing countries (ibid., p. 560).
- Any choice of standard gives an artificial advantage to countries that already adopted this standard, working as an implicit subsidy to firms operating in these countries (ibid., p. 284).

MNEs, Ethics, and Consumers' Position

To the extent MNEs actively or passively contribute to the "race to the bottom" in terms of labor standards, thus enhancing modern slavery, these actions raise questions regarding corporate culture, truth, integrity, value, and differentiation:

Corporate culture – Do we, as consumers, want to encourage such extreme capitalist corporate culture, bluntly ignoring workers' interests for the sake of profit? To what extent cheap products "bribe" us, thus turning us indifferent to the true social price? To what extent do we passively accept this culture due to its geographically distant implications? To what extent is our indifference or even worship of MNEs' economic and financial success a result of the Western capitalist culture?

Truth and integrity – Could consumers globally (e.g., through social networks) join hands (thus circumventing their governments) to require that such MNEs respect truth and integrity as a condition for buying their products?

Value – What are the values that we, as a global consumers society, share? International agreements and declarations as well as national legislation and regulation seem to enshrine some of these core values. Yet, for the reasons specified above, their enforcement seems to be insufficient. To what extent and at what price are we – as a global society – ready to defend them? Should society in strong countries take measures to defend society in weak countries, or might such acts be perceived by the latter as patronizing acts with adverse effects?

Differentiation – Is differentiation between labor conditions in weak, poor countries and strong, rich countries discriminating against the former, or does it have an economic justification?

Weak Enforcement

Of all international legal instruments mentioned above, only the European Convention on Human Rights accords individuals the right to file claims against signatory countries to the European Court on Human Rights (ECtHR) in Strasbourg, France, for infringing this convention (including the slavery and servitude prohibitions). Access of individuals to this court may form a strong enforcement instrument, since it circumvents political considerations that may prevent states from filing such claims, or from enforcing such legal prohibitions. Surprisingly, however, ECtHR cases reflect that most of the complaints individuals file refer to private, individual employers, rather than to employing MNEs (Shachor-Landau, 2015, pp. 61–70; cf., European Convention on Action against Trafficking in Human Beings, 2005).

A Glance into the Future

The robots' age is not science fiction anymore. Autonomous cars will be in common use by 2020 (*10 million self-driving cars will hit the road by 2020*, 2017). Robots with artificial intelligence, already performing bank tellers' functions and even medical operations, threaten to completely replace many common professions, for example, drivers, lawyers, and doctors (Will robots replace human drivers, doctors, and other workers?, 2017).

Robots' developers market them as solely developed to improve human standards of living by releasing humans from the duty to perform many exhausting and sometimes boring tasks, freeing them to perform tasks that demand high-level human skills like critical thinking, problem solving, etc., and freeing time for enjoyable human interaction and leisure.

Assuming that in the future, MNEs may be no less driven by capitalist motivation than currently, they may find the use of robots very tempting: For a relatively cheap cost (avoiding pension funds, insurance schemes, vacations, rest breaks, etc.), they would be able to obtain obedient laborers who are not affected by feelings and human needs, who do not go on strikes, who's performance is stable and predictable, and as artificial intelligence develops, may offer far greater effective and efficient output than humans. MNEs thus may prefer robots over human workers. Globalization is expected to enhance and support this process.

The Global Slavery Index website (2017) notes that vulnerability to modern slavery is

> affected by a complex interaction of factors related to the presence or absence of protection and respect for rights, physical safety and security, access to the necessities of life such as food, water and health care, and patterns of migration, displacement and conflict.
>
> (n.p.)

The robots' age may blur current reality to create more such uncertainties that might trigger new forms of slavery.

This future prospect implies great concerns to the human race. Does current regulation and legislation offer any comfort?

Current Legislation and Regulation: A Valuable Starting Point?

As the development of robots and their capacities probably will be gradual, analysis should address short-, medium-, and long-term scenarios separately.

Short Term

Paradoxically, replacement of workers by robots may solve current modern slavery to a great extent.

In addition, the image of a robot shopping for you in Tokyo, which you direct through your computer, while you sit comfortably in your house in London (Tilden, 2017), may be very appealing.

However, multiplied by hundreds of times, and operated by the wrong hands, it could imply "private armies" serving strong interest groups, even aggressive MNEs, in obtaining goals that might not meet common human values.

Heavy dependence on robots may turn the society lazy and passive, and helpless in cases robots mal-function or cease to function (or in cases of intentional sabotage).

The combination of a broadly unemployed population thus suffering poverty might broadly undermine the leisure dream and produce a bored, frustrated, and even violent society.

While economically rich countries' citizens may have to learn how to make a living of relatively small "maintenance allowances" replacing their current salaries, economically poor countries may not afford supporting their citizens with "maintenance allowances" altogether. Consequently, the use of robots to replace human workers may deteriorate economically and socially poor communities even further, making them more vulnerable and willing to work in even worse conditions than now, just to survive.

Luckily, the process of replacing human workers with robots in poor countries may be slower than in rich countries, since employers in these countries, who are not MNEs, may find robots more expensive than human workers, at least in early stages.[8]

Although current national legislation in most countries potentially offers tools to prevent, or deal with large-scale potential hostilities that such a situation may invoke, the pragmatic test of these tools will occur in real time. Currently, national and global legislation does not assume any responsibility on MNEs or other rich companies that may trigger this situation by their economically motivated choices.

Adjustment of national or global regulation may authorize governments to finance their citizens' "maintenance allowances" – and strengthen national enforcement mechanisms – by taxes MNEs and other strong enterprises operating in their territory will be required to pay, but effectiveness of such

---

Check Your Understanding

Cyborg

Cyborg, short for "Cybernetic Organism," is an organism (not necessarily a mammal) with both organic and biomechatronic body parts. Manfred Clynes and Nathan S. Kline coined this term in 1960. Unlike bionic entities, biorobots, or androids, cyborgs' enhanced abilities result from an integration of an artificial component or technology that relies on some sort of feedback. Cyborgs are common in fiction, where they often are portrayed with physical or mental abilities far exceeding a human counterpart.

laws would depend on determinant enforcement that, as mentioned above, most governments currently prefer to avoid.

Medium Term

As cyborgs may turn out to perform better than human beings, trafficking and abduction of human beings in order to transform them into such cyborgs may take place. Current national and global regulation against slavery and servitude prohibits such conducts, but its effectiveness would depend on determinant national and international enforcement (currently insufficient).

Desperate (or even ambitious) unemployed human beings may volunteer to become cyborgs, to perform better or to be more attractive as laborers. Such voluntary action, although current anti-slavery regulation does not prohibit implying many ethical questions (unless the interpretation for "coercion" is very broad).

Assumption of external control over the minds of people transformed to cyborgs (Harari, 2015, pp. 324–327) may present even greater ethical challenges that current regulation may not cover, giving new meaning to the term "forced labor."

New, autonomous vehicles (airplanes? ships? spaceships?) and advanced means of communication may facilitate globalization, further eroding governments' ability to regulate, in favor of international standards. This, in turn, would strengthen MNEs' dominance of the global arena (which their strong financial position, and ownership of most innovative technologies that would appeal both to governments and international players, reinforces), encouraging them to leverage their effect on global decision-making, to enhance their interests.

Long Term

Artificial intelligence may prevail over human intelligence, attempting to dominate it, assuming dominance over human decision-makers, wholly or partly. This might turn into a blessing, if artificial intelligence balances the different interests involved better than human players, avoiding emotional and other human biases and mistakes.

However, artificial intelligence may attempt to challenge human values, thus endangering them, depending on the way it would define its future goals and the role of human kind (if at all) in this scenario (Harari, 2015, pp. 345–377). This is still an unknown zone, which current legal instruments (above) still do not cover. It is clear that if and when such events take place, humankind might find it is too late to impose its values and defend them. Thus, ethical and legal thinking regarding how to control and constrain this process should take place before that irreversible stage.

Conclusion

Economic considerations form MNEs major motivation. Globalization has opened tempting opportunities for MNEs to increase their profits, taking advantage of the comparative advantages of different countries. This practice has encouraged a "race to the bottom," serving economic and political interests at the expense of laborers experiencing modern slavery.

While future optimist prospects promise more convenient human life, as robots will perform most of current human labor, one cannot ignore the prospects for severe ethical challenges such developments may involve.

Current regulation and legislation prohibiting modern slavery, which is already insufficient and insufficiently enforced, does not cover many of these future challenges.[9]

Without global restraint, there is no reason why MNEs would not take full advantage of the technological developments to assume more economic and political power globally, without any ethical commitment to the communities that such aggressive behavior may severely hurt.

Without immediate action, communities in economically strong countries soon may find themselves in a position quite similar to that of communities in economically weak countries: poor, suffering unemployment, and vulnerably exposed to exploitation. Thus, communities globally should better join forces to assume political pressure on governments and MNEs, to reach global agreement regarding the ethical constraints that should regulate these developments, balancing the global interest of benefitting from modernization with the global interest to protect human beings from future, large-scale forms of modern slavery.

Discussion Questions

1   What might be the due balance of these interests?
2   What checks and balances may ensure that this balance of interests is respected globally?
3   How can consumers' power work to make MNEs respect this balance of interests globally?
4   How can consumers' power work to engage MNEs in making a real, substantial contribution to the global effort to abolish modern slavery, servitude and other forms of laborers' exploitation?

To Cite This Chapter

Munin, N. (2018). Slavery, chocolate, and artificial intelligence: Brands ethical dilemmas in a modern world. In H. Gringarten, & R. Fernández-Calienes (Eds.). *Ethical branding and marketing: Cases and lessons* (pp. 143–158). Routledge Management and Business Studies Series. London and New York: Routledge.

Notes

1 The eight "millennium goals" UN Millennium Declaration (UN, 2000) specifies, aiming at eradicating extreme poverty and enhancing freedom and equality do not include slavery eradication as a separate goal.
2 See discussion on the legal link between slavery and trafficking in Kyriazi, 2015.
3 According to the OECD (Ucnikova, 2014), between 2003 and 2012, 12 donor countries (OECD members) contributed a combined average of USD$124 million annually, predominantly funding projects in Southeast Asia, Eastern Europe, and Sub-Saharan Africa.
4 In 2011, authorities initiated an investigation against Zara for running "sweatshops" in Brazil (Zara investigated for sweatshops, slave labor practices in Brazil, 2011).
5 Bangladesh, Chile, China, Colombia, Honduras, Kenya, Morocco, Sri Lanka, South Africa, Thailand, the UK, and the USA.
6 Business codes including non-discrimination provisions were adopted, for example, by Nike (2017), Coca Cola (2018), and Nestle (n.d.).
7 See the list of brands which joined the Fair Labor Association code (2017), retrieved from: http://www.fairlabor.org/affiliates/participating-companies
8 The product life-cycle theory (Vernon, 1966) suggests that new products are always very expensive at first, to finance the investment made in their development. Thus, only the rich can afford them. In later stages, they come into common use, and their price decreases, respectively.
9 The European Commission (2017) recently acknowledged the need to make the most of the new opportunities whilst mitigating any negative impact they may have and "for the roll-out of new social rights to accompany the changing world of work."

References

10 million self-driving cars will hit the road by 2020. (2017). *Forbes.* Retrieved from https://www.forbes.com/forbes/welcome/?toURL=https://www.forbes.com/sites/oliviergarret/2017/03/03/10-million-self-driving-cars-will-hit-the-road-by-2020-heres-how-to-profit/&refURL=https://www.google.co.il/&referrer=https://www.google.co.il/

Anderson, G. W. (2005). *Constitutional rights after globalization.* Oxford, England, and Portland, Oregon: Hart Publishing. doi:10.5040/9781472559715

Coca Cola. (2018). *Integrity: The essential ingredient: Code of business conduct.* Retrieved from https://www.coca-colacompany.com/content/dam/journey/us/en/private/ fileassets/pdf/2018/Coca-Cola-COC-External.pdf

Dahan, N., Doh, J., & Guay, T. (2006). *The role of multinational corporations in transnational institution building: A policy network perspective.* London, Thousand Oaks, CA, and New Delhi, India: Tavistock Institute and Sage Publications. Retrieved from http://journals.sagepub.com/doi/abs/10.1177/0018726706072854

European Commission. (2017). *White paper on the future of Europe: Reflections and scenarios for the EU27 by 2025.* Retrieved from https://

ec.europa.eu/commission/sites/beta-political/files/white_paper_on_the_future_of_europe_en.pdf

European Convention on Action against Trafficking in Human Beings. (2005). Retrieved from https://rm.coe.int/168008371d

European Convention on Human Rights. (1953). Retrieved from http://www.echr.coe.int/Documents/Convention_ENG.pdf

Fair Labor Association. (2017). Retrieved from http://www.fairlabor.org/

Finland trials basic income for unemployed. (2017, January 3). *The Guardian*. Retrieved from https://www.theguardian.com/world/2017/jan/03/finland-trials-basic-income-for-unemployed

Food Empowerment Project. (2017). Child labor and slavery in the chocolate industry. Retrieved from http://www.foodispower.org/slavery-chocolate/

The Global Slavery Index. (2017). Retrieved from https://www.globalslaveryindex.org/

Harari, Y. (2015). *Homo Deus: A brief history of tomorrow*. Tel Aviv, Israel: Kinneret, Zmora, Bitan, Dvir Publishing House Ltd.

How can data help bankrupt the billion-dollar slavery industry. (2017, February 3). Thomson Reuters. Retrieved from https://blogs.thomsonreuters.com/answerson/data-bankrupt-slavery-industry/

ILO Abolition of Forced Work Convention, no. 105. (1957). Retrieved from http://www.ilo.org/dyn/normlex/en/f?p=1000:12100:0::NO::P12100_ILO_CODE:C105

ILO Convention no. 182 on the Worst Forms of Child Labour, no. 182. (1999). Retrieved from http://www.ilo.org/dyn/normlex/en/f?p=NORMLEXPUB:12100:0::NO::P12100_ILO_CODE:C182

ILO Forced Labor Convention, no. 29. (1930). Retrieved from http://www.ilo.org/dyn/normlex/en/f?p=NORMLEXPUB:12100:0::NO::P12100_ILO_CODE:C029

International Labor Rights Forum. (2013). *Sweatshops*. Retrieved from http://www.laborrights.org/creating-a-sweatfree-world/sweatshops

Jansson, D. B. (2014). Modern slavery: A comparative study of the definition of trafficking in persons. Leiden, Netherlands: Brill. doi:10.1163/9789004281073

Kyriazi, T. (2015). Trafficking and slavery: The emerging European legal framework on trafficking in human beings – Case law of the European Court of Human Rights in perspective. *International Human Rights Law Review*, *4*(1), 33–52. doi:10.1163/22131035-00401002

Munin, N. (2013, Spring). NGOs, multinational enterprises, and gender equality in labor markets: A political economy of conflicting interests? *Journal of Multidisciplinary Research*, *5*(1), 5–26. Retrieved from http://www.jmrpublication.org/portals/jmr/ Issues/JMR5-1.pdf

Nestle. (n.d.). *Code of business conduct*. Retrieved from https://www.nestle.com/asset-library/documents/library/documents/corporate_governance/code_of_business_conduct_en.pdf

Nike. (2017). *Commitment is everything: The Nike code of conduct*. Retrieved file:///C:/Users/%D7%92%D7%9C%D7%A2%D7%93/Downloads/Nike_Code_of_Conduct_2017_English.pdfOxfam. (2004). *Trading away our rights: Women working in global supply chains*. Retrieved from https://policy-practice.oxfam.org.uk/publications/trading-away-our-rights-women-working-in-global-supply-chains-112405

Oxfam. (2004). *Trading away our rights: Women working in global supply chains.* Oxford, England: Author. Retrieved from https://www.oxfam.org/sites/www.oxfam.org/files/rights.pdf

Qiu, J., & Lin, L. (2017, February 23). Foxconn: The disruption of iSlavery. *Asiacape: Digital Asia, 4*(1–2), 103–128. doi:10.1163/22142312-12340070

Shachor-Landau, C. (2015). *The European Convention on Human Rights (ECHR) – A Guide including a comparison with Israeli law.* Tel Aviv, Israel: Bursi [Hebrew].

Slave Free Chocolate. (2017). Ethical chocolate companies. Retrieved from http://www.slavefreechocolate.org/ethical-chocolate-companies/

Tilden, M. W. (2017). Robotics can – and will – change our lives in the near future. *The Guardian.* Retrieved from https://www.theguardian.com/zurichfuturology/story/0,1920335,00.html

Trebilcock, M. J., & Howse, R. (2005). *The regulation of international trade* (3rd ed.). Oxford, England, and New York, NY: Routledge.

Ucnikova, M. (2014). OECD and modern slavery: How much aid money is spent to tackle the issue? *Anti Trafficking Review, 3.* Retrieved from http://www.antitraffickingreview.org/index.php/atrjournal/article/view/68. doi:10.14197/atr.20121437

United Nations Convention on the Rights of the Child. (1989). Retrieved from http://www.ohchr.org/EN/ProfessionalInterest/Pages/CRC.aspx

United Nations Millennium Declaration. (2000). Retrieved from http://www.un.org/millennium/declaration/ares552e.htm

United Nations Protocol to Prevent, Suppress, and Punish Trafficking in Persons, especially Women and Children. (2000).

United Nations Slavery Convention. (1926). Retrieved from http://www.ohchr.org/EN/ProfessionalInterest/Pages/SlaveryConvention.aspx

United Nations Universal Declaration on Human Rights. (1948). Retrieved from http://www.ohchr.org/EN/UDHR/Documents/UDHR_Translations/eng.pdf

United States Department of State. (2017). What. Retrieved from https://www.state.gov/j/tip/what/

United States Federal Victims of Trafficking and Violence Protection Act. (2000). Retrieved from https://www.state.gov/j/tip/laws/61124.htm

Vernon, R. (1966). International investment and international trade in the product cycle. *The Quarterly Journal of Economics, 80*(2), 190–207. Retrieved from doi:10.2307/1880689

Veseth, M. (n.d.). What is international political economy? An excerpt from an article. University of Puget Sound, p. 12. Retrieved from http://www2.ups.edu/ipe/whatis.pdf

Will robots replace human drivers, doctors, and other workers? (2017). *VOA News.* Retrieved from https://www.voanews.com/a/will-robots-replace-human-drivers-doctors-workers/3810706.html

Women. (2004, February). *World Socialist.* Retrieved from http://www.wsws.org/articles/2004/feb2004/wome-f25.shtml

Woods, N. (2000). *The political economy of globalization.* In Woods, N. (ed.), (2000), *The political economy of globalization.* Basingstocke, England: Macmillan. Retrieved from http://www.globaleconomicgovernance.org/wp-content/uploads/Political%20Economy %20of%20Globalization.pdf

Zara investigated for sweatshops, slave labor practices in Brazil. (2011). *The Gloss.* Retrieved from http://thegloss.com/fashion/zara-investigated-for-sweatshops-slave-labor-practices-in-brazil/

11 Jardine Matheson
Drugs, War, and Empire

Stan Neal

Introduction

This chapter will examine the transformation of the British merchant firm Jardine Matheson from illicit opium smugglers in nineteenth century China to a modern, multi-national group of companies that is involved in a range of legal business activities. In doing so, it will examine the firm's historical activities as a classic case study of unethical business and look at how the modern business represents this history. Even British contemporaries in the nineteenth century, who often shared similar assumptions about Western superiority and wanted to open Qing China to free trade, criticized Jardine Matheson's opium smuggling operation and advocacy for British military action against China. But, by the 1870s, Jardine Matheson was no longer involved in the opium trade, and the firm has continued to diversify its business activities up to the present day. For the modern firm, this connection to the past raises a number of questions about the role of company history in modern day branding.

In 1832, business partners William Jardine and James Matheson re-branded the trading firm Magniac & Co. as Jardine Matheson. This new firm became notorious for smuggling opium grown in British India into China beyond the limits of the "Canton system." The "Canton system" limited the access of Western traders to the port of Canton and ensured that they could trade only with the carefully selected and regulated Cohong merchants. This system prohibited the importation of opium into China.

Jardine Matheson re-invested capital raised through its illegal opium smuggling operations into the legal tea trade. Effectively, the firm acted as a go-between for business clients who lacked the resources to smuggle opium themselves. The firm offered 16 different "agency" services that revolved around brokering for buyers and sellers of goods to and from Asia (Connell, 2004, p. 6). The services provided included sales, arranging insurance, chartering ships, obtaining freight, and transhipping goods. Jardine Matheson traded in a range of imported or exported products, such as tea or silk, but the firm's most important customers were figures like the Parsee merchant Jamsetjee Jejeebhoy. Based in

Bombay (Mumbai), Jejeebhoy supplied the firm with Indian-grown opium for sale on the China coast, which accounted for the bulk of its business growth in the 1830s (Le Pinchon, 2006, pp. 3–5). The firm made profit through the commission charged on sales made on behalf of sellers such as Jejeebhoy.

The firm's opium voyages served multiple purposes. They were also channels for circulating biblical literature, recruiting tea cultivators, sourcing valuable plant samples, and disseminating various forms of "useful knowledge" (Berg, 2006; Chen, 2012). Thus, beyond gaining a reputation as drug runners, the firm became a symbol of Western economic, colonial, and cultural incursions into the isolationist Qing Empire in the nineteenth century.

An Unethical History

In Britain, firms like Jardine Matheson were "country traders" – private firms that distributed opium grown in British India into China. The East India Company used intermediate firms, such as Jardine Matheson, to avoid directly circumventing the Chinese state's prohibition of the highly addictive drug and risking a diplomatic confrontation between Britain and China. This illegal trade ensured the profitability of the legitimate trade in Chinese tea to Britain. In turn, excise duties on tea imports into Britain accounted for 7% of Britain's public revenue and raised £4 million per annum for the East India Company by the 1830s (Lawson, 1993, p. 157). So, whilst illegal under China law and officially disassociated from the British state, the opium trade in which Jardine Matheson were engaged was crucial to Britain's domestic and colonial finances.

However, by 1839, the profitable system of Anglo-Chinese trade faced a crisis. For decades, the Qing state had issued increasingly hostile edicts against Western firms importing opium into China. In March 1839, Commissioner Lin Zexu famously forced the foreign merchants at Canton to destroy their opium stores. This seizure took place as William Jardine was en route to London. On his arrival, he urged the Foreign Secretary, later Prime Minister, Viscount Palmerston to take military action against China. The Royal Navy dispatched a squadron to seek redress for the perceived insult of Commissioner Lin's activities, and the First Opium War (1839–1842) ensued. The firm was a consistent voice in favor of military action against the Qing Empire with the aim of opening China to foreign trade. By directly lobbying senior politicians and publishing the first English language China coast newspaper, the *Canton Register*, Jardine Matheson was moving beyond involvement in the opium trade and into making justifications for war.

Jardine Matheson also was influential in the development of the British colony of Hong Kong. During the First Opium War, the firm relocated from the China coast to Hong Kong and seized prime geographical locations as the colony developed. In 1844, Jardine Matheson relocated its main office from Macao to Hong Kong. The Treaty of Nanking (1842) granted Hong Kong to the British, opened five "treaty ports" to Western traders, made the Qing pay indemnities for costs incurred and granted legal extraterritoriality to Westerners in China. This was the beginning of "gunboat diplomacy": a strategy by which industrialized Western nations forcibly opened closed markets to trade through the nineteenth century. The economic philosophy of Adam Smith justified this course of action. Both Jardine Matheson and commentators in Britain presented this conflict as a moral contest between modern British economic freedom and archaic Chinese despotism (Grace, 2014). The representation of China as backwards, uncivilized, and savage, in contrast to Britain and the Western, imperial powers in general served as a justification for the opium trade and the conflict it led to.

However, there were limits to Jardine Matheson's commitment to free trade. Following the Treaty of Nanking, which neglected to mention opium explicitly, the firm was actively against the legalization of the opium trade. Along with Dent & Co., Jardine Matheson had a virtual monopoly on the importation of opium into China. Abolition of the smuggling system would lower the delivery costs of the trade and increase competition from firms with small capital (Le Fevour, 1968). Similarly, the Opium War had increased Jardine Matheson's supply advantage as the increase in piracy along the China coast made the trade a risk for firms without armed vessels. Even after the First Opium War, the opium trade remained both profitable and risky. Continued tensions over the opium trade and the instability of the Taiping Rebellion (1850–1864) led to the Second Opium War (1856–1860), after which Britain and France forced further concessions from China, including the legalization of opium, in the Convention of Peking (Feige & Miron, 2008).

Whilst Britain used gunboat diplomacy to force China open to Western trade, and opium by extension, many British commentators criticized opium traders like Jardine Matheson. In 1840, the Tory politician William Gladstone, who would later serve as Prime Minister, criticized the First Opium War as "a war more unjust in its origin, a war calculated in its progress to cover this country with a permanent disgrace, I do not know and have not read of" (Hanes & Sanello, 2002, p. 78). Beyond the Opium War, the main criticism of the opium trade was that it operated at the expense of legitimate trade in China and consumed Chinese capital. This, in turn, reduced the potential market for legal British exports like cotton. Criticism also came from religious groups. In 1848, Donald Matheson left the firm and actively campaigned against the opium trade due to its perceived immorality (Keswick, 1982). His conversion became a publicity coup for the Society for the Suppression of the Opium Trade, which led an increasingly vocal public campaign against the trade in the late nineteenth century (Gelber, 2004). This criticism of opium consumption sat within a broader Victorian concern with moral, physical, and mental purity that also was manifest in the temperance movement against alcohol consumption.

Orientalist discourse shaped the representation of the Chinese opium addict (Said, 1978). The defining image of the Chinese people in nineteenth-century Britain was that of the opium wreck. As the Opium Wars opened China, Chinese migrants moved into British settler colonies – Australia, New Zealand, South Africa, and Canada – and the USA from the 1850s onwards. These migrants subsequently encountered viscous anti-immigrant rhetoric from White settlers. These racially motivated exclusion movements drew heavily on the imagery of opium by equating Chinese immigrants with drug addiction, immorality, and crime. As a result, whilst public condemnation of the opium trade itself was common, Western observers did not see Chinese opium addicts as victims. Instead, British traders saw opium addiction as part of a flawed Chinese character that explained China's civilizational decline and justified the Western opening of China.

Most importantly, the damaging effects of opium addiction were common knowledge in the nineteenth century. Criticism of Jardine Matheson's historical activities is not the projection of modern moral standards onto a specific historical context with different norms and conventions. The contemporary criticism of the opium trade as unethical makes it more difficult for modern observers to insulate the firm from criticism. Moreover, for historians and scholars of the nineteenth century, the name Jardine Matheson is synonymous with the addiction of the opium trade, the violence of the Opium War, and the expansion of the British Empire.

Justifying the Opium Trade

In the face of resistance in China and criticism in Britain, Jardine Matheson invested heavily in publishing and managing the firm's public image. Through these publishing networks, the firm was keen to emphasize that their interests were aligned with that of the British state and its vast Empire. They expended considerable resources on shaping public opinion and constructing a narrative of their trading operations as bringing Western civilization, modernity, and freedom to the backward, despotic and corrupt Qing Empire. In many ways, this was an attempt at branding by invoking the prevailing assumptions and ideas about the superiority of Western civilization and the British Empire to justify their unethical business practices.

The core of Jardine Matheson's communication strategy was its newspaper: the *Canton Register*. The *Register* was the first English-language newspaper on the China coast. With an average population of around 30, the foreign merchant community in Canton was not the intended audience. The newspaper was intended to influence opinion in Britain, India and across the Empire. Articles from the *Register* were commonly reprinted in Britain's provincial titles. According to Matheson, the newspaper was a "recorder of facts" and not a "vehicle for controversy" (King, 1965, p. 41). It was this aversion to controversy that led Mathe-

> **Check Your Understanding**
>
> *Opium*
>
> *Opium* is produced from poppy seeds and contains morphine, which can be used to produce heroin. In nineteenth-century Britain, opium mixed with alcohol, known as laudanum, was commonly used as pain relief. At the same time, Chinese opium users smoked the drug mixed with tobacco, which made it much stronger.

son to remove the American editor William Wood in February 1828 and replace him with the British Missionary Robert Morrison. Wood had publicly criticized the East India Company's monopoly of the China trade. In contrast, Matheson kept the *Register's* editorial position on the monopoly debate neutral until 1834, when the British state removed the East India Company's monopoly of the China trade. At this point, the paper became openly anti-regulation and pro-free trade.

The need to avoid controversy, despite its potential benefits in terms of an increased audience, was clearly demonstrated in a letter from Alexander to James Matheson: "I mean to disavow any connection with the paper ... The offensive paragraph will, I have not the smallest doubt, give notoriety to the paper, and gain it many subscribers in India" (Le Pinchon, 2006, p. 68). In spite of the acrimony with Wood, the paper's future seemed bright. Specifically, the newspaper could offer unparalleled specialist knowledge of China: "the field for a newspaper is certainly extensive, and if the *Register* is properly conducted it may be made the most popular journal in the East" (Le Pinchon, 2006, p. 68). Matheson had identified a gap in the provision of news and information about China. By making use of his connections to contemporary China experts, Matheson used the *Register* to reach an audience beyond the Western Canton community. Matheson was so successful that by 1850 Shanghai merchants published the *North China Herald* so they could similarly advocate their interests (Bickers, 2011, p. 108).

The need to de-legitimize the Qing Empire in order to justify the opium trade affected the *Register's* editorial angle (Hillemann, 2009, pp. 83–85). Much of the *Register's* content concerned the implications of Chinese law for the foreign community and the prejudice that Western merchants faced. For example, this concern was evident in an 1828 article on the linguistic debate over Chinese words for foreign residents and whether they were offensive:

> everyone knows that in ordinary speech they use to each other ... the most contemptuous language: such as foreign devil; red bristled

devil; black devil; a devil; flower flagged devil ... (to refer to) not
only the poor ignorant people, but the Gentleman merchants.
(Canton Register, 24 May 1828)

The idea that the Chinese did not treat foreign, and most importantly
British, merchants with adequate respect was a common accusation –
the inference being that Chinese restriction of trade was not targeted on
opium, but connected to a wider anti-British prejudice. The dismissive
attitude of Chinese officials to the wants and desires of British firms was
especially hard to accept given the contemporary attitudes of civilizational superiority and hierarchy: "the superiority of Europeans in some
of the mechanical arts, and physical sciences, does not elevate them
as rational beings in the estimation of the Chinese" (Canton Register,
17 July 1830).

In addition to the *Canton Register*, Jardine Matheson was also integrated into broader information networks. For example, the firm
employed the Protestant missionaries Robert Morrison and Charles Gutzlaff, who were some of the most prolific China experts of the 1830s, as
interpreters. In some cases, the firm had direct control over the activities
of China experts and facilitated or funded their research and writing.
A letter from Gutzlaff to James Matheson in 1834, demonstrated the
role Matheson played in the book publishing process. Gutzlaff, working on an opium clipper on the China coast for the firm, gave Matheson specific instructions to publish his *General Description of China*
through the firm's London agent Thomas Weeding (Le Pinchon, 2006,
p. 218). Through these connections, the firm was not just opening China
to opium but to Christianity.

The firm also had an important involvement in Chinese language publishing. William Jardine paid for the publication of Gutzlaff's *Dong-Xi*
as part payment for his interpreting work on the firm's opium vessels
(Chen, 2012, p. 1711). Gutzlaff also distributed this Chinese language
magazine – which brought news of Western science, geography, government, and history for a Chinese audience – during his voyages along
the China coast. Perhaps most significantly, given Jardine Matheson's
economic interests, Gutzlaff published texts titled *Outlines of Political
Economy* and *Treatise on Commerce* in Chinese in 1840, both of which
advocated free and open markets (Trescott, 2007, p. 23). Similarly,
during Robert Morrison's editorship of the *Canton Register,* he saw the
dissemination of information into China as important as the acquisition
of knowledge: "were instructive papers and books, printed in Chinese,
they would no doubt gradually find their way to every part of the Empire... and convey new ideas, calculated to benefit every country of East-
ern Asia" (Canton Register, 16 August 1828). The firm's involvement
in publishing on China in the 1830s was widespread, combining direct
ownership of the *Register* and specific firm-funded publications, as well

as more surreptitious associations. As a result of these associations, the firm's interests in uninhibited trade were heavily reflected in contemporary discourse on China.

Defense of the firm's economic interests in the 1830s provided the rationale, particularly for James Matheson, for such an involvement in publishing. After the removal of the East India Company monopoly the firm advocated a European-style diplomatic relationship with the Chinese government, a relaxing of Chinese trading regulations and, ostensibly, the liberalization of the despotism that oppressed the Chinese populace (Keswick, 1982, p. 21). Chinese government edicts prohibiting the opium trade regularly targeted Jardine Matheson, and this fed into a sense of victimhood at the hands of Chinese authorities. On his return to Britain in 1835, Matheson lamented how foreigners had to deal with "ignominious surveillance and restrictions" (Matheson, 1836, p. 3). As the Chinese officials aimed to curtail the opium trade – which was Jardine Matheson's main income – it was in the firm's economic interests to present Chinese trade restrictions alongside broader critiques of the Qing tyranny. Attempts to control the opium trade were equated with resistance to Christianity, freedom of movement, the rights of women, and the expansion of legal trade. This was particularly important for the firm as it meant that the blame for poor British export sales could also be attributed to the regressive Chinese authorities. It was in the firm's economic interest to portray the Qing Emperor's legal edicts as despotic and against the natural laws of humanity. The firm's connection to the publishing network of China experts was not coincidental. Jardine Matheson both offered unparalleled access to China and had a vested interest in supplementing the criticism of the Qing Empire that became a significant narrative of writing on China in the 1830s and 1840s.

Check Your Understanding

Orientalism

In 1978, the Palestinian American academic Edward Said published *Orientalism*. Said argued that Western observers had historically represented the East as fundamentally different and inferior to the West. Crucially, these "orientalist" representations of the East were influenced by colonialism and continue to influence the modern world.

Friends in High Places

In addition to Jardine Matheson's publishing connections, its commercial and political links ensured that their narrative of Western and Chinese victimhood at the hands of the despotic Qing Empire was also visible in British political discourse in the 1830s. Due to their perceived expertise on China and the China trade, the opinion of members of the firm was sought in Britain. William Jardine and Alexander Matheson,

Check Your Understanding

Gunboat Diplomacy

Gunboat Diplomacy refers to the use of displays of military power to intimidate less powerful nations into diplomatic agreements. Most historical examples of gunboat diplomacy involve Western powers, such as the UK or USA, forcing economic concessions from weaker nations with the threat of military force.

as well as other notable Canton merchants, were called to give evidence to the 1840 *Select Committee on the Trade with China,* which had been appointed in a direct response to Commissioner Lin Zexu's seizure of British-owned opium (British Parliamentary Papers, 1840). Similarly, Magniac, Smith & Co. and the veteran Whig MP John Abel Smith represented Jardine Matheson in London through the 1830s (Price, 2004). An even more direct connection to parliament came from the careers of prominent members of the firm after their time on the China coast. After returning to Britain, William Jardine was elected as Whig MP for Ashburton in 1841 (Keswick, 1982, p.24). Upon Jardine's death in 1843, James Matheson ran for, and won, Jardine's seat and subsequently sat on the 1847 *Select Committee on Commercial Relations with China* (British Parliamentary Papers, 1847). Throughout the 1830s and 1840s, the firm was well connected with the political elite in London.

The lobbying of Viscount Palmerston in favor of military action against China demonstrated the firm's ability to influence senior British statesmen. As Foreign Secretary for most of the 1830s, Palmerston was instrumental in determining British policy toward China. John Abel Smith engineered the first meeting between the firm's partners and Palmerston, which took place in 1835 when James Matheson returned to Britain with the widowed Lady Napier. In light of the diplomatic failure and death of the first Superintendent William Napier in 1834, Matheson urged an aggressive stance toward the Qing Empire. At this meeting, Matheson was unsuccessful in convincing Palmerston to take military action in defense of the interests of British subjects at Canton (Napier, 1995, p.214). In March 1839, Commissioner Lin seized British-owned opium in Canton. At the same time, William Jardine was travelling to London. On his arrival, Jardine had a private meeting with Palmerston. He advised Palmerston on the necessary size of naval force and the strategic advantages of seizing Hong Kong – information which would later be acknowledged as essential by Palmerston (Le Pinchon, 2006, p.43). The firm had become a vital point of information on China by both British legislators and senior statesmen.

Beyond the firm's direct political links, Jardine Matheson were also integral to new commercial networks and organizations developing in the 1830s, which were designed to articulate the interests of China trade merchants as a collective. Over the 1830s, British merchants across

Asia established Chambers of Commerce: in Canton (25 August 1834), Bombay (22 September 1836), Madras (29 September 1836), Singapore (8 February 1837), and Ceylon (25 March 1839) (Webster, 2006, p. 757; Nish, 1962, p. 75). Given the prominence of Jardine Matheson in Canton's foreign merchant community, it is of little surprise that the firm was instrumental in the formation and coordination of these organizations. The Canton Chamber of Commerce elected James Matheson as its first president in 1834, and several heads of the firm filled this role over subsequent decades. The Chamber acted as an important lobbying device, which aimed "to protect the general interests of the foreign trade with China" (Chinese Repository, 1838, p. 44).

Using their publication networks, lobbying of senior politicians and commercial organizations, Jardine Matheson was able to maintain the support of the British state and, to some extent, public in spite of contemporary criticism of opium addiction and the opium trade.

Change and Diversification

Whilst the name Jardine Matheson became synonymous with opium, one of the firm's strengths lay in its ability to diversify and adapt. Over the nineteenth century, many of its competitors ceased to exist, yet the Jardines Group still exists today. The diversification of business interests began early. On an individual level, one of the firm's founders, James Matheson, became Chairman of the Peninsula and Oriental Steam Navigation Company (Grace, 2014). Similarly, Hugh Matheson, James Matheson's nephew, was the first President of the Rio Tinto Company in 1873. Over the nineteenth century, the opium trade became less lucrative, and Jardine Matheson scaled back its opium smuggling operations through the 1860s. After opium imports into China were legalized in 1860, the firm faced much more competition. Importantly, competitors like Sassoon & Co. controlled their own opium supplies in India and were able to match Jardine Matheson's competitive advantage. The firm had withdrawn completely from the opium trade by 1872 (Keswick, 1982). From the firm's base in Hong Kong, it was able to transition successfully from an agency house, to an investment house, to a multinational corporation.

As one of the first merchant houses to move to Hong Kong, Jardine Matheson was instrumental in the colony's development. By 1881, the firm was described as 'controlling the Hong Kong dockyards,' and in 1889, it founded the Hong Kong Land Company, which exists as Hongkong Land in the present day. From Hong Kong, Jardine Matheson also increased its involvement and investment in mainland China. For example, in 1867, the firm gave a loan of £400,000 to the Chinese government (Keswick, 1982). Of course, the irony was that decades of conflict around the opium trade had caused China's money troubles.

The opening of China to Western trade also opened the Chinese economy to investment and modernization. In 1898, Jardine Matheson and the Hong Kong Shanghai Banking Corporation formed the British and Chinese Corporation for the financial exploitation of Chinese railways. This contracting firm was equipped to build railways, and supply engines and rolling stock, and staff to work the train lines. As with the Opium Wars, this Western involvement led to resistance and political turmoil in China. By the end of the nineteenth century, the proto-nationalist, anti-colonial Boxer Rebellion (1899–1901) swept China before the military intervention of a coalition of Western powers.

Overtime, Jardine Matheson also expanded its operations geographically. In 1859 – following Commodore Perry's opening of Japan to American trade in an infamous episode of US "gunboat diplomacy" – the firm opened an office in Yokohama. As the firm's representative, William Keswick arrived in Yokohama with "cotton goods, sugar candy, elastic bands and 40,000 Mexican dollars" (Keswick, 1982, p. 154). The firm's success in late-nineteenth-century Japan again represented its ability to adapt. For example, in 1863, Jardine Matheson exploited the global cotton shortages during the US Civil War by engaging in the export of Japanese cotton (Keswick, 1982, p.159). Similarly, the firm became involved in banking when high prices damaged the profitability of the silk trade. Rather than specialize in one particular business area, Jardine Matheson were able to adapt to specific geo-political and market conditions.

By 1930, Jardine Matheson had offices across China, Japan, London, and New York, with staff numbering 113,000 (Keswick, 1982). The spread of operations also allowed the firm to adapt to geo-political challenges. For example, after the fall of Hong Kong in 1941, operations continued to be supervised from Calcutta and later Bombay, and the head office moved to Shanghai in 1950. In the present day, Jardines comprises a group of companies with extensive operations across Asia and the world, including engineering and construction, transport services, motor trading, property, retailing, restaurants, hotels, and insurance broking.

Controlling History

The comprehensive archive of commercial, and personal, letters and records at Cambridge University has made Jardine Matheson an attractive topic of study for historians. Access to the Jardine Matheson Archive requires approval from the Jardines Group's London agents Matheson & Co. After using the archive, scholars also require the firm's consent to publish material arising from their research. That the modern-day Jardines Group maintains editorial control over the historical archive demonstrates an awareness of the significance of Jardine Matheson's history.

The centrality of Jardine Matheson to historical themes of war, colonialism, trade, opium, and migration also makes the firm an important topic of study. For example, Alain Le Pinchon's *China Trade and Empire* provides a selection of letters from the archive that traces the evolution of the firm in the nineteenth century. But, this text also offers an insight into Anglo-Chinese exchange, colonial life, business culture, and global economic changes. There are also more problematic histories. Maggie Keswick's *The Thistle and Jade* is more a celebration of the firm than an analytical history, though it is laden with fascinating images and items of material culture. But whilst Keswick takes a positive tone and Le Pinchon provides primary sources, the specter of opium smuggling, inevitably, looms large in these and other histories of the firm.

Typically, the firm's founders are either characterized as drug-dealing agent provocateurs or celebrated as enterprising pioneers of free trade. Richard Grace's recent biography of William Jardine and James Matheson *Opium and Empire*, which seeks to look beyond the firm's infamous reputation, summarizes this historical problem. Grace describes how, as individuals, William Jardine and James Matheson have been:

> Caricatured by writers who mention them briefly, depicting them as one-dimensional villains whose opium commerce was 'ruthless' and whose imperial drive was 'war-mongering'. Such cardboard figures fail to represent with any adequacy the complex, multifaceted personal and business histories of Jardine and Matheson.
>
> (Grace, 2014, p. viii)

Scholars have often portrayed this firm, which has left such a visible and searchable wealth of sources, on a variety of historical topics, as an evil corporation. This is clearly an issue for historians, but why is access to the firm's archive such a concern for the Jardines Group?

In Chinese history, Jardine Matheson represents the West's forcible domination of China through drug addiction, military power, and colonial control. Historically, the Treaty of Nanking is the start of a "century of humiliation" in which foreign powers dominated and exploited China until the creation of the People's Republic in 1949 (Lovell, 2011, p. 9). The colonial history, to which the "Jardine Matheson" name is so closely connected, is of deep, national significance. The diplomatic discomfort between Britain and China over Beijing's interference in Hong Kong's affairs since the handover of sovereignty in 1997 is a good example of how the colonial past can cause controversy in the present. In 2017, Chinese President Xi Jinping suggested that Britain and China should "shelve differences" over Hong Kong in order to maintain a strong trading relationship post-Brexit (Reuters, 2017). In this context, multi-nationals like Jardine Matheson must navigate a precarious relationship with the colonial past.

Today, the Jardines Group website consciously alludes to a broader history. It refers to an "unsurpassed experience in the region, having been founded in China in 1832" (Jardine Matheson, 2017). This reference to the past skillfully acknowledges the firm's history whilst neglecting to mention opium, conflict, or even the cession of Hong Kong. Similarly, the firm's history is a potential selling point: "affiliates benefit from the support of Jardine Matheson's extensive knowledge of the region and its long-standing relationships" (Jardine Matheson, 2017). This attempt to construct a positive narrative around the firm's history mirrors the way that the original firm used its publishing networks to justify the opium trade as part of a wider philosophical conflict. In a competitive global marketplace, Jardines attempts to promote longevity and stability, whilst disassociating the modern company name from the controversial activities of its nineteenth-century founders. Operating in post-colonial Asia, the Jardines Group is anxious to preserve its history selectively.

Discussion Questions

1   To what extent can companies distinguish between their modern business operations and their historical activities?
2   What is the role of company history in a brand?
3   What is the relationship between businesses, academics, and consumers?
4   To what extent have companies always managed and manipulated their public image?
5   What ethical issues do war and colonization raise?

To Cite This Chapter

Neal, S. (2018). Jardine Matheson: Drugs, war, and empire. In H. Gringarten, & R. Fernández-Calienes (Eds.). *Ethical branding and marketing: Cases and lessons* (pp. 159–172). Routledge Management and Business Studies Series. London and New York: Routledge.

References

Berg, M. (2006). Britain, industry and perceptions of China: Matthew Boulton, 'useful knowledge' and the Macartney Embassy to China. *Journal of Global History, 1*(2), 269–288. doi:10.1017/s1740022806000167

Bickers, Robert. (2011). *The scramble for China: Foreign devils in the Qing empire, 1832–1914.* London, England: Allen Lane.

British Parliamentary Papers. (1840). *Report from the select committee on the trade with China.* 359.

British Parliamentary Papers. (1847). *Report from the select committee on commercial relations with China; together with the minutes of evidence, appendix, and index.* 654.

Chen, S. (2012). An information war waged by merchants and missionaries at Canton: The society for the diffusion of useful knowledge in China, 1834–1839. *Modern Asian Studies, 46*(6), 1705–1735. doi:10.1017/s0026749x11000771

Canton Register. (24 May 1828).

Canton Register. (16 August 1828).

Canton Register. (17 July 1830).

Chinese Repository. (1838).

Connell, C. (2007). *A business in risk: Jardine Matheson and the Hong Kong trading industry.* London, England: Praeger.

Feige, C., & Miron, J. (2008). The opium Wars, opium legalization and opium consumption in China. *Applied Economics Letters, 15,* 911–913. doi:10.3386/w11355

Gelber, H. (2004). *Opium, soldiers, and evangelicals: Britain's 1840–42 war with China, and its aftermath.* New York, NY: Palgrave Macmillan.

Grace, R. (2014). *Opium and empire: The lives and careers of William Jardine and James Matheson.* Montreal and Kingston, Canada: McGill-Queen's University Press.

Hanes, W., & Sanello, F. (2002). *The opium Wars: The addiction of one empire and the corruption of another.* Naperville, IL: Sourcebooks.

Hillemann, U. (2009). *Asian empire and British knowledge: China and the networks of British imperial expansion.* New York, NY: Palgrave Macmillan. doi:10.1057/9780230246751

Jardine Matheson. (2017). *Jardines: Introduction.* Retrieved 15 August 2017 from http://www.jardines.com/the-group.html

Keswick, M. (1982). *The thistle and the Jade: A celebration of Jardine, Matheson & Co.* London, England: Octopus.

King, F. H. H. (1965). *A research guide to China-Coast newspapers, 1822–1911.* Cambridge, MA: Harvard University Press.

Lawson, P. (1993). *The East India company: A history.* London, England; New York, NY: Longman.

Le Fevour, E. (1968). *Western enterprise in late Ch'ing China: A selective survey of Jardine, Matheson & Company's operations, 1842–1895.* Cambridge, MA: Harvard University Press.

Le Pinchon, A. (2006). *China trade and empire: Jardine, Matheson & Co. and the origins of British rule in Hong Kong, 1827–1843.* Oxford, England: Oxford University Press.

Lovell, J. (2011). *The opium war: Drugs, dreams and the making of China.* London, England: Picador.

Matheson, J. (1836). *The present position and prospects of the British trade with China.* London, England: Smith, Elder & Co.

Napier, P. (1995). *Barbarian eye: Lord Napier in China, 1834 the prelude to Hong Kong.* London, England: Brassey's.

Nish, I. (1962). British Mercantile cooperation in the India-China trade from the end of the East India company's trading monopoly. *Journal of Southeast Asian History, 3*(2), 74–91. doi:10.1017/s0217781100001253

Price, J. M. (2004). *Smith, John Abel (1802–1871).* Oxford Dictionary of National Biography. Oxford University Press. Retrieved 14 September 2017 from http://www.oxforddnb.com/view/article/25854. doi:10.1093/ref:odnb/25854

Reuters. (2017). *China's Xi says should 'shelve differences' in meeting with Theresa May*. Retrieved 15 August 2017 from https://uk.reuters.com/article/uk-g20-germany-china-britain-idUKKBN19T03U

Said, E. (1978). *Orientalism*. New York, NY: Vintage Books.

Trescott, P. B. (2007). *Jingji Xue: The history of the introduction of western economic ideas into China, 1850–1950*. Hong Kong: The Chinese University Press.

Webster, A. (2006). The strategies and limits of gentlemanly capitalism: The London East India agency houses, provincial commercial interests, and the evolution of British economic policy in South and South East Asia 1800–50. *Economic History Review, 59*(4), 743–764. doi:10.1111/j.1468-0289.2006.00366.x

12 Ethics and Celebrity Advertising

Cases in the Indian Advertising Industry

Gurbir Singh and Abhishek Mishra

Introduction

Consumers are rational decision-makers only to a limited extent, and emotions play a larger role in their purchase decisions (Simon, 1955, 1956; Zeelenberg, Nelissen, Breugelmans, & Pieters, 2008). The idea of bounded rationality states that the people desire to make good decisions with minimum resources, something achievable by converting rational decisions to emotional ones (Afuah & Tucci, 2012). Celebrities make the purchase decisions of customers easy. Hence, brands associate with them to draw positive meanings and emotional responses (Halonen-Knight & Hurmerinta, 2010). Research supports the idea that celebrities have a greater influence on the public at large. Celebrity endorsements have an impact on the purchase decisions of customers (Choi & Berger, 2010).

Perceived expertise (Eisend & Langner, 2010) and trustworthiness (Spry, Pappu, & Bettina, 2011) of a celebrity for a product category largely influence consumers' perception of an advertised message's effectiveness. Different celebrity dimensions like credibility, performance, personality, feelings, physical appearance, cogent power, and values lead to the transfer of celebrity characteristics to the product and from the product to the consumer (Jain & Roy, 2016). In such circumstances, it is essential to understand the role celebrities play in the branding of offerings. India ranks as one of the largest consumer markets in the world, where 60% of all advertisements in India use celebrities when the global average is around 25% (Saxena, 2008; Shimp, 2003). Indian celebrities help promote and advertise various brands for a long period and charge a large fee for the same.

Even though brand endorsements contribute a major share to the earnings of celebrities, those endorsements have some negative implications too (Keel & Nataraajan, 2012). Some celebrities, for money, become part of advertisements that provide misleading information or are for products harmful to end consumers. Normally, celebrities avoid their moral responsibility toward customers and shift them to the brands they advertise. They claim to make their decisions based on the research data and information those brands share. Although their rationale may have legal validity, they are devoid of morality, and such celebrities end up promoting unethical advertising practices for their personal benefit. Such behavior is directly in conflict with the American Marketing Association's code of ethics, which promotes honesty and fairness as basic values for marketing practices (American Marketing Association, n.d.).

Many instances of celebrity endorsements exist in India in which the advertisements were unethical because of misrepresentation of facts, surrogate advertisements, puffery advertisements, unverified claims, and exaggerated representations. In this chapter, we will discuss a few cases in which Indian celebrities were on a wrong footing while promoting certain brands. In some of the cases, celebrities faced legal cases, while in the rest, they faced flak in print and online platforms. The focus of these cases is to identify various unethical nuances of celebrity endorsements and implications for the public at large.

Case 1

Emami is a leading Indian company in the personal and healthcare sector. It has a product, 'Fair and Handsome,' for which the brand ambassador was Mr. Shahrukh Khan, a popular film personality. In its advertisement, Emami claimed fairer skin for users in three weeks. The advertisement misrepresented the product as the one making the skin fairer. It was a clear exaggeration of benefits accruing from the use of the product. Mr. Shahrukh Khan reportedly charged a large fee for promoting Fair and Handsome. In 2012, a consumer filed a case against Emami in a District Consumer Court (Sengupta, 2015). The complainant used Fair and Handsome for four weeks, just like Shahrukh Khan mentioned in the advertisement. The user did not find any difference in his skin color and went through mental agony, and he decided to file a suit against the company to save other people from similar negative emotions. The legal battle went on for two and a half years before the court imposed a fine of INR 15 lakhs on Emami for misrepresentation of facts ("Fair & Handsome Ad Removed," 2015; Sengupta, 2015). Consequently, the company withdrew that advertisement featuring Shahrukh Khan, yet Emami drew flak on various online and offline platforms ("Fair & Handsome Ad Removed," 2015). However, Shahrukh Khan is not the only one involved in endorsing skin fairness products in India.

There are many other film personalities like John Abraham (Garnier), Ileana D' Cruz (Ponds), Vidya Balan (Dabur), Shahid Kapoor (Vaseline), Deepika Padukone (Garnier), and Sonam Kapoor (L'Oreal) endorsing skin fairness brands ("Abhay Deol Calls Out," 2017). Although there are many Indian celebrities who have time and again declined offers to promote a skin fairness brand, most of the times, celebrities are least concerned about the ethicality of the advertisements when they decided to promote a brand.

It was unethical on Mr. Khan's part to promote Fair and Handsome for two reasons. First, he made a claim that was false and led to mental distress for the consumers. No one has the right to exploit and play with the emotions of others for his or her material benefits. Second, India is a country where most of the people are brown skinned. The promotion of skin whitening cream signals the supremacy of white-skinned people. Such advertisements are equivalent to promoting racism in the country. When a popular face like Shahrukh Khan testifies the need for fair skin, the thought process of his fans and public at large becomes biased. In the long run, such advertisements can have a very adverse impact on the society as they create discrimination toward dark-skinned people.

Case 2

Surrogate advertising is indirect advertising in which the purpose is to promote one product in the guise of another (Sharma & Chander, 2007). Entities use surrogate advertising to promote banned products like liquor, cigarettes, and tobacco. In the Indian context, surrogate advertising is a major ethical issue. Liquor companies nowadays are using music CDs, drinking water, and soda for surrogate advertisements of their brand. Similarly, cigarette and tobacco companies engage in surrogate advertisements through sponsorships, socially responsible messages, and allied products. This problem of surrogate advertising of liquor and tobacco products becomes more intense when celebrities become part of such advertisements. Ajay Devgn, a famous film personality, became associated with Bagpiper, a renowned whiskey brand, in 2006 and featured in an advertisement of Bagpiper Soda (Dhillon, 2015; Vaj, 2006). Similarly, famous cricketers like Yuvraj Singh, MS Dhoni, and Harbhajan Singh signed an advertisement contract for Seagram, owner of Royal Stag whiskey, for promoting music CDs under the brand name of Royal Stag (Bag, 2014). Surrogate advertisement for promoting liquor brands is a clear violation of law in spirit, if not words. Celebrities help brands in making consumers not only attend to the information (Wei & Lu, 2013) but also retain it (Erdogan, 1999; Misra & Beatty, 1990). When a celebrity shares information about a socially harmful product in the form of surrogate advertisement, that information remains for a long period and increases the sale of such products. Moreover, when celebrities become brand ambassadors for promoting liquor in a disguised fashion, they are setting a very poor example for people as their role models. Adolescents idolize celebrities featuring in advertisements and purchase such products to be like them (Chia & Poo, 2009). Celebrities justify consumption of liquor, which has a negative impact on such vulnerable consumers.

Case 3

It is considered unethical to compare a brand with competitors on the basis of unsubstantiated claims. In 2017, the first Indian celebrity yoga guru, Baba Ramdev, head of his homegrown FMCG company Patanjali, landed in the middle of a controversy. In a radio advertisement, Baba Ramdev claimed the products of foreign companies are dangerous for the people and the country, as they take their wealth abroad. He also claimed that foreign companies' products are sub-standard (Gupta, 2017). He blamed them for selling adulterated food items and drinks, hair oils with cancerous elements, and cosmetics with chemicals in them (Gupta, 2017). Many companies raised objections to the claims Baba Ramdev made. It is clearly unethical on the part of Baba Ramdev to make such false allegations against other companies without any proof. All the products of companies like Hindustan Unilever Limited and Proctor & Gamble comply with all the rules and regulations of the country. Moreover, multinational companies around the world are contributing to the Indian economy by making investments in the country, providing employment, and raising the standard of living. Extant literature terms Patanjali's strategy to promote its products as negative advertising, and negative advertisers promote their product by establishing the superiority of their brand and focusing on negative aspects of a competitor brand (Vijayalakshmi, Laczniak, & Muehling, 2015). Although the normal application of negative advertising strategy is for a zero-sum game situation, in which the loss of one competitor is others' gain (Merritt, 1984); however, Patanjali effectively categorized the available brands in the FMCG sector in two categories, Indian and foreign. As the major shareholding in the FMCG sector in India lies with Unilever and Proctor & Gamble, this strategy was successful in branding all their competitors as foreign brands. People find negative advertisements more credible and believable, even when they do not like the negativity in the information (Robideaux, 2013). The fortunes twisted in favor of Patanjali, and it had sales of INR 105 billion in FY 2016–17 from around INR 20 billion in 2014–15 (Sarkar, 2017). The celebrity, in this case, engaged in unethical practices for multiple reasons. First, it is immoral for any local brand to incite feelings of nationalism in a wrong way for its own benefit. The repercussions of such negative campaigns can have a detrimental impact on all the Indian companies doing business in foreign lands. Second, unsubstantiated claims featured in the campaign. Third, the presence of a celebrity further increased the salience of negative information for the public. Indeed, the established practice inscribed in the American Association of Advertising Agencies (AAAA) declares "the advertising agency should compete on merit and not by attempts at discrediting or disparaging a competitor agency" (n.p.). Although negative advertisements have legal validity, many ethical concerns remain, and the presence of celebrities in such campaigns further aggravates those concerns.

Case 4

Many celebrities promote brands whose target customers consist of vulnerable populations of society, like children or elderly people. Vulnerable customers believe in claims of such advertisements more as compared to regular customers, and hence, it is the duty of the celebrities to ensure they behave in an ethical fashion while promoting brands to this section of society. Many Indian celebrities also endorse products meant for children. Trouble erupted for Maggi, a Nestle noodles product, in 2015 when food regulators found lead and monosodium glutamate over and above the permissible limits in it (Anand, 2015). The government intervened and immediately stopped the sale of Maggi noodles. An Indian court summoned three celebrities, namely, Amitabh Bachchan, Madhuri Dixit, and Preity Zinta, who appeared in the advertisement of Maggi noodles (Mehta, 2015). They received charges of misrepresentation of facts and promoting an unhealthy food product. This controversy was a huge embarrassment for Nestle and the celebrities involved in their advertisements.

Even if this controversy did not happen, there are problems with the promotion of products for vulnerable consumers. The first problem is that advertisements influence and lure the children in the purchase and consumption of food items (Hamilton-Ekeke & Thomas, 2007; Halford, Boyland, Hughes, Oliveira, & Dovey, 2007). Childhood food preferences remain with people throughout their lives, and thus, advertising can affect a child's future health status (Skinner, Carruth, Bounds, & Ziegler, 2002). The negative effects of advertisements on younger population increase with the presence of celebrities. Advertisements featuring celebrities have a greater influence on children food consumption (Birch, 1999). Children prefer to consume products that celebrities endorse, unconcerned about their own health. We argue that in such circumstances, the onus of verifying their advertised claims about a product lies with the celebrity, and the celebrities cannot shun their responsibility toward children.

The second problem starts when celebrities support unverified claims about a product and project it as a healthy option for children. In many cases, children start believing the celebrity-promoted products are healthier than they actually are (Phillipson & Jones, 2008). Even in the case of Maggi, celebrities made tall claims about its nutritious value. In reality, Maggi noodles are a type of fast food that are not good for health. Children perceive Maggi as a healthy food option due to celebrity endorsements, and this amounts to a misrepresentation of facts by these celebrities. Celebrities' appearance in food advertisements has damaging and confusing effects on children's understanding of healthy food. Children lose their competence to differentiate between healthy and unhealthy foods and often resort to overconsumption (Boyland et al., 2013).

They consume more than required, which leads to health problems like obesity and stress among children. In the present case discussion, even when the celebrities are working within the legal framework, they are still morally responsible toward society. They should never promote anything directed toward children unless they are confident about the effect of such endorsements.

Case 5

Another problem with celebrity advertising is that of exaggerated claims they make. It is grossly unethical on the part of a celebrity to project a brand in a way that overstates its functionalities. Hindustan Unilever Limited developed an advertisement featuring actor Ranbir Kapoor for promoting its new deodorant under the brand name Axe. In the advertisement, the actor keeps a record of a number of times he is able to grab female attention in a day. The advertisement makes an exaggerated claim when it projects that applying Axe deodorant can always attract females toward a man ("Axe Gets Ranbir," 2013). In a huge embarrassment to Hindustan Unilever Limited, a 26-year-old filed suit against it for cheating and causing mental agony (Kamral, 2011). He claimed he had been using Axe deodorant for the previous seven years but still was not able to find a girlfriend.

The involvement of celebrities in such exaggerated claims enhances the problem as customers buy brands under false promises and feel cheated. Such advertisements easily influence non-users and waste their money on products they do not require. Such advertising, which makes customers acquire products with false or misleading beliefs, falls under the category of deceptive advertising (LaTour & LaTouor, 2009; Xie, Madrigal, & Boush, 2015). Deceptive advertising is a morally objectionable act because it is wrong to rob anyone of his or her financial resources for one's own benefit. Celebrities must avoid being part of such advertisements. Another common unethical practice most celebrities follow is they promote products they never use. While endorsing a brand, they may make an impression that the product benefits them in one way or another but in reality, they themselves are not actual consumers. Again, it is unethical on their part to endorse something they have not personally experienced.

In all the cases above, our purpose is to understand the morality of celebrities involved in such branding initiatives. Celebrities are brands in themselves, and they have the potential to amplify the impact of advertised brands (Buttle, Raymond, & Danziger, 2000). So, it is pertinent to comprehend the kind of role celebrities play while endorsing brands. Celebrities get celebrity status because of their fans and people at large. They are successful because other people support them, and they at least owe to society not promoting brands without looking into all the important claims. They cannot hide behind the companies they endorse for any such misdeeds. From a virtue-based ethics perspective, every individual and organization needs to improve its character and contribute to the betterment of society at large (Melé, 2009). A virtue ethics framework provides us with a standard to measure the ethicality of celebrity behavior in an advertising context. Celebrities, thus, need to understand the social impact of their decision as part of an advertisement campaign.

Celebrity endorsements are known for improving the financial health of companies (Chung, Derdenger, & Srinivasan, 2013; Elberse & Verleun, 2012). Advertising practitioners are the third party involved in celebrity advertising. They are the main entities that conceive and execute a campaign. Research indicates that advertising practitioners themselves suffer from "moral myopia" (Drumwright & Murphy, 2004). Their decision-making process is devoid of ethical considerations (Bakir & Vitell, 2010). In such circumstances, the onus of proving the ethicality of their act lies mostly on the celebrities. There is no strictly defined law in India to regulate endorsements by celebrities. Even when the Food Safety and Standards Act (FSSA), 2006, states that "any person who publishes, or is a party to the publication of an advertisement, which falsely describes any food, or is likely to mislead as to [its] nature or substance or quality... or gives a false guarantee" (p. 45), there are many legal loopholes that make it difficult to make celebrities clearly accountable for promoting a wrong product. In such circumstances, it is the responsibility of celebrities to check for the morality of the decisions they make while promoting any brand.

Recently, in a major development in the Indian advertising sector, the Advertising Standards Council of India (ASCI) came up with guidelines making celebrities responsible for the claims in the advertisements (Bhusan, 2017). As per new ASCI guidelines, the celebrity endorsements or opinions should reflect the genuine and current opinions based on their actual experience with the products. In another development, a parliamentary panel is pondering on strict punishment for celebrities featuring in misleading advertisements ("Celebrity endorsers could face 10 Lakhs fine," 2016). The panel is likely to recommend a jail term up to five years and a fine up to INR 5 million for celebrities found guilty. The point here is that when citizens to not voluntarily fulfill the moral obligations, it leads to the birth of strict formal rules and regulations, which in itself is not good. People in society do not need rules for each and every transaction, and one should be aware morally of his or her duties toward other members of society and act accordingly.

Thus, in a nutshell, celebrities need to depict more ethical behavior while endorsing different brands. They are representatives of society, and choices they make have an impact on the society. They cannot pass on blame to brands if something goes wrong. They are accountable for the decisions they make. Celebrities should endorse only products they have experienced personally and should verify the genuineness of the claims in brand advertising to the best of their knowledge. There should not be any misrepresentation or exaggeration of facts under any circumstances. All celebrities should avoid promoting socially undesirable products like liquor or cigarettes through surrogate advertising. Last, celebrities should take the utmost care when they decide to promote a brand targeting vulnerable consumers like children or elderly people. We expect a better future for consumers and companies in which celebrities behave in a more socially responsible manner.

Discussion Questions

1   Do you think celebrities involved in advertising have some responsibilities toward consumers? If so, what are they? If not, why not?
2   Discuss the effectiveness of rules and regulations in governing advertising scenarios around the world.
3   Who should be more responsible toward consumers, the celebrities or the brands?
4   How should the celebrities decide which brand to endorse?
5   What should be the repercussions of a product failure on the celebrity endorser?
6   In the race to achieve higher sales, how should brands set the boundary of what is ethical advertising?

To Cite This Chapter

Singh, G., & Mishra, A. (2018). Ethics and celebrity advertising: Cases in the Indian advertising industry. In H. Gringarten, & R. Fernández-Calienes (Eds.). *Ethical branding and marketing: Cases and lessons* (pp. 173–184). Routledge Management and Business Studies Series. London and New York: Routledge.

References

Abhay Deol calls out Bollywood's obsession with fair skin; Disses SRK, Deepika. (2017). *News 18*. Retrieved from http://www.news18.com/news/ movies/abhay-deol-calls-out-bollywoods-obsession-with-fair-skin-disses-srk- deepika-1371577.html
Afuah, A., & Tucci, C. L. (2012). Crowdsourcing as a solution to distant search. *Academy of Management Review, 37*(3), 355–375. doi:10.5465/ amr.2010.0146
American Marketing Association. (n.d.). Statement of ethics. Retrieved from https://www.ama.org/AboutAMA/Pages/Statement-of-Ethics.aspx

Anand, U. (2015). Are the endorsers of Maggi culpable? Law sweeping, no legal precedent yet. *Indian Express*. Retrieved from http://indianexpress.com/article/explained/are-the-endorsers-of-maggi-culpable-law-sweeping-no-legal-precedent-yet/

Axe gets Ranbir going with clicker, without Axe. (2013). *Campaign India*. Retrieved from http://www.campaignindia.in/video/axe-gets-ranbir-going-with-the-clicker-without-axe/418767

Bag, A. (2014). Surrogate advertisement of liquor in India: How Indian liquor companies game the rules? Retrieved from https://blog.ipleaders.in/surrogate-advertisement-of-liquor-in-india-how-indian-liquor-companies-game-the-rules/

Bakir, A., & Vitell, S. J. (2010). The ethics of food advertising targeted toward children: Parental viewpoint. *Journal of Business Ethics, 91*(2), 299–311. doi:10.1007/s10551-009-0084-2

Bhusan, R. (2017). Advertisements for products being reworked after ASCI puts the onus on benefit-based claims on celebs. *The Economic Times*. Retrieved from https://economictimes.indiatimes.com/industry/services/advertising/advertisements-for-products-being-reworked-after-asci-puts-onus-of-benefit-based-claims-on-celebs/articleshow/58707116.cms

Birch, L. L. (1999). Development of food preferences. *Annual Review of Nutrition, 19*(1), 41–62. doi:10.1146/annurev.nutr.19.1.41

Boyland, E. J., Harrold, J. A., Dovey, T. M., Allison, M., Dobson, S., Jacobs, M. C., & Halford, J. C. (2013). Food choice and overconsumption: Effect of a premium sports celebrity endorser. *The Journal of Pediatrics, 163*(2), 339–343. doi:10.1016/j.jpeds.2013.01.059

Buttle, H., Raymond, J. E., & Danziger, S. (2000). Do famous faces capture attention? *Advances in Consumer Research, 27,* 245. Retrieved from http://www.acrwebsite.org/volumes/8395/volumes/v27/NA-27

Celebrity endorsers could face 10 Lakhs fine, 2-year jail for misleading ads. (2016). *NDTV*. Retrieved from https://www.ndtv.com/india-news/celebrity-endorsers-could-face-10-lakhs-fine-2-year-jail-for-misleading-ads-1395273

Chia, S. C., & Poo, Y. L. (2009). Media, celebrities, and fans: An examination of adolescents' media usage and involvement with entertainment celebrities. *Journalism & Mass Communication Quarterly, 86*(1), 23–44. doi:10.1177/107769900908600103

Choi, C. J., & Berger, R. (2010). Ethics of celebrities and their increasing influence in 21st-century society. *Journal of Business Ethics, 91*(3), 313–318. doi:10.1007/s10551-009-0090-4

Chung, K. Y., Derdenger, T. P., & Srinivasan, K. (2013). The economic value of celebrity endorsements: Tiger Woods' impact on sales of Nike golf balls. *Marketing Science, 32*(2), 271–293. doi:10.1287/mksc.1120.0760

Dhillon, A. (2015). Bollywood icons who endorse irresponsibly. *The National*. Retrieved from https://www.thenational.ae/arts-culture/bollywood-icons-who-endorse-irresponsibly-1.122209

Drumwright, M. E., & Murphy, P. E. (2004). How advertising practitioners view ethics: Moral muteness, moral myopia, and moral imagination. *Journal of Advertising, 33*(2), 7–24. doi:10.1080/00913367.2004.10639158

Eisend, M., & Langner, T. (2010). Immediate and delayed advertising effects of celebrity endorsers' attractiveness and expertise. *International Journal of Advertising, 29*(4), 527–546. doi:10.2501/S0265048710201336

Elberse, A., & Verleun, J. (2012). The economic value of celebrity endorsements. *Journal of Advertising Research, 52*(2), 149–165. doi: 10.2501/JAR-52-2-149-165

Erdogan, B. Z. (1999). Celebrity endorsement: A literature review. *Journal of Marketing Management, 15*(4), 291–314. doi:10.1362/026725799784870379

Fair & Handsome ad removed after this student fought for two and half years. (2015). *The Logical Indian.* Retrieved from https://thelogicalindian.com/news/this-student-fought-for-two-and-half-years-to-get-fair-handsome-ad-removed/

Food Safety and Standards Act (FSSA), 2006. (2006, August 23). New Delhi, India: Ministry of Law and Justice (Legislative Department). Retrieved from http://www.fssai.gov.in/home/fss-legislation/food-safety-and-standards-act.html

Gupta, R. (2017). #Recap 2016: Most controversial ads of the year. *AdAge India.* Retrieved from http://www.adageindia.in/advertising/recap2016-most-controversial-ads-of-the-year/articleshow/56259411.cms

Halford, J. C., Boyland, E. J., Hughes, G., Oliveira, L. P., & Dovey, T. M. (2007). Beyond-brand effect of television (TV) food advertisements/commercials on caloric intake and food choice of 5–7-year-old children. *Appetite, 49*(1), 263–267. doi:10.1016/j.appet.2006.12.003

Halonen-Knight, E., & Hurmerinta, L. (2010). Who endorses whom? Meanings transfer in celebrity endorsement. *Journal of Product & Brand Management, 19*(6), 452–460. doi:10.1108/10610421011085767

Hamilton-Ekeke, J. T., & Thomas, M. (2007). Primary children's choice of food and their knowledge of balanced diet and healthy eating. *British Food Journal, 109*(6), 457–468. doi:10.1108/00070700710753517

Jain, V., & Roy, S. (2016). Understanding meaning transfer in celebrity endorsements: A qualitative exploration. *Qualitative Market Research: An International Journal, 19*(3), 266–286. doi:10.1108/QMR-03-2015-0020

Kamral, D. (2011). Deo ads face the Axe effect. *The Times of India.* Retrieved from https://timesofindia.indiatimes.com/tv/news/hindi/Deo-ads-face-the-axe-effect/articleshow/8585331.cms

Keel, A., & Nataraajan, R. (2012). Celebrity endorsements and beyond: New avenues for celebrity branding. *Psychology & Marketing, 29*(9), 690–703. doi:10.1002/mar.20555

LaTour, K. A., & LaTour, M. S. (2009). Positive mood and susceptibility to false advertising. *Journal of Advertising, 38*(3), 127–142. doi:10.2753/JOA0091-3367380309

Mehta, A. (2015). Maggi noodles in soup: Can actors who endorse products be held liable? *Hindustan Times.* Retrieved from http://www.hindustantimes.com/india/maggi-noodles-in-soup-can-actors-who-endorse-products-be-held-liable/story-2i1mxjj5ticxPDyMqiw1oJ.html

Melé, D. (2009). Integrating personalism into virtue-based business ethics: The personalist and the common good principles. *Journal of Business Ethics, 88*(1), 227–244. doi:10.1007/s10551-009-0108-y

Merritt, S. (1984). Negative political advertising: Some empirical findings. *Journal of Advertising, 13*(3), 27–38. doi:10.1080/00913367.1984.10672899

Misra, S., & Beatty, S. E. (1990). Celebrity spokesperson and brand congruence: An assessment of recall and affect. *Journal of Business Research, 21*(2), 159–173. doi:10.1016/0148-2963(90)90050-N

Phillipson, L., & Jones, S. C. (2008). I eat Milo to make me run faster: How the use of sport in food marketing may influence the food beliefs of young Australians. In D. Spanjaard, S. Denize, & N. Sharma (Eds.), *Proceedings of the Australian and New Zealand Marketing Academy Conference* (pp. 1–7). Sydney, Australia: Australian and New Zealand Marketing Academy.

Robideaux, D. (2013). Credibility and television advertising: Negative and positive political ads. *Journal of Marketing Development and Competitiveness, 7*(3), 68. Retrieved from http://www.na-businesspress.com/jmdcopen.html

Sarkar, J. (2017). Ramdev's fast food chain to take on MNC's. *The Times of India.* Retrieved from https://timesofindia.indiatimes.com/business/india-business/ramdevs-fast-food-chain-to-take-on-mncs/articleshow/58524814.cms

Saxena, R. (2008, April 22). It's not working. *Business Standard, The Strategist.* Retrieved from http://www.business-standard.com/article/management/it-s-not-working-108042201018_1.html

Sengupta, A. (2015). Emami fined Rs 15 lakh after executive feels cheated. *ABP Live.* Retrieved from http://www.abplive.in/india-news/emami-fined-rs-15-lakh-after-executive-feels-cheated-239938

Sharma, R. R., & Chander, S. (2007). Consumer psychographics and surrogate advertising: An application of multiple discriminant analysis. *ICFAI Journal of Consumer Behavior, 2*(4), 25–47.

Shimp, T. A. (2003). *Advertising, promotion, & supplemental aspects of integrated marketing communication.* Mason, OH: Thomson South-Western.

Simon, H. A. (1955). A behavioral model of rational choice. *The Quarterly Journal of Economics, 69*(1), 99–118. doi:10.2307/1884852

Simon, H. A. (1956). Rational choice and the structure of the environment. *Psychological Review, 63*(2), 129. doi:10.1037/h0042769

Skinner, J. D., Carruth, B. R., Bounds, W., & Ziegler, P. J. (2002). Children's food preferences: A longitudinal analysis. *Journal of the American Dietetic Association, 102*(11), 1638–1647. doi:10.1016/S0002-8223(02)90349-4

Spry, A., Pappu, R., & Bettina Cornwell, T. (2011). Celebrity endorsement, brand credibility, and brand equity. *European Journal of Marketing, 45*(6), 882–909. doi:10.1108/03090561111119958

Vaj, J. (2006). Ajay Devgan signed as Bagpipers brand ambassador. *Business of Cinema.* Retrieved from http://businessofcinema.com/bollywood-news/ajay-devgan-signed-as-bagpipers-brand-ambassador/15882

Vijayalakshmi, A., Laczniak, R. N., & Muehling, D. (2015, January). Measuring consumers' responses to negative advertising: The tolerance of negativity (ton) scale. In *American Academy of Advertising. Conference. Proceedings (Online)* (p. 123). American Academy of Advertising. Retrieved from http://www.aaasite.org/proceedings

Wei, P. S., & Lu, H. P. (2013). An examination of the celebrity endorsements and online customer reviews influence female consumers' shopping behavior. *Computers in Human Behavior, 29*(1), 193–201. doi:10.1016/j.chb.2012.08.005

Xie, G. X., Madrigal, R., & Boush, D. M. (2015). Disentangling the effects of perceived deception and anticipated harm on consumer responses to deceptive advertising. *Journal of Business Ethics, 129*(2), 281–293. doi:10.1007/s10551-014-2155-2

Zeelenberg, M., Nelissen, R. M., Breugelmans, S. M., & Pieters, R. (2008). On emotion specificity in decision making: Why feeling is for doing. *Judgment and Decision Making, 3*(1), 18. Retrieved from http://journal.sjdm.org/vol3.1.htm

List of Contributors

Ya'akov M. Bayer holds a Ph.D. in economics from ýBen-Gurion University of the Negev and has training in both economics and anthropology. He lectures in a wide range of fields within economics (health economics, behavioral economics, economics and culture, finance, etc.). He teaches economics in the Department of Health Systems Management of Ben-Gurion University and serves in managerial position in the Israeli Ministry of Health. His research relates to health economics, decision-making, and behavioral economics, with an emphasis on the connections between economics and culture, religion, beliefs, cognition, health condition, and old age. In addition, he researches the anthropology of Jewish communities in South America and the structure of their collective memory.

Thomas F. Brezenski, M.S., Ph.D., is an Associate Professor of Political Science at St. Thomas University with expertise in the areas of firearms and mental health public policy and is a member of the 23rd Congressional District (FL) Gun Violence Task Force, chaired by the Hon. Rep. Debbie Wasserman-Schultz. His research interests focus on firearms policy at the state and federal level, and he is also an expert on presidential politics, serving as a major-market radio political analyst in that area. Dr. Brezenski is the recipient of three university teaching awards over the course of a 21-year undergraduate teaching career and has taught or developed, or both, more than 30 courses. He is a two-time tournament champion in karate and enjoys playing the guitar. He resides in Plantation, Florida, with his wife, Kristine, and their five children.

Antonella Capriello, Ph.D., is an Associate Professor of Marketing at the Universita del Piemonte Orientale in Italy. She graduated in Economics and Commerce from the University of Turin in 1996; at the same University, she earned the title of Doctor of Philosophy in Business Administration in 2004. She is involved in international research networks in the field of tourism and marketing, being a part of the debate on the potentials of qualitative methods. The research activities include studies on networking processes in tourist destinations and event management. She has collaborated with the Business Incubator of the University of Piemonte Orientale, resulting the winner of the START CUP – Piedmont Region – Tourism and Innovation Special Award in 2007 for the "Innoviaggiando" project, and in 2009 for the "GEO4MAP" project (in collaboration with the de Agostini Group). She has published more than 60 research papers, including articles in the *Journal of Business Research, Current Issues in Tourism,* and *Tourism Management.*

Timothy Dewhirst, M.A., Ph.D., is an Associate Professor of Marketing & Consumer Studies in the College of Business and Economics at the University of Guelph in Canada. Previously, he was Visiting Associate Professor at the University of California, San Francisco, as a Canada-U.S. Fulbright Scholar. He has been awarded numerous research grants and funds from such organizations as the Canadian Institutes of Health Research and the U.S. National Institutes of Health/U.S. National Cancer Institute. His work has appeared in the *Encyclopedia of Major Marketing Strategies* as well as the *Journal of Advertising,* the *Journal of Historical Research in Marketing,* the *Journal of Public Policy and Marketing,* and the *Journal of Business Ethics.*

Raúl Fernández-Calienes, the Reverend Professor, M.Div., M.A.R., M.S.-TESOL, Ph.D., is a sought-after researcher, writer, and editor. At St. Thomas University, he is Adjunct Professor of Management Ethics in the Gus Machado School of Business, Senior Research Fellow at the Human Rights Institute, and formerly Visiting Associate Professor in the School of Law. For other authors, he has been the manuscript or production editor of more than two dozen books and monographs published by Cambridge University Press, the University of California Press, Praeger, HarperCollins*Religious,* the Christian Literature Society (India), and others. He also has served as Deputy Editor of the American Bar Association Section of International Law, *The Year in Review.* He is co-editor of the three-volume series *Women Moving Forward* and Managing Editor of the peer-reviewed *Journal of Multidisciplinary Research.*

Robert Jeffery Foran, M.A., Ed.D., is a Professor of Economics at Miami-Dade College in Florida. His experience includes teaching at a university in China, serving as a field examiner for the International Baccalaureate Organization based in the United Kingdom, and currently serving as a program evaluator for the American Council of Education based in Washington, D.C.

Hagai Gringarten, M.B.A., Ph.D., is a Professor and a branding expert. He teaches branding and marketing at St. Thomas University's Gus Machado School of Business, and he is a Visiting Professor at Harbin

Finance University in China. He has served as president of the American Marketing Association South Florida chapter and co-authored a bestselling book about coffee. He also pursued postgraduate studies at Harvard Graduate School of Business and the Kellogg School of Management. Dr. Gringarten serves as a faculty advisor to the American Marketing Association chapter at STU and is the founder and Editor-in-Chief of the *Journal of Multidisciplinary Research*, a peer-reviewed academic journal. He is also co-founder and faculty advisor of the *Journal of Student Research* and serves on the editorial board of the *Journal of International & Interdisciplinary Business Research*, a California State University system publication.

Punam Gupta, Ph.D., is an Associate Professor at Dev Samaj College for Women, Chandigarh, India. She has written many research papers and participated in seminars on gender sensitization, green economics, environment studies, value education, media, and society.

Rohail Hassan, Ph.D. in Management Sciences, works as a Graduate Research Assistant at Universiti Teknologi PETRONAS in Malaysia. Rohail received his undergraduate education in Management Sciences at the University of the Punjab in 2010 and earned his Master of Philosophy degree there in 2012. He earned a Doctor of Philosophy in Management Sciences degree in 2018 from Universiti Teknologi PETRONAS in Malaysia. His research on corporate governance, women's empowerment, gender-related issues, diversity management, financial management, marketing management, firm performance, and strategy has been published in several academic journals – more than 30 refereed journal articles to date. Rohail also serves as an International Reviewer to several academic journals.

Larry Hubbell, Ph.D., is a Professor and the Director of the Institute of Public Service at Seattle University. He previously served as a faculty member at the University of Wyoming for 25 years. As a Fulbright scholar, Larry taught in Lithuania and Sierra Leone. In addition, he taught, consulted, and conducted research in Cambodia, China, Taiwan, Indonesia, Russia, South Africa, England, Italy, Dominica, and Panama. He has published 60 articles in peer-reviewed journals as well as a novel called *Almost Dysfunctional*. Larry worked at the U.S. Environmental Protection Agency and ACTION, the agency that formerly administered Peace Corps and VISTA. His primary research interests are higher education administration, problems facing emerging democracies, and organization development.

Jeffrey Kleeger, Esq., M.B.A., Ph.D., teaches criminal justice law classes for the Department of Justice Studies in the College of Arts & Sciences at Florida Gulf Coast University in Fort Myers, Florida. He is an attorney with real property law transactional experience. His research interests include conflict between state authority and private rights, the economically driven privatization of law and its impact on private rights, economic development in land use, conflict resolution, sustainability in economic and environmental factors, the pedagogy of law study, and ethical considerations in business, law, and organizational development.

Dinesh Kumar, M.B.A., Ph.D., is the Director of The Winning Edge Training Consultants in India. His publications include *Consumer Behaviour* (Oxford University Press), *Rural Marketing* (Sage Publications), and *Marketing Channels* (Oxford University Press). He has 15 years of industry experience, and since joining academia, he has taught at business schools and universities in India, Norway, and Switzerland. He has written several papers and presented them in international conferences.

Wonkyong Beth Lee, M.A., Ph.D., is an Assistant Professor, DAN Department of Management & Organizational Studies, Western University, in Canada. Previously, she was a Visiting Scholar at the School of Public Health at the University of Sydney in Australia as well as the Department of Advertising and Public Relations in the College of Communications at Hanyang University in South Korea. Her work has appeared in the *Journal of Business Ethics, Tobacco Control,* the *Journal of Health Communication,* and *Health Psychology.*

Abhishek Mishra, M.B.A., Ph.D., is an Assistant Professor at the Indian Institute of Management (IIM), Indore. He did his Ph.D. in the area of Product Design and its implications on Brand Equity from IIM Lucknow. He has publications in leading marketing journals, and his research interests are in the areas of New Product Development, Product and Brand Management, and Fuzzy Sets and Systems. He has conducted academic research in Canada, and his work has been published in the *Academy of Marketing Science Review,* the *Journal of Brand Management,* and the *Journal of Business Research.*

Nellie Munin, LL.D., Adv., is a lawyer and legal expert in European Union economic law and international trade law. Previously, she was an Associate Professor at the law school of the Zefat Academic College, in Israel, as well as the Minister of Economic Affairs in the Israeli Mission to the European Union. She also was the Chief Legal Advisor with the State Revenue Administration in the Israeli Ministry of Finance.

Stan Neal, M.Res., Ph.D., FHEA, is the John Springhall Post-Doctoral Lecturer in Modern British/Imperial History at Ulster University. He has previously lectured in History at the University of Leicester, Northumbria University, and the University of Sunderland. His research interests focus on issues of race, empire, and globalization. Of particular interest are the migration and information networks that spanned the British Empire in Asia in the nineteenth century.

Gurbir Singh, M.B.A., is a doctoral student at the Indian Institute of Management in Indore, India. He holds a Bachelor's degree in Commerce and an M.B.A. in Marketing from UBS, Panjab University, Chandigarh. He is a Fellow of the Insurance Institute of India. His work experience includes nine years in the financial and education sector. His research interest lies in consumer behavior. More specifically, he works on understanding (1) the ethical decision-making process, (2) the impact of control desires on consumer behavior, and (3) the impact of emotions on decision making. He has attended many national and international conferences and workshops.

Further Readings

Specific Works

Brenkert, George G. *Marketing ethics*. Malden, MA: Blackwell Pub., 2008, xii, 256 pages, ISBN: 9780631214236, 0631214232; 9780631214229, 0631214224.

Chonko, Lawrence B. *Ethical decision making in marketing*. Thousand Oaks, CA: Sage, 1995, 314 s.; ISBN: 0803955456, 9780803955455; 0803955464 9780803955462.

Laczniak, Eugene R., & Murphy, Patrick E. *Marketing ethics: Guidelines for managers*. Lexington, MA: Lexington Books, 1985, xv, 182 pages, ISBN: 0669108332 9780669108330, 0669108324 9780669108323.

Murphy, Patrick E., & Laczniak, Eugene R. *Marketing ethics: Cases and readings*. Upper Saddle River, NJ: Pearson Prentice Hall, 2006, xii, 172 pages, ISBN: 0131330888, 9780131330887.

SAGE Brief guide to marketing ethics. Thousand Oaks, CA: Sage Publications, 2012, 218 pages, ISBN-13: 978-1412995146, ISBN-10: 1412995140.

Saucier, Rick D. *Marketing ethics*. Lewiston, NY: Edwin Mellen Press, 2008, xv, 162 pages, ISBN: 0773451161, 9780773451162.

Schlegelmilch, Bodo B. *Marketing ethics: An international perspective*. London, England: International Thomson Business Press, 1998, ISBN: 186152191X, 9781861521910.

Smith, N. Craig, & Murphy, Patrick E. *Marketing ethics*. Los Angeles, CA, and London, England: SAGE, 2012, 5 volumes, ISBN: 9781446208106 1446208109.

Van de Ven, Bert. *Responsible marketing: Marketing ethics*. London, England: Routledge, 2005, 232 str. ISBN: 0415349680, 9780415349680, 0415349672, 9780415349673.

General Works

Boatright, J., & Smith, J. (2016). *Ethics and the conduct of business*. Pearson Education, 408 pages, loose leaf, ISBN 978-0134167657.

Brooks, L. (2017). *Business & professional ethics for directors, executives & accountants*. South-Western College Pub., 670 pages, paperback, ISBN 978-1305971455.

Ferrel, O. C., Fraedrich, J., & Ferrel, O. C. (2016). *Business ethics: Ethical decision making & cases*. South-Western College Pub., 654 pages, hardcover, ISBN 978-1305500846.

Jennings, M. (2011). *Business ethics: Case studies and selected readings.* South-Western Legal Studies in Business Academic, 640 pages, hardcover, ISBN 978-0538473538.

Lawrence, A., & Weber, J. (2016). *Business and society: Stakeholders, ethics, public policy.* McGraw-Hill Education, 592 pages, hardcover, ISBN 978-1259315411.

Shaw, W. H. (2016). *Business ethics: A textbook with cases.* Wadsworth Publishing, 480 pages, hardcover, ISBN 978-1305582088.

Shaw, W. H., & Barry, V. (2015). *Moral issues in business.* Wadsworth Publishing, 656 pages, hardcover, ISBN 978-1285874326.

Stanwick, P. A., & Stanwick, S. D. (2015). *Understanding business ethics.* Thousand Oaks, CA: Sage Publications, 600 pages, hardcover, ISBN 978-1506303239.

Trevino, L. K., & Nelson, K. A. (2013). *Managing business ethics: Straight talk about how to do it right.* Wiley, 480 pages, hardcover, ISBN 978-1118582671.

Velazquez, M. G. (2012). *Business ethics: Concepts and cases.* Pearson Education, 504 pages, hardcover, ISBN 978-0205017669.

Index

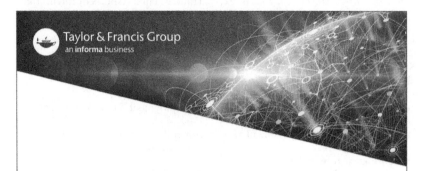

Made in United States
Orlando, FL
20 August 2023

36253606R00117